A Chalcolithic Marble Workshop at Kulaksızlar in Western Anatolia

An analysis of production and craft specialization

Turan Takaoğlu

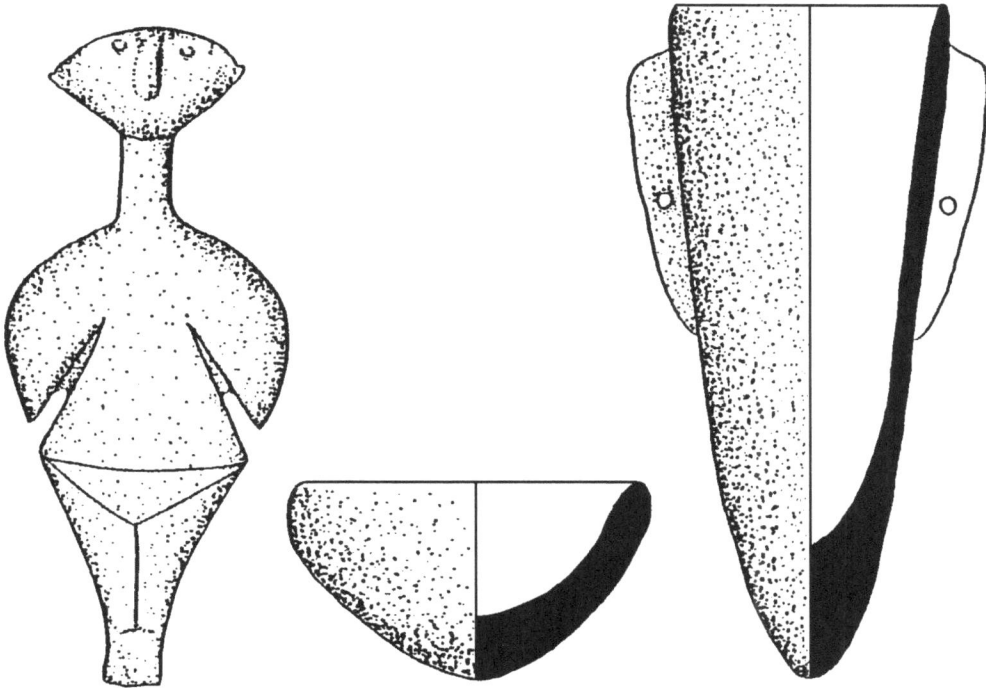

BAR International Series 1358
2005

Published in 2016 by
BAR Publishing, Oxford

BAR International Series 1358

A Chalcolithic Marble Workshop at Kulaksızlar in Western Anatolia

ISBN 9781841718033 paperback
ISBN 9781407327884 e-format
DOI https://doi.org/10.30861/9781841718033
A catalogue record for this book is available from the British Library

BAR Publishing is the trading name of British Archaeological Reports (Oxford) Ltd.
British Archaeological Reports was first incorporated in 1974 to publish the BAR
Series, International and British. In 1992 Hadrian Books Ltd became part of the BAR
group. This volume was originally published by Archaeopress in conjunction with
British Archaeological Reports (Oxford) Ltd / Hadrian Books Ltd, the Series
principal publisher, in 2005. This present volume is published by BAR Publishing,
2016.

BAR

PUBLISHING

BAR titles are available from:
      BAR Publishing
      122 Banbury Rd, Oxford, OX2 7BP, UK
EMAIL   info@barpublishing.com
PHONE +44 (0)1865 310431
FAX   +44 (0)1865 316916
      www.barpublishing.com

Kulaksızlar eserlerini zor günümde doktora tez konusu olarak bana devreden Rafet Dinç'e armağandır

Acknowledgments

I owe a great depth of gratitude to the faculty of the Department of Archaeology at Boston University, Curtis Runnels, Julie Hansen, and Paul Zimansky, for allowing me to study archaeology with them and jointly supervising my Ph.D. dissertation on Chalcolithic marble working at Kulaksızlar in central-western Turkey, slightly modified version of which forms the basis of this study. With this occasion, I would like to express my graditude to professors James Wiseman, Murray McClellan, Norman Hammond, Kathryn Bard, Ricardo Elia, Kenneth Kvamme, and Paul Goldberg for shaping my scholarship in their seminars and courses that I attended at Boston University.

I am grateful to Rafet Dinç, who made the material from the 1994 and 1995 Kulaksızlar surveys available to me and encouraged me to carry out further research on this site and its remains. Hasan Dedeoğlu, the director of the Manisa Museum, kindly allowed me to re-examine the surface assemblage in his care in 1999. I am also thankful to Mehmet Söylemez, archaeological representative from the *Department of Antiquities and Museums* of Turkey, for accompanying me during the survey that I carried out at the site during June, 1999. I thank Jurgen Seeher for sharing their thoughts on the marble beaker fragments from Beşik-Sivritepe and Demircihöyük and to Utta Gabriel for explaining me the material remains from Kumtepe 1a and Beşik-Sivritepe. The information obtained from the recent excavtions of the present author at the fifth millennium B.C. site of Gülpınar on the coastal Troad, which I carried out under the supervision of Coşkun Özgünel from the Ankara University, are used to clarify the issues related to the cultural affiliation of the site.

I will always feel privileged to be a student of Curtis Runnels, who has long been a role model for me, as he has been for many of his students. I am, however, responsible for any shorthcomings and erors that may be found in this study.

Turan Takaoğlu

Table of Contents

List of Tables

List of Figures

List of Plates

Part One

INTRODUCTION

Almost every prehistoric village community probably included at least one skilled craftsman who differed from ordinary people pursuing tasks associated with the immediate needs of daily life. Scholars such as Gordon Childe (1951: 25) and Colin Renfrew (1972: 340) recognized the role of individuals with technical skills in their views of early village societies. It was believed that specialists with high levels of technical skills worked on a part-time basis at their crafts when specific needs arose for specialist goods and during the spare time left over after the essential occupation of carrying out basic subsistence activities, such as farming, fishing, and hunting had been completed (Childe 1951: 62). The difficulties involved in identifying the organizational and technological contexts of their production in the archaeological record prevented archaeologists from intensively exploring the specialized craft production systems of pre-urban times. The ways in which pre-urban specialists organized their production and the motivation behind the crafting of prestige objects requiring a high level of craftsmanship are still poorly understood. Consequently, the question of whether pre-urban specialists obtained agricultural surplus so that they could practice their special skills or a particular craft production constituted the major part of the village economy presents a problem of interpretation for archaeologists studying prehistoric craft specialization.

Craft production carried out by pre-urban specialists was to a large extent structurally less complex than that carried out by full-time specialists in urban or state societies, owing mainly to the nature of control over production. This basic distinction employing an element of control resulted in the development of a wide range of models positing a causal link between political complexity and craft specialization (e.g. Brumfiel and Earle 1987; Peregrine 1991). According to these models, elites employed craft specialists to produce prestige or wealth objects that were important components of the power or administrative structures of the society, the ownership of which helped to differentiate elites from the rest of the society. Attached specialists working for the elite were withdrawn from subsistence pursuits and supported by agricultural surplus so that that they could work full-time at their crafts (Childe 1950; Evans 1978: 115). Because most archaeological studies of craft specialization have been directed towards the study of urban or state societies, the study of specialized craft activities in pre-urban cultures has received relatively little attention in the literature. The relative paucity of information available on specialized production systems of pre-urban societies is primarily due to a lack of relevant data in the archaeological record. Recognizing this prompted me to concentrate on the issue of pre-urban craft

specialization. I believe that a model outlining the life of craft specialists working in a cultural environment where no political structure existed to support them can provide us with a picture of what pre-urban craft specialization was like. Because production does not occur independently of wider processes, this model also incorporates the social, economic, and symbolic relations of production, by integrating exchange and consumption systems into the study. The spatial distribution of source-specific artifacts creates a framework with which the role of exchange in the development and maintenance of specialized craft activities during pre-urban times can be investigated. The nature of exchange is important in determining whether production was oriented towards the supplementation of basic subsistence or to maintenance of social alliances through inter-personal or inter-communal exchanges. Understanding how specialist-produced artifacts were used is also important in revealing both economic and non-economic components of production. Consequently, in order to provide a comprehensive picture of the environment in which pre-urban craftsmen produced special classes of artifacts, such as technically elaborated prestige objects of high value, the reconstruction of the social, economic, and symbolic relations of production remains essential.

The recent recovery of an early example of marble working from the Chalcolithic site of Kulaksızlar in central-western Anatolia (Fig. 1.1) presents an opportunity to develop a model showing what form craft specialization may have taken in a pre-urban setting. Archaeological evidence from Kulaksızlar is invaluable as it dates to the second quarter of the fifth millennium BC, a period with no signs of internal political differentiation and which was characterized by small self-sufficient agricultural village societies. The evidence for marble working at the site of Kulaksızlar has been derived from high concentrations of manufacturing debris that were recorded during survey studies carried out in 1994, 1995, and 1999. The manufacturing debris found on the surface comprises nearly two thousand artifacts that consist largely of blanks, waste byproducts, manufacturing errors, and stone tools associated with multiple stages of marble working. Analysis of the surface finds from the site reveals that the workshop was oriented towards production of the so-called Kilia figurines and stone vessels (pointed beakers and bowls), although several fragments attest to the manufacture of globular jars, flat-based bowls, and other types of schematic figurines. The enormous quantity of artifacts associated with marble working (90%), relative to artifacts relating to daily life such as pottery and food processing implements (10%), implies that marble working occupied a central role in the lives of the site's population. Placement of the site in the less fertile foothills rather than in the alluvial plain or on the gently sloping hills encircling it is striking since most of the pre-Bronze Age sites of the region were located in the plains where land was more suitable for agriculture. The locus of the site was most likely chosen for access to marble sources as well as rocks such as gabbro, basalt, and sandstone used to shape marble. The diversity of geologic sources close to the site allowed non-agricultural craft production to emerge and develop at this locality.

Specialized production behavior prior to the Early Bronze Age II, a period that saw the emergence of complex societies, has rarely been documented in the archaeological record of western Anatolia. The Chalcolithic period in western Anatolia was a time of change that contributed to the rise of complex societies during the Early Bronze Age. Reliance on specialist-produced artifacts, which resulted from increased social differentiation and the increasing role of goods in the communication system, probably had an impact on the emergence of specialized craft production at Kulaksızlar. Analysis of this manufacturing debris from the marble workshop is important because it also provides information on technological aspects of production such as how the marble figurines and vessels were made, where the raw materials were acquired, what kinds of tools were used, and how craftsmen utilized these tools. Although marble artifacts were in use in western Anatolia as early as the Late Neolithic period, how these artifacts were manufactured and how their production was organized have not been archaeologically documented so far. In the absence of excavated evidence for production of Chalcolithic artifacts from western Anatolia, a model showing the technological aspects of specialized craft production will be an important contribution to our understanding of pre-Bronze Age western Anatolia. The marble products from the workshop seem to constitute a special class of artifacts that were unlikely to have been used in mundane tasks associated with everyday life. The distribution of the marble products of this workshop over great distances clearly shows that these artifacts were highly valued in most parts of western Anatolia. Studies of the distribution of finished artifacts allow the patterns of exchange involving prestige or symbolic artifacts to be reconstructed, while information regarding the use of these marble artifacts can partially inform us on the social and economic roles of the specialist-produced artifacts.

Information derived from the study of Kulaksızlar marble working can also be used to define what constitutes a "craft specialist" and to reconstruct the factors that result in the emergence of specialized craft production in pre-urban times. The problems in defining craftsmen with high levels of technical skills operating in pre-urban times as "craft specialists" seem to arise from uncertainty about their social role and viewing

their craft activities as purely economically motivated. Reconstruction of the social and economic relations of the marble working at Kulaksızlar complements our understanding of why skilled individuals pursued laborious, time consuming, and risky non-agricultural production such as stone working instead of adopting less complex production strategies.

This archaeological study of village-based marble production also contributes to theories of specialized behavior in pre-urban contexts, enabling this behavior to be recognized in the archaeological record. Identifying specialized production and reconstructing its organizational context from data obtained through surface surveys present particular problems of interpetation, mainly due to discard behavior and post-depositional processes. The parameters applied in the analysis of marble working debris may be applied to other categories of artifacts, and can be useful in identifying specialized production involving other goods found among the surface remains. Thus, the Kulaksızlar data contributes to our knowledge of both archaeology (pre-Bronze Age production, exchange and consumption systems) and theory (presence of craft specialization in pre-urban times). The fact that Kulaksızlar temporally belongs to the transitional stage between the early and late Chalcolithic periods in western Anatolian archaeology makes this production system very significant. This is because there is a significant culture change observed between the early and Late Chalcolithic periods in western Anatolia. The appearance of a new cultural tradition during the Late Chalcolithic period had something to do what happened during the preceding transitional Middle Chalcolithic period, to which Kulaksızlar assemblage probably belonged to. Thus, reconstructing the nature of production, exchange, and use involved in the products of the Kulaksızlar workhsop will also enhance our understanding of the cultural evolution of Chalcolithic western Anatolia.

It is also argued in this study that the Chalcolithic marble working at Kulaksızlar was an example of village-based craft specialization. Technological and organizational indicators such as the separation of production into different work units, standardization of artifact forms and production methods, volume of output, and the level of technical investment display a complex pattern of production that distinguish the village-based Kulaksızlar specialization from domestic production. Productive utilization of local environment, technological innovations, and socio-economic constraints provided incentives for specialized craft production to emerge and develop in this part of western Anatolia. I suggest that marble working formed a major part of the village economy and that agriculture was only supplemental. This assertion argues against approaches that see specialization in pre-urban times as a simple or casual activity carried out by individuals in spare time left over after they had completed agricultural activities. The idea that marble working dominated the Kulaksızlar economy is supported by the location of the site near or in the forest on the foothills rather than in the alluvial plain, where most agricultural populations of the region preferred to live during the Chalcolithic period. There was enough arable land suitable for farming activities in the alluvial plain, so the location of the site did not result from competition for land. It was the abundance of marble that induced these people to settle at the locality and adopt a manufacturing strategy involving non-agricultural production. Basic subsistence needs could have been obtained in exchange for marble products manufactured using their special skills. This does not mean that agriculture was not practiced at all on the perennial spring-watered lower ends of the slopes by members of the Kulaksızlar village who were not involved in marble working.

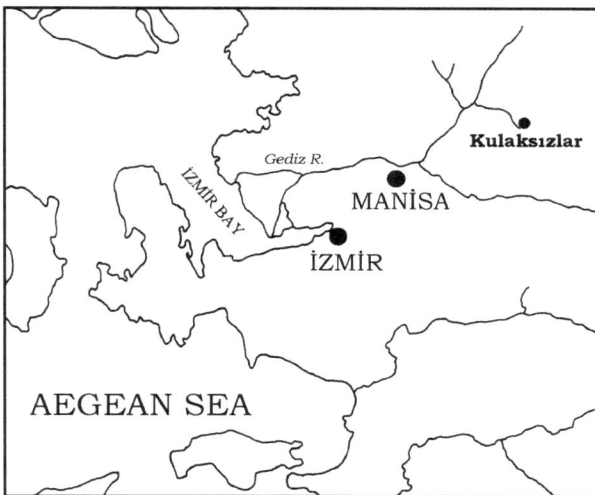

Fig. 1.1. Map locating Kulaksızlar in central- western Turkey

Although marble working formed the central part of Kulaksızlar economy, the reason for adopting marble working had also non-economic components. It is resonable to suggest that social and symbolic relations of production were also important for craftsmen to adopt a non-agricultural strategy. Kulaksızlar craftsmen concentrated their attention on the production of prestige or symbolic objects. It is believed that Kilia figurines were important within the belief system of the western Anatolian communities because a single deity was embodied in this form. Because of the symbolism attached to the Kilia figurines, they were highly valued and in great demand. It was probably the social and symbolic relations of production that led Kulaksızlar craftsmen to collaborate and adopt a specialized production strategy rather than pursuing agricultural production as most contemporary Chalcolithic settlements did. It was this demand for figurines and prestige marble vessels used in mortuary rituals that created an economic strategy involving non-agricultural production. Exchange of these special artifacts could have led Kulaksızlar people to maintain social relationships with their neighboring settlements in central-west Anatolia. This suggests that social,

economic, and symbolic relations of production determined the intensity of marble working, resulting in the collaboration of several craftsmen on a village basis. Therefore, the idea that craft activities of pre-urban specialists were supported from surplus may not always be the case. This is one of the most important contributions of this research to the study of specialized production systems in non-urban societies In this context, it is argued that both direct and indirect exchange were responsible for the distribution of Kulaksızlar marble figurines and beakers, following a pattern similar to that involved in rare and exotic goods such as precious stones, marine shells, obsidian, and copper objects. These artifacts appear to have moved along the already existing trade routes that tied the sub-regions of western Anatolia together. The presence of these artifacts at sites along or at the end of these land-based trade routes suggests a down-the line-exchange carried out on inter-personal or inter-communal level during the Chalcolithic period.

Archaeological evidence for marble working from Kulaksızlar reveals the characteristics of specialized behavior that have often been accepted are concomitant with the emergence of urban societies. Technological and organizational indicators of Kulaksızlar production, however, reveal a complex pattern of production. Standardization in the forms of artifacts and technology adopted in their manufacture, the high level of technical investment, the internal work division among the craftsmen, the distribution of finished artifacts over great distances, and their non-utilitarian associations all indicate that Kulaksızlar production was a village-based form of specialized activity. The nature of the Kulaksızlar evidence leads me to believe that pre-urban craft specialization can take a very complex form. Because what constitutes craft specialization in a pre-urban context appears to have been determined by the social, economic, and symbolic relations of production, archaeologists differentiating specialized craft activity from a domestic production must first identify the associations of the finished artifacts. In other words, the intended function of specialist-produced artifacts determines the degree and kind of a given specialized production behavior in pre-urban contexts. Those prestige or wealth items used in social display and objects used in household or communal cults or rituals often display distinctive features characterized by the quality of material, high craftsmanship, or technical elaboration.

Craft specialization here is not viewed as a phenomenon whose existence exclusively depended on agricultural surplus. It is suggested that craft specialization could become the major source of income for a given pre-urban community even in an environment where land shortage does not occur or at places where the natural environment was optimal for pursuing basic subsistence activities. Because economic factors are not necessarily the only motivation for non-agricultural production to occur, social and symbolic relations of production are viewed as elements that conditioned the patterns of pre-urban specialized behavior. The symbolic role of the Kulaksızlar artifacts and social relations of production characterized by their exchange relationships in an interpersonal or intercommunal level were important factors for the emergence of craft specialization in the pre-urban western Anatolian context. Therefore, the idea that craft specialization helped to create interpersonal ties and redefined differences in status and power (Cross 1993: 80) is valid for the arguments presented in this dissertation. Moving from the economic, social, and symbolic role of production, craft specialization can be defined as home- or village-based production, organized in order to supplement the local economy and maintain social alliances through inter-personal or inter-communal exchanges of the items produced with special skills.

Reconstruction of the behavioral patterns of Kulaksızlar craft production is not a single research objective. It is predicated on a complex set of closely interrelated theoretical and methodological questions with social, economic, environmental, organizational, and aesthetic components. Kulaksızlar presents a problem of interpretation since there is no architectural context with which to associate the manufacturing debris. All avenues of inquiry are used in this study for a proper understanding of this prehistoric marble working evidence within the broader framework of western Anatolian cultural history and within the theories of craft specialization. In this context, part Two provides a critical assessment of the two main approaches adopted for studying prehistoric craft specialization, namely those that accept craft specialization as a characteristic feature of only urban or state societies and those that place this notion into a wider context that includes non-urban or non-state societies. Then, the differences between the structures of specialized and domestic (non-specialized) production systems is underlined in light of current archaeological models. This general theoretical background underscores the main reasons why Kulaksızlar marble working must be classified as village-based specialized production, in spite of the fact that it occurred in a pre-urban context dating roughly to the second quarter of the fifth millennium BC. Part three, on the other hand, attempts to reconstruct the natural and cultural environment in which the site of Kulaksızlar functioned. Because the selection of this locality was due the availability of suitable raw materials, it is important to understand the natural characteristics of the site and its environs, including topographical features, geological, and climatic conditions that prevailed in the region during the time of the site's occupation. In this chapter, I also make a general assessment of the material culture derived from the surface studies in order to reconstruct settlement patterns as well as the production and exchange systems of the region. This enables me to determine whether the Kulaksızlar culture resulted from local development or was derived from such factors as cultural interactions, demic movements, and social reorganization.

Part Four presents a general picture of the surface finds recovered at Kulaksızlar. First, it describes and classifies the surface assemblage by providing a general description of the main marble products of the workshop in reference to overall morphology and their functional characteristics. Then, it describes the stone tools associated with the various stages of marble vessel and figurine production according to the functions they may have served. Use-wear observed on the stone tools complements the reconstruction of the sequences of production and craftsmen's tool use. The delineation of the surface artifacts also includes the study of pottery, the evaluation of which provides cultural and chronological affiliations of this site, and the marble products of the workshop within the broader framework of Chalcolithic western Anatolia.

Part five reconstructs the patterns of Kulaksızlar marble working, in relation to processes such as the choice of the raw material to be utilized, prospecting and extracting strategies involved in their acquisition, and the sequences of manufacture. The archaeological evidence is supplemented with ethnographic analogies and replication experiments to aid in the interpretation of the technological and socio-economic aspects of this prehistoric production system. The ways in which the finished marble artifacts might have been exchanged and used in western Anatolian village communities are also discussed. This perspective is important for reconstructing the patterns that structured Kulaksızlar marble working.

Part Six attempts to demonstrate why Kulaksızlar marble working must be classified as village-based craft specialization instead of less complex domestic production by using four parameters to highlight this distinction: 1) separation of production activities into stages and different spatial units; 2) volume of output; 3) technical elaboration; and 4) standardization in the forms of artifacts and the methods of production. Patterning of the distribution of surface finds, technological analysis of use-wear patterns, and a series of statistical analyses of surface finds are undertaken to determine the character of this specialized production.

Part Seven discusses this specialized craft production evidence within the wider framework of western Anatolian cultural history. Because specialized economic behavior has not been documented in the archaeological record of Chalcolithic western Anatolia previously, It also discusses what this production system means for our understanding of pre-Bronze Age culture and what a prehistoric craftsman's life was like in western Anatolia during this period. First, a model of specialized craft production centered on marble working is provided to shed new light on one of the least known aspects of western Anatolian cultural history. Kulaksızlar reveals the most visible example of prehistoric lithic craft specialization in western Anatolia, with patterns of production otherwise documented archaeologically.

Part Two
CRAFT PRODUCTION AND SPECIALIZATION

The notion of craft specialization has long been considered a theme by archaeologists studying the evolution of prehistoric societies. The available literature on this subject reveals two different approaches to craft specialization. The first approach limits the term craft specialization to urban or state societies with a complex political structure. In contrast, the second approach opens this term to a wide range of societies with different levels of social organization, including early village societies with no internal political differentiation. The former perspective originates in the writings of V. Gordon Childe, who first identified craft specialization as one of the criteria essential for urbanization and the "emergence of civilization" (1950: 16). Childe referred to craft specialization as an occupational specialization associated with the development of stratified social organization in pre-state and early state societies (1950). Childe based his argument on the assumption that craft specialization occurred in history only after humankind had mastered subsistence techniques and could produce a surplus to support craftsmen (1936: 118). In this context, the urban revolution enabled temple-based theocratic elites to concentrate a sufficient surplus to support craft specialists, who were attached to those elites and worked full-time. Childe argued that irrigation-based agriculture in Mesopotamia yielded food surpluses at a large level enough to support urban centers. Therefore, ruling elites released a dependent class of full-time craft producers from food production enabling them to perform their special skills. Full-time specialists do not produce food themselves, but are fed from the social surplus in return for the products of their special skills (Childe 1951: 63). Childe further suggested that the surplus from irrigated agriculture was concentrated in the hands of a temple-based theocratic elite, who supported and controlled this emergent class of attached craftsmen (Childe 1942: 77; Wailes 1996: 7).

In his final work, *The Prehistory of European Society* (1958), Childe drew a distinction between full-time and part-time craft specialization. It was the use of metal artifacts as luxury items that led to the first true full-time specialization, mainly because metal artifacts were in such great demand that production required full-time attention (Childe 1942: 77). Elites wanted prestige items such as metal artifacts to bolster their internal and external political position. In contrast to full-time specialization in the Near East, Childe proposed independent specialization for the societies of Europe. In Bronze Age Europe, there could have been no attached specialists since there was neither a class structure, nor elites to support craftsmen or sufficient population to support full-time metalworkers (Childe 1958: 167). Because those prehistoric European metalworkers were itinerant, they were unable to produce their own food, and instead, obtained their food in return for their crafts. This distinction, based on control over the craft production activities of the full- and part-time specialists, formed an important contribution to the study of specialized production among prehistoric societies. For instance, Timothy Earle (1981: 230) highlighted this distinction by separating special, high-value goods produced for elite consumption (attached production) from utilitarian goods produced for broader distribution (independent production) in order to clarify differences in sociopolitical and economic origins of demand (Earle 1981). Elites maintain key social distinctions through the ownership of status-legitimizing objects and by controlling the production of politically charged items, which are often made from highly valued, rare and expensive materials (Brumfiel and Earle 1987: 5). Elites provide specialists with raw materials, work facilities, and subsistence support in return for the goods produced, so by definition, attached specialists are supplied with subsistence support in return for their services through craft production. In contrast, independent specialists operate autonomously, producing goods in response to economic, social, or political demand. Independent specialization does not arise out of the elite's desire to control the political economy (Brumfiel and Earle 1987). Independent specialists assume all the risks of production and are expected to provide the raw material and support themselves during the manufacturing process. The distinction between attached and independent specialization echoed in numerous studies (e.g. Clark and Parry 1990; Lewis 1986).

In a similar way, Sinopoli (1981: 581) created a tripartite typology to differentiate the modes of production according to the degree of elite or administrative management of production: administered production, centralized production, and non-centralized production. Administered production, which can be equated with attached specialization, is defined as production that is directly regulated by some powerful institution under the control of the political and/or religious elite. Craft producers are attached specialists, spatially and economically bound to the institutions that control production. Administered production is expected to focus on certain classes of goods such as rare and precious objects that convey social standing or more common goods crucial to the acquisition of wealth and power. Sinopoli's centralized production refers to large-scale and spatially segregated production by specialists without any direct involvement from the administrative apparatus of the state. Market conditions such as supply and demand, and tradition play major roles in regulating the workshop organization. This kind of specialization is very similar to independent specialization. Non-centralized production, on the other hand, refers to specialized production that takes place on a smaller scale and in more dispersed locations. Goods are produced by specialists, working either full- or part-time at their crafts, but the workshops are small and output is comparatively low. Nuclear or extended families are the typical production groups in these contexts (Sinopoli 1988: 582).

Most of the archaeological models concerning craft specialization that were developed after Childe's work appear to have placed special emphasis on the causal relationship between productive specialization and political administration. According to these political models, elites employ craft specialists to produce politically valued items to differentiate themselves from the rest of the society (e.g. Peregrine 1991: 2; Helms 1993: 69). The scholars formulating these models see craft specialization as a result of increasing social complexity together with the formation of hierarchies.

There is also a tendency to acknowledge the presence of craft specialization in rural parts of urban contexts. For example, recent archaeological evidence from the Ubaid period in Mesopotamia (ca. 5500-3900 BC) demonstrates that independent specialization was an important component of the earliest complex societies in the Ubaid period (Stein 1996: 27). Although the Ubaid period was a time when ideologically linked chiefdoms, economic differentiation, irrigation-based agriculture, regional centralization, and ceremonial elaboration were in existence, craft specialization was not attached to those elites. Stein (1996: 28) argues that specialized pot-making took place in numerous in dependent workshops at the site of Tel Abada, rather than under the control of elites. High concentration of manufacturing facilities within the site of Tel Abada led Stein to view pot-making as a large scale decentralized specialized craft activity (1996: 28). Despite the presence of socioeconomic differentiation in Ubaid Mesopotamia, there appears to have been no sign of either attached craft specialists or exotic prestige goods.

This pattern of developing specialized craft production independent of elites can also be documented among the urban societies. Metric and compositional and analyses of the pottery from Tell Leilan in northern Syria show that pottery was mass-produced by independent specialists based in a relatively large number of non-centralized workshops. This non-centralized nature of ceramic production argues against elite control of pot-making (Stein and Blackman 1993: 55), and probably arose from the fact that the social role of pottery declined in the Early Bronze Age relative to preceding stages of the region's culture, when pottery conveyed more social meanings. The centralized institutions of this period controlled the production of goods such as metals or textiles that were considered essential to maintaining political status. Independent specialists produced a wide variety of utilitarian goods

within the non-elite sectors of the settlement or rural parts close to it. The rural village communities located far from the urban centers in third millennium north Syria exchanged their products with other communities in order to supplement the economy of their villages (Blackman and Stein 1993: 54). The evidence showing the presence of independent craft specialization in both urban and pre-urban settings implies that specialized craft production can occur without any political intervention.

In his work *Social Evolution* (1951: 62), Childe recognized the presence of specialists among some generally self-sufficient pre-urban societies such as those of Neolithic Europe. He saw this kind of pre-urban specialization as a relatively small-scale intensification of skills common to the society. Part-time specialists in this framework worked at their crafts during times they were not following basic subsistence pursuits. Childe (1951: 62) stated that "In the ethnographic record specialists, in the sense of experts who are specially skilled in carving weapons, net-making, potting, or some other craft, have been reported at all economic levels, save the lowest. But generally such are only part-time specialists; they are primarily hunters, or fishers, or farmers, and exercise their special skill not in place of getting their own food directly, but in addition there to, and in return merely for a supplement to the produce of their own labor. Such part-time craft specialists could not be recognized in the archaeological record." This argument was primarily based on ethnographic analogies drawn from part-time pot-makers on the Amphlett islands and pouch-makers on the Trobriands in the Pacific. Childe (1951: 63) inferred from these ethnographic parallels that specialists of the Pacific only worked on their crafts during their spare time, after they had completed the task of obtaining sufficient food. He assumed that prehistoric flint-miners in England and western Europe remained part-time specialists by combining flint-mining activities with cultivating and herding. According to this model, part-time specialists still had to feed themselves through a combination of farming, fishing, herding, and hunting activities, and could only work at their crafts during any time that was available after they had satisfied their subsistence requirement.

Nearly two decades later, Colin Renfrew (1972: 340) also argued in favor of the presence of casual and part-time specialists among Neolithic Aegean village societies. He viewed these specialists as individuals with high levels of technical skill. The products of these Neolithic Aegean craftsmen were classified as specialist-products based on a number of archaeological studies dealing with chipped stone (Perlès 1992), pottery (Vitelli 1989, Kalogirou 1995), and *Spondylus* shells (Miller 1996). For example, C. Perlès (1992) suggests that the majority of lithic production in the early stages of the Neolithic period was specialized. The criteria she adopts are the use of non-local and highly circumscribed sources of raw material, the utilitarian use of most flaked stone tools, the high level of technical expertise needed to produce them, and the large-scale distribution of finished tools to distant areas. The lithic specialists were itinerant knappers, who worked for economic purposes and with minimal social constraints (Perlès 1992: 149). The Neolithic Aegean evidence derived from the lithic studies confirms the existence of independent specialization during non-urban periods in the Aegean. Strategies of specialized production appear to have been determined to a large degree by the social context in which the finished artifact functioned (Perlès and Vitelli 1999: 96). The Neolithic Aegean evidence adds much to our knowledge of specialized production in non-urban environments, because earlier views of this phenomenon were primarily derived from ethnographic analogies or implicit interpretation of available archaeological evidence.

Over recent years, scholars have increasingly begun to recognize the presence of specialist-produced artifacts in non-urban societies. As a consequence, the number of descriptive models has been augmented accordingly (Kenoyer et al. 1991: 44; Hayden 1994: 196; Lewis 1996: 374; Stark 1991: 73). The organization of craft production in non-state or non-urban societies exhibits considerable variation in its structure, hence the wide range of models. Cross (1993) argues that specialist production in small scale societies occurs as highly variable and part-time production with low output, which operates in a non-market system. It is the interpersonal relationship between the part-time specialists and the consumers that maintain such craft activities among early societies (Cross 1993: 64), rather than elite demand for politically desired objects.

A. Domestic versus Specialized Production

Archaeologists studying prehistoric production systems often make a distinction between specialized and domestic craft activities. The organizational context of specialized production differs from that carried out in domestic settings. Domestic production is defined as the manufacture of utilitarian products for personal uses, and consequently, is not oriented towards the acquisition of additional income through exchange (Rice 1987: 184). A single individual often carries out all of the steps involved in domestic production from the extraction of raw materials to the fabrication of the finished product (Sahlins 1972: 77). It is characterized by the use of simple technology, exploitation of locally available raw materials, a relatively poor quality of manufactured goods, and a lack of standardization in the forms of products. Domestic production occurs on a part-time basis during breaks in the agricultural calendar or when specific needs arise. For potters, specific needs could include the replacement of broken pots or a demand for additional pots due to population increase. Lithic producers would need to replace broken blades by knapping cores in their households or courtyards, while textile producers would weave in their households during any spare time left over from their everyday tasks. The lack of motivation oriented towards exchange appears to be a defining criterion that separates domestic production from specialized production, with products being consumed in the household in which they were made.

Domestic production differs from individual-based specialization in which the craftsman derives his or her livelihood solely from craft production, and often has a significant amount of capital invested in tools or raw materials (e.g. kilns and wheels for pot-making) (Rice 1987: 184). Parameters such as labor input, time invested in production, technical elaboration, distribution of finished artifacts, and associations of the products help to distinguish the product of specialized craftsmen from those produced in domestic settings. Individual-based specialized production is organized for exchange, which contrasts to domestic production oriented towards local consumption.

There are cases in which production was carried out by a certain number of autonomous individuals within a single site, who produced goods for unrestricted regional consumption. The cooperation of a group of craftsmen for economic or social reasons is a more complex phenomenon than a production of artifacts for local consumption by single individual. Sahlins (1972: 77) stated that "I do not suggest that the household everywhere is an exclusive work group, and production merely a domestic activity. Local techniques demand more or less cooperation, so production may be organized in diverse social forms, and sometimes at levels higher than the household. Members of one family may regularly collaborate on an individual basis with kith and kin from other houses; certain projects are collectively undertaken by constituted groups such as lineages or village communities."

This kind of a group-based specialization, showing the collaboration of craftsmen, was also identified by Childe as "intercommunal specialization" in his reconstruction of Neolithic society (1951: 63). Childe provides ethnographic evidence by citing the Melanesian pot- and basket-makers who worked at their crafts in addition to tilling their fields and fishing (Childe 1951:63). "Intercommunal specialization" appears to have been classified under part-time specialization in Childe's reconstruction of non-urban European society. Other modes of production observed from the archaeological and ethnographic record that share similarities with intercommunal specialization include "rural nucleated industries" (Peacock 1982: 103), "site specialization" (Rice 1987: 187), "community based-specialization" (Stark 1991; Costin 1991), and "village specialization" (Hayden 1994: 196). Village communities operate independently to produce goods in response to economic, social, or political demands from a variety of resources. Therefore, their products can be utilitarian in character, for broader distribution or symbolic for non-utilitarian use. The specialist-produced crafts are oriented towards the acquisition of additional income through exchange. This kind of specialization was often organized by lineage, kin, or household-based social groups (Rice 1987: 187). Production activities are undertaken on a part-time or seasonal basis that complements agricultural activities. In this production system, craftsmen also utilize local raw materials and elaborate technology, standardize their products and methods of manufacture to be more cost-effective, produce a high density of manufacturing debris, and spatially segregate production within the site.

Community-based specialization often evolves under conditions of unequal resource distribution, especially when individuals or communities lack subsistence resources to sustain themselves (Rice 1981). Earle (1981: 230) explained the presence of independent specialists in non-state societies by a modified formalist perspective derived from Hagget's (1965: 114-35) "central place theory", according to which a specialist producer requires a certain aggregate population that has access to his or her products. The efficiency of production is the primary factor that determines the scale of production (Costin 1991: 15). Thus, an estimation of the number of people involved in production would indicate the scale of production. Estimates of the number of people involved were often determined by the nature of demand. In community-based specialization, the costs are lowered through dividing tasks among many workers and standardizing the forms of artifacts and technology of manufacture.

Because manufacturing debris often tends to be spread throughout a given site, identifying site-specialization in the archaeological record is not an easy task. Indirect evidence employing a number of parameters, however, can help to reconstruct the organizational context of community-based specialization among non-urban societies. In particular, information drawn from studies of similar community-based production systems among remote villages can help establish a framework enabling study of craft activities involving the collaboration of family or kin groups. The comparative ethnographic record indicates that site specialization has been an important component of Anatolian villages. For example, numerous villages located in the Sardis region of central-western Anatolia have been economically dependent upon pot-making for several centuries. Here the villagers maintained their tradition of pot-making for generations to supplement their economy. Pot-making was undertaken solely by women, while men were involved only in the acquisition of the raw materials for tempering (Crane 1988). The villagers produce and exchange large quantities of pottery to meet their households' subsistence needs. A very similar type of site-level specialization production occurs at the Central Anatolian village of Sorgun, where most of the community is involved in pot-making (Steele 1971; Yakar 2000: 122). Pot-making was a long

tradition that was passed down from generation to generation, forming a major part of the economy in the village. The production strategies are to a large degree determined by seasonal, ecological, and cultural conditions, as well as supply and demand conditions. The community produces coarse black cooking ware, with little variability in form, on a very large scale and supplies it to the populations of the region. The distribution of pots produced by these village communities has been undertaken by a middleman. Although the agricultural pursuits play a secondary role for the economy of the village, it has flourished no less than successful farmers. Preparation of flint-blades (Döven) for threshing sledges near the village of Çakmak in northwestern Anatolia also involves much of the community (Bordaz 1959; Weiner 1981). These farmers/specialists work seasonally to supplement their economy during the breaks in the agricultural cycle and to fulfill their own requirements for threshing wheat after the harvest. In a similar way, bead-making out of black amber was practiced in a community level by numerous villages located close to the raw materials in north east Anatolia (Gündoğdu 2004). The Anatolian ethnographic record shows that village-based specialization emerges as an alternative strategy to basic subsistence practices. Similar economic factors probably motivated prehistoric craftsmen to cooperate and fulfill the requirements of their villages.

B. Summary

It is reasonable to infer from the evaluation of the current approaches that craft specialization has become a more complex notion than that discussed by Childe several decades ago. Most models of craft specialization developed since the days of Childe have placed special emphasis upon the causal relationship between craft specialization and political complexity. These models posit craft specialization as a result of increasing social complexity, the formation of social hierarchies, and population growth. Attached specialists working for political elites or institutions (either part- or full-time) were withdrawn from agriculture and supported by agricultural surplus. It is now becoming clear that craft production also occurred in non-urban settings, which was most likely shaped by both economic, social, and symbolic constraints. The common belief is that specialists in pre-urban societies were independent and worked at their crafts during time left over from pursuing basic subsistence activities such as farming, hunting, herding, or fishing. The crafts they manufacture were exchanged for both economical and social reasons on an inter-personal or inter-communal basis. This kind of specialization associated with non-urban contexts was less complex in structure than that of urban societies. As a consequence, it is more difficult to document patterns of the craft activities of pre-urban specialists than that of attached specialists of urban times.

Part Three

THE SITE AND ITS SETTING

An evaluation of the characteristics of the site, its environs, and the region's topographic, climatic, and hydrological features is essential in understanding the environmental context in which the Kulaksızlar marble workshop functioned. This is important because the productive strategies of a certain site often augmented the opportunities that the local environment presents. Non-agricultural production such as stone working is more likely to occur in areas where suitable geological deposits abundantly exist, while the availability of cultivable land, climate, and water supplies would more likely to be utilized for agriculture and supporting populations and craftsmen dependent upon agricultural surplus.

Fig. 3.1. General view of the site from the south (the arrow on the left shows the perennial spring that crossed the site)

The site of Kulaksızlar, which derived its name from a modern village nearby, is located ca. 16 km south of the town of Akhisar in Manisa Province at about 39° 30′ East Longitude, and about 38° 40′ N Latitude. Kulaksızlar was a flat settlement located on a natural rise on the eastern part of the alluvial Selendi plain, at an elevation of 115 m above sea level. The surface of the site slightly undulates towards a perennial spring which flowed across crossed the site in a NW-SE direction during the time of its occupation (Fig. 3.1). It is likely that the site was located in a forested area, implying in an implicit way that agriculture was secondary for the site's economy. This assumption is supported by remnants of original natural vegetation such as pine (*Pinus brutia* and *Pinus nigra*), oak (*Quercus sp.*), and juniper (*juniperus sp.*) trees that are still encountered on the rising mountains, several hundred meters northeast of the site (Hoşgören 1983). The location of the site on the foothills of the mountains is not a common feature for habitation sites, as most prehistoric populations preferred to settle in the alluvial plains. The lower end of the slopes of the hills that face the alluvial plain from the east, however, are well-watered by perennial springs that flow at several hundred meter-intervals from one another.

Because Kulaksızlar was a flat settlement located on a slightly undulating area, erosion has had little negative impact on the site formation process. The lack of post-depositional erosion, combined with the very shallow layer of cultural deposits overlying virgin soil, indicates that the settlement was short-lived. Settlements occupied longer duration have different site formation processes. A thick calcareous incrustation cover (2-4 mm) can be observed on only one side of most marble artifacts. Since its formation takes a very long period of time, the manufacturing debris was more or less *in-situ*. The argument that this site saw a short-term occupation can be supported by the homogeneity in the forms and manufacturing techniques of the pottery documented over the surface of the site. It is unfortunate that our archaeological knowledge about Kulaksızlar is derived entirely from the evaluation of surface finds, since no excavations have been carried out there that would have allowed the association between the manufacturing debris and architectural forms. This need not hinder our evaluation of the data, however, since the clustered distribution pattern of marble artifacts over the surface further supports the inference that geomorphic factors did not alter the archaeological record significantly since the time of habitation. The clustering of different artifact groups in spatially distinct areas within the site usually implies that archaeological finds are close to their original locations. For example, no artifacts representing other major artifact groups such as beakers and figurines were found in the area where the fragments of marble bowl preforms were found. (The spatial distribution of surface finds is discussed in detail in part seven).

Fig. 3.2. Pointed beaker fragments broken during the drilling process

Evaluation of the surface finds provides information about the function of this site. Almost 90 % of the surface finds are marble-working debris. Pottery and food processing implements such as querns, pestles, and handstones, constitute only 10 % of the surface assemblage. In addition to these food processing implements, the recovery of several sling-balls may be viewed as additional archaeological evidence indicating the presence of subsistence activities. The greater quantity of unfinished marble fragments, however, indicates that marble working formed the major part of the site's economy. Agriculture can be envisioned as a complement to marble working. This high ratio of marble artifact to other artifacts groups such as pottery and food processing implements is not documented for other Chalcolithic sites in the region, where survey data from pre-Bronze Age sites reveal pottery as the most dominant artifact group.

A. Natural Environment

The Akhisar region, in which Kulaksızlar is located, is for the most part a limestone-floored graben encircled by mountains rich in metamorphic rocks. The region forms part of a structural landform that has a complex geological history. Tectonic, alluvial, and colluvial movements have had very important effects upon the formation of the geomorphological features of the region that are still visible within the present day landscape. The region, composed of a group of flat plains, lies in a lowland area surrounded by rising mountains. The main line of the relief features of this lowland area began to appear in the middle of the Miocene epoch, at a time when tectonic movements formed grabens in a west-east direction throughout western Anatolia. The Gediz (ancient *Hermos*) River valley was one of the most distinctive of these grabens located in the central part of western Anatolia, lying perpendicular to the coastline after the post-Glacial rise of sea levels worldwide. The resultant transgression formed longer indentations along the coasts of western Anatolia (Erinç 1978). During the Quaternary period, new tectonic movements occurred and the Gediz River settled in the long tectonic depressions. The greater part of the Miocene formation was subsequently eroded and the resultant alluvial and colluvial accumulations formed wide alluvial lowlands, among which the Akhisar region is the most notable. The Selendi plain occupies the southeastern part of this geomorphological feature.

The region is rich in metamorphic, igneous, and sedimentary rocks, and this coexistence of various geological formations offered various alternatives for the populations of the region. The range of naturally occurring rocks could have been used to manufacture items for food processing (e.g. querns, hand-stones, and sickle-blades) or non-utilitarian objects (e.g. marble vessels and figurines). Metamorphic rocks were formed by the transformation and/or crystallization of pre-existing rock due to changes in temperature, pressure, and chemistry. The geological map illustrated in Figure 3.3 shows that marble, a typical metamorphic rock that consists predominantly of calcite and/or dolomite, was rich in the region (Hoşgören 1983). The area that surrounded the village of Kedikuyusu, located about 2 km southeast of the workshop, is the nearest marble source that could have been exploited by the prehistoric Kulaksızlar population. The region was also

rich in igneous rocks, which were formed when molten rocks cooled and solidified. Because their textures are determined by the rate of cooling, igneous rocks are subdivided into two categories: intrusive rocks (or plutonic rocks) and extrusive rocks. Intrusive igneous rocks such as gabbro, radiolarite, and serpentine are present in the area to the northeast of the site of Kulaksızlar. Extrusive igneous rocks (e.g. basalt) are also found abundantly in the form of cobbles within region. These igneous rocks of ophiolite sequence are found to the west of Kulaksızlar. In addition, sedimentary rocks are common in the vicinity of Kulaksızlar. Sandstone is the predominant sedimentary rock in the area, which were formed by the precipitation and subsequent lithification of sand from surface waters, of which quartz was the predominant mineral. The sandstone from this source contains a small amount of calcite. The nearest sandstone source to the site is located along a southeast-northwest band near the villages of Sarıçalı and Kulaksızlar.

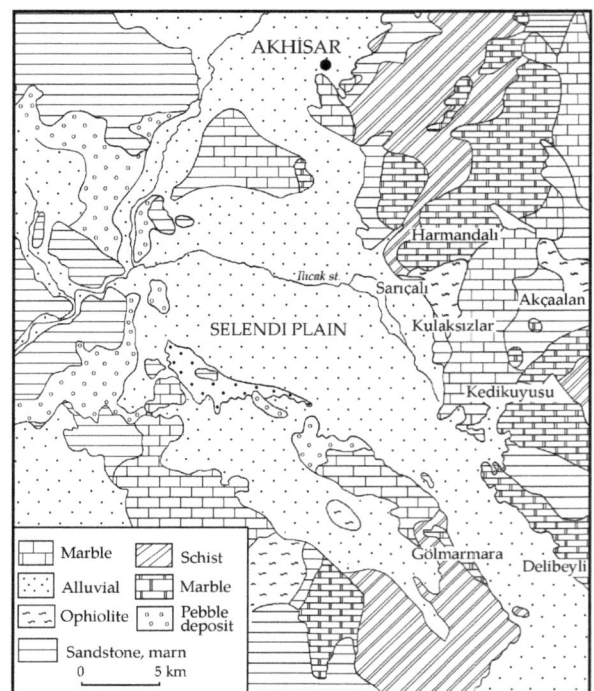

Fig. 3.3. Geologic map of the vicinity of Kulaksızlar

The coexistence of different rock groups within a circumscribed area, in which Kulaksızlar was located, apparently played a major role in the site's economy. Marble, ophiolite sequence rocks, and sedimentary rocks such as sandstone occur abundantly in most parts of the Akhisar region. The natural occurrence of marble, gabbro, basalt, and sandstone on the surface in the immediate vicinity of the site (e.g. in cobbles) probably did not escape the notice of the prehistoric populations living in the region. The area of Kulaksızlar in this sense can be seen as a liminal zone that had easy access to rocks with different chemical and physical properties. The rocks utilized at the workshop were primarily acquired from an area radiating roughly several kilometers from the site.

The fertile alluvial Selendi plain and the slightly sloping terraces of the hills encircling it were also optimal for agriculture due to the mild temperature, the perennial supply of water and the ample rainfall, and the quality of soil. The suitability of the land to farming would have resulted in crop yields that could satisfy the subsistence requirements of pre-Bronze Age population. The present-day villagers benefit from the well-drained alluvial plain and the slightly sloping areas by crop cultivation and horticulture of primarily grapes, olives, tobacco, and wheat (Hoşgören 1983: 73; Günal 1987: 93). The previous patterns of agricultural production probably remained constant for millennia until the introduction of tobacco production in the 1890s. In addition to this dramatic change in land-use strategies, the arrival of Turkish newcomers from Balkan countries as part of a population exchange after the First World War dramatically changed settlement patterns in the region. For example, the site of Moralı ("one from Mora") was resettled in the late 1920s by those newcomers from the Mora Peninsula (Peloponnese) in Greece. The number of settlements and the population of each settlement prior to the introduction of tobacco plantations and the arrival of new peoples were probably similar to those of prehistoric times in the Akhisar region. The number of pre-1890s villages in the area with an economy based on wheat cultivation (İzdem 1944) appears to have been similar to the pre-Bronze Age one documented through archaeological surveys covered in this dissertation. It is noteworthy that an Ottoman document dating to 1531 mentions the presence of seventeen villages in the Akhisar region (Satış 1994), a number that is very similar to that of pre-Bronze Age ones documented during the surveys.

Climate was another factor that conditioned prehistoric production systems. The climate of the Akhisar region is currently a dry semi-continental variant of the Mediterranean climate, or forms a transition between Mediterranean and temperate continental (Mesothermal) climates (Hoşgören 1983: 50). Remnant floral groups such as pine trees and juniper also suggest a Mediterranean climate, with rainy winters and hot dry summers. It is unfortunate that no paleoclimatic data such as pollen studies exist for the region in which prehistoric populations lived. The mean temperature is 16 ° C, the area today receives an average annual precipitation of 610 mm. Rainfall currently varies seasonally, with the maximum rain falling in winter and spring. In addition to the high amount of direct rainfall, water from the hill slopes also accumulates in the alluvial plain. If we accept that the climate and the rainfall regime in the Chalcolithic period was very similar to that of the present-day, then one may argue that the climatic conditions complemented an agricultural way of life in the region.

B. Material Culture

The Akhisar region was one of the most heavily populated areas of prehistoric western Anatolia. The region occupied a key point along a natural trade route that tied the western Anatolian coast with the hinterland (Mellaart 1964: 4; Meriç 1993: 146; Takaoğlu 2004a). Because no excavations have so far been carried out in the Akhisar region, the cultural sequence is archeologically very little known. Surface surveys identified fifteen sites with pre-Bronze Age pottery (French 1961, 1965, and 1969; Dinç 1996b). Of these fifteen, twelve are mounds situated on alluvium, while the remaining three are represented by two low mounds and one flat settlement on higher ground in the foothills. These mounds are composed primarily of anthropogenic sediments rather than being natural hillocks on the plain. The small number of flat sites recorded is in part due to their burial by alluvial sediments. Since most archaeologists looked for mound sites that were easily visible on the surface, many flat settlements with a short period of occupation were probably ignored as they are difficult to detect archaeologically. The discovery of flat settlements such as Kulaksızlar has tended to occur purely by chance. The accumulation of thick alluvial deposits in the plains of Akhisar resulted in the partial burial of a number of Late Neolithic or Early Chalcolithic mounds, including large mound settlements such as Moralı and Kayışlar. The available surface pottery from the pre-Bronze settlements illustrated in Figure 3.4 indicates that the Akhisar region was settled as early as the Late Neolithic period. Sites such as Moralı, Nuriye Arpalı II, Alibeyli, and Kayışlar yielded monochrome pottery, characterized predominantly by lustrously burnished thin-walled jars and bowls with curved sides and vertically placed tubular lugs. Their surfaces were coated with red, buff, or crimson color wash, which was then very finely burnished. Dissimilarities evident in the surface color apparently occurred due to the variations in the firing temperatures (French 1965: 18 and 1969: 47). Moreover, several sherds of red-on-cream painted pottery were also found at Moralı and Kayışlar (e.g. French 1965: fig. 5.4 and 1969: fig. 8.2). This type of painted pottery also finds its closest parallels in the pot-making tradition of Lakes District in southwest Anatolia (Mellaart 1970: 101).

The homogeneity of the fabric, shapes, and the manufacturing techniques of the monochrome pottery demonstrate that a local Late Neolithic/Early Chalcolithic culture existed in the Akhisar region. Because the shapes and the surface treatment of the monochrome burnished pottery can be viewed as contemporary to that of the Lakes Distict in southwest Anatolia. This may be the result of a parallel development based on the pottery tradition of the Lakes District. The Neolitihic villages of the Akhisar region developed their own Neolithic tradition based primarily upon that of the Lakes District of the southwest Turkey, characterized by the excavated sites of Hacılar, Bademağacı, Höyücek, and Kuruçay. However, whether the Neolithic culture was introduced fully developed from the Lakes District or it was a result of a local line of development with roots in the earlier periods remains unclear. The arrival of elements from the Lakes District into the Akhisar region is not surprising since was attested as far away as at the eastern Aegean islands such as Chios and Imbros (Duru 1999; Hood 1981: 15; Harmankaya and Erdoğu 2003: 464) and at the Thracian sites such as Hoca Çeşme and Hamaylıtarla (Özdoğan 1999: 217; Erdoğu 2000: 162). The widespread distribution of this distinctive ware peculiar to the Lakes District in southwest Anatolia clearly shows the complex level of cultural interactions during these periods. Although elements of the Lakes District in southwestern Anatolia were very evident in the Akhisar region, surface finds imply that the societies occupying areas on the fringes of the Neolitic culture zone of the Lakes District came in casual contact with that of the Neolithic Fikirtepe culture of the Marmara Region For example, the report of a footed rectangular vessel fragment with incised decoration at Moralı, peculiar to Fikirtepe culture, (Dinç 1996b: fig. 20) shows that the early populations of the region also interacted with the cultures of northwest Anatolia. In addition, the occurrence of Melian obsidian blades at Moralı (Renfrew et. al. 1968: 226) reveals the coexistence of maritime and land-based long distance exchange during the Late Neolithic and Early Chalcolithic periods.

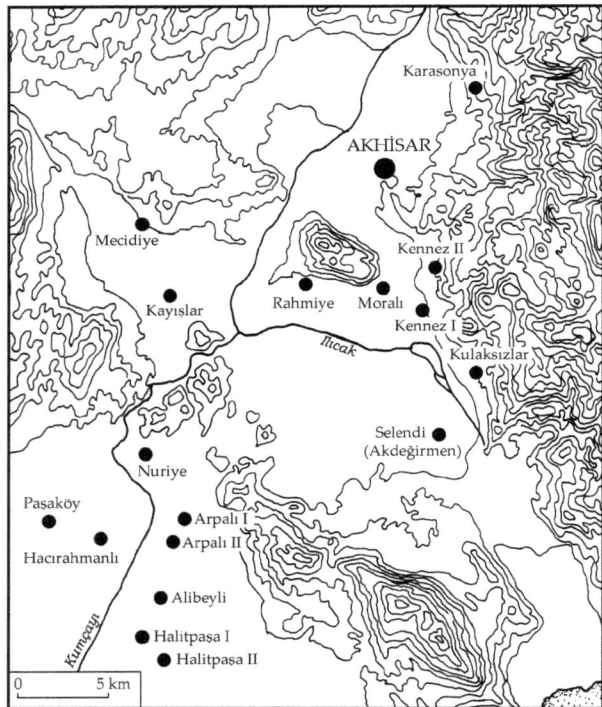

Fig. 3.4. Major pre-Bronze age sites in the Akhisar region (on the basis of available surface data)

Although the cultural boundaries between the Neolithic cultural traditions of the Lakes Districts of the southwest and Fikirtepe culture of the Marmara region cannot be established with certainty, the area covering roughly the Akhisar region, coastal strip of western Turkey, and adjacent eastern Aegean islands can be viewed another cultural zone with its own right, in the formation of which cultural interactions and exchange played significant roles (Takaoglu 2004b). With material culture sharing similarities with both of the Lakes District and the Marmara region, Moralı, Kayışlar, Nuriye, Alibeyli, and Arpalı II remain important sites illustrating the nature of Neolithic culture in the Akhisar region. The acquaintance with the cultural assemblages of the Lakes District to the southeast and the Fikirtepe culture of northwest Anatolia highlights the importance of the strategic location of the Akhisar region for the arrival of foreign elements and ideas. Regardless of multi-directional contact, however, the impact of southwest Anatolia on the formation of the Late Neolithic/Early Chalcolithic tradition in the Akhisar region is evidently much stronger than any other region.

Site	LN	EC	MC	LC	Location + size
Moralı	●	●			in the plain (150 m x 3 m)
Kayışlar	●	●		●	on a natural ridge (80 x 4 m)
Nuriye	●	?			on a natural ridge (90 x 4 m)
Alibeyli	●			●	in the plain (80 m x 6 m)
Arpalı II	●	?		●	in the plain (80 m x 3 m)
Arpalı I				●	on a sloping ground (80 x 6m)
Kulaksızlar			●		on the foothills (120 m x 1 m)
Karasonya				●	in the plain (80 m x 2 m)
Selendi			?	●	in the plain (?) Destroyed
Rahmiye				●	in the plain (80 m x 3 m)
Kennez II				●	on a natural (ridge 50 x 3m)
Mecidiye				●	in the plain (100 m x 5 m)
Hacırahman				●	in the plain (80 m x 4 m)
Halitpaşa II				●	in the plain (90 m x 3 m)
Paşaköy				●	in the plain (90 m x 4 m)

Table 3.1. Temporal tabulation of the sites in the Akhisar region (on the basis of available surface pottery)

An increase in settlement numbers appears to have occurred from Late Neolithic/Early Chalcolithic (five) to Late Chalcolithic (thirteen). Only three of those mounds with early pottery provided evidence showing their reoccupation during the Late Chalcolithic period (Table 3.1). Late Chalcolithic populations of the region looked towards the northwest for ideas rather than southwest as their Late Neolithic and Early Chalcolithic predecessors did. In terms of pottery, it seems that each village society of the region had its own potters and particular tradition, within the general ceramic tradition of western Anatolia, which is characterized by hand-made and grit tempered pottery. The lack of standardization in the forms of the pots, the lack of technical investment, the poor quality of firing, and the low volume of output seems to indicate that the pottery of this period resulted from non-specialized household production. Although local imitations of exported pottery may have led to the diffusion of elements related to pot-making outside of their area of manufacture, there were individualistic traits that were peculiar to the pot-making in the Akhisar region. Beycesultan type pottery, which is a regional subgroup that characterizes the Late Chalcolithic period in southwest Anatolia, has rarely been documented at the sites of the Akhisar region so far, except several examples representing painted pottery found at

Kayışlar near Kulaksızlar (Lloyd and Mellaart 1962: 109). Conversely, thirteen mounds in the Akhisar region yielded Kumtepe 1b type pottery, which is a distinct pottery group that defines the later stages of the Late Chalcolithic period of northwest Anatolia. The Kumtepe 1b type pottery is a regional subgroup characterized by handmade, smooth, black-burnished bowls with rolled rims (Renfrew 1972: 162; Yakar 1985: 123). This pottery tradition differs from the Late Neolithic/Early Chalcolithic one in terms of manufacturing techniques, shapes, and the surface treatment. The widespread presence of the distinctive Kumtepe 1b pottery in the Akhisar region can be accepted as evidence tho show that there was a large cultural interaction sphere that encompassed northwestern Anatolia and the Akhisar region in central-western Anatolia.

The shift in focus from southwest to northwestern Anatolia may provide a reason for the cultural gap between the Late Neolithic/Early Chalcolithic and Late Chalcolithic periods. Middle Chalcolithic pottery evidence that would fill the gap is scarce in the Akhisar region, as in many parts of western Anatolia during this period. This incompleteness of the Chalcolithic sequence, combined with the difference between the material cultures of the early and late periods of the western Anatolian Chalcolithic confirms the presence of an intermediate phase in the Akhisar region. This problem will probably not be solved until one of the mounds n the Akhisar region is excavated. Kulasızlar remains one of the most likely sites to fill the gap between the Early and Late Chalcolithic periods, since its pottery strikingly does not share similarities with those of the Late Chalcolithic sites. The evidence from Late Chalcolithic period reveals the coexistence of two different modes of production each driven by different socio-economic motives. The first mode concerns the production and distribution of utilitarian goods such as pots and lithics, which formed an essential component of the local economy. The second mode of production involves prestige goods, such as metal artifacts, shells, stone beads, and stone artifacts. The motivation behind the production of these prestige artifacts was probably not only economic but also social and political in nature. It is unlikely that the agricultural communities of the region also invested a great amount of time and energy in direct long-distance trade. Uneven distribution of prestige or exotic artifacts among the village communities of this period appears to correspond to that associated with indirect trade. The production and exchange strategies prevailing during the Late Chalcolithic period might have been different than that of the Middle Chalcolithic period. Thus, what we can learn about the production, exchange and use involving the Kulaksızlar marble working is of great archaeological significance in reconstructing the nature of cultures that prevailed in western Anatolia during this poorly understood transitional stage of the Chalcolithic period (See the section on pottery in chapter four).

C. Summary

Evaluation of the site in its natural and cultural contexts provides a useful picture of prehistoric human activity in the region. Both natural and cultural factors were suitable for a small community like Kulaksızlar to concentrate on stone working since they could use the raw materials at hand and take advantage of the cultural interactions occurred during the site's occupation. The natural environment was productive because it provided opportunities for pursuing both agricultural and non-agricultural production. The Kulaksızlar people preferred to settle in a location that differed from contemporary settlements. The abundance of geologic deposits on the foothills juxtaposed with fertile land and stream beds made this locality attractive to Kulaksızlar people. It seems likely that they were specialized in marble working from the outset rather than changing from agriculture to marble working. The access to rich metamorphic, igneous, and sedimentary rocks in the region apparently played a major role in adopting a non-agricultural production strategy. The fertile soil and the year-round water supplies generated by these perennial springs on the lower ends of the slopes of the hills could have enabled the population to fulfill their subsistence needs in addition to marble working or could have supported craftsmen withdrawn from agricultural activities. This is probably why most Chalcolithic sites occurred in the alluvial plain or on the low ridges encircling it.

Geography was another factor that played a major role in the development of the site's economy. The Akhisar region was located on a land-based trade route running between the western coast and hinterland of Anatolia and another that reached to the region of Troad in the northwest. We know from an evaluation of the surface finds that the populations of the region benefited from the strategic location on the trade routes as early as the Neolithic period (Meriç 1993: 146), and this seems to have continued down to the Late Chalcolithic period and later. The Kulaksızlar pottery proves that the later stages of the Middle Chalcolithic also existed in this geographically important region. A noticeable increase occurred in the number of settlements from the Early Chalcolithic to the Late Chalcolithic period. Changes observed in the cultural assemblages and settlement numbers in the region probably resulted from increasing intensity of cultural interactions and the arrival of newcomers from the north during this poorly understood Middle Chalcolithic period. The cultural interaction zone at this early stage of the Chalcolithic period was comprised of an area that extended as far as the eastern Aegean islands. Kulaksızlar evidence indicates that whatever happened during the Middle Chalcolithic period had caused significant changes during the culturally important Late Chalcolithic period. Therefore, the opportunities provided by the environment, combined with region's strategic location on the natural trade routes, probably stimulated these changes and led to the diversification of and search for alternative economic strategies.

Part Four

SURFACE ASSEMBLAGE

The aim of this part is to present a synthesis of the surface finds and to describe the survey methodology adopted in their documentation and collection. This part is divided into four parts accordingly. The first section explains the methodology used in recording the density and concentration of the surface finds and the methods applied in their collection. The second section provides a general description of the main marble products of the workshop, which are classified into two categories, stone vessels (beakers and bowls) and Kilia figurines on the basis of the analysis of finished and unfinished fragments. The third section describes the stone tools that were used in the manufacture of marble vessels and figurines. Terms such as percussive, abrasive, and polisher are assigned to the stone tools according to the function that they are believed to have served. The use-wear patterns observed on these stone tools, and their functional categorization, are used to reconstruct the various sequences of production and craftsmen's tool use. The final section describes the surface pottery. Evaluation of basic pottery features such as shape, fabric, decoration, and manufacturing techniques enables reconstruction of the cultural and chronological affiliations of the site, allowing Kulaksızlar to be placed within the broader framework of western Anatolian cultural history.

A. Survey Method

The archaeological materials utilized in this study are primarily derived from surface studies carried out at Kulaksızlar during the summers of 1994, 1995, and 1999. The first two survey studies were undertaken by a team under the leadership of Rafet Dinç from the Adnan Menderes University in Turkey (Dinç 1996a, 1996b). Preliminary analysis of the material remains from these two survey studies raised a number of questions regarding the organization of production and the methods involved in marble working. With the permission of the *Department of Antiquities and Museums*, I re-surveyed the site and its environs in the summer of 1999 obtaining as much information as possible to address these questions. Rafet Dinç kindly accompanied me during the 1999 surface study to discuss the problems of interpreting such the task of comparing and combining the results obtained from all three surveys. The methodology used in the collection of surface finds in the workshop area was straightforward. The creation of a contour map of the study area was the first step in the study of the density and concentration of artifacts and the relationships of different artifact groups to one another. For this purpose, the area was divided into twenty by twenty meter squares using a Total Station and the NetCAD mapping program. In order to record the concentration and frequency of the fragments of marble vessels,

figurines, stone tools, and pottery over the surface, each find was plotted on a large contour map (Figs. 4.1 and 4.2). Once all of the artifacts had been mapped, 50 % of the specimens were collected for analysis; the other half of the artifacts were left in the field, although they were inspected for information relating to the sequence of production. This recovery procedure consisted of maintaining a basic count of all material recovered from the collection units. The amount of time required for walking, plotting, and collecting the diagnostic specimens varied according to the density of artifacts in the squares, but on average, nearly two hours were necessary for a single individual to document, plot, and collect the surface finds from a single square. Together, the three seasons of surveys, covering an area of approximately 200 x 300 m, yielded almost two thousand specimens representing the multiple stages of production of marble vessels and figurines, stone tools, and pot sherds.

The artifacts related to marble working consist largely of manufacturing rejects together with stone tools used in the production of figurines and vessels. Almost 90% of the marble assemblage is represented by pieces discarded due to manufacturing errors that occurred during flaking, pecking, and drilling. The remaining 10% of the entire marble assemblage include finished products or those broken during the final stage of manufacturing, commonly termed is the refinement process. The breakage pattern observed on these faulty or discarded pieces is very useful in reconstructing the sequences of marble vessel and figurine production and the craftsmen's tool use. Considering that the site measures only 200 x 300 meters, and the time spent in surveying the site was limited, the 2000 artifacts collected form a representative sample. A precise statistical study of the collected surface finds collected and those left in the field is a very difficult task to carry out. Only a rough estimate of the percentage of certain artifact groups within the site can be calculated, because the number of available surface artifacts is a portion of entire debris generated in marble working. The basic count of the surface finds collected from three seasons of survey indicates that fragments of marble vessels and figurines quantitatively dominate the total surface assemblage (ca. 1400 pieces, 72%). Stone tools constitute 17% of the surface assemblage with 330 pieces, including tools used in flaking, pecking, and drilling, and smoothing works. Pottery forms the smallest group, constituting only 11% of the assemblage with 220 pieces. The majority of the marble artifacts (ca. 900 specimens) demonstrate various stages of Kilia figurine production from the initial stages to the end product. The pointed beaker form is represented by 400 and pointed bowls are represented by 120 diagnostic specimens.

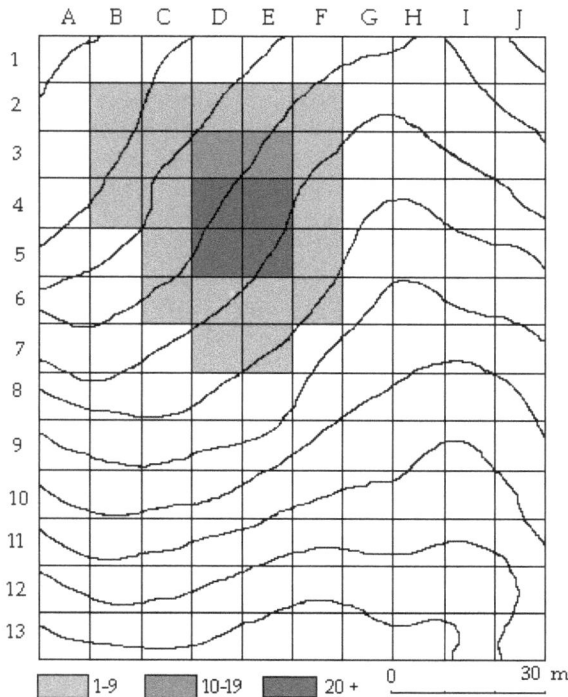

Fig. 4.1. Map showing the surface density of pottery fragments over the surface of the site

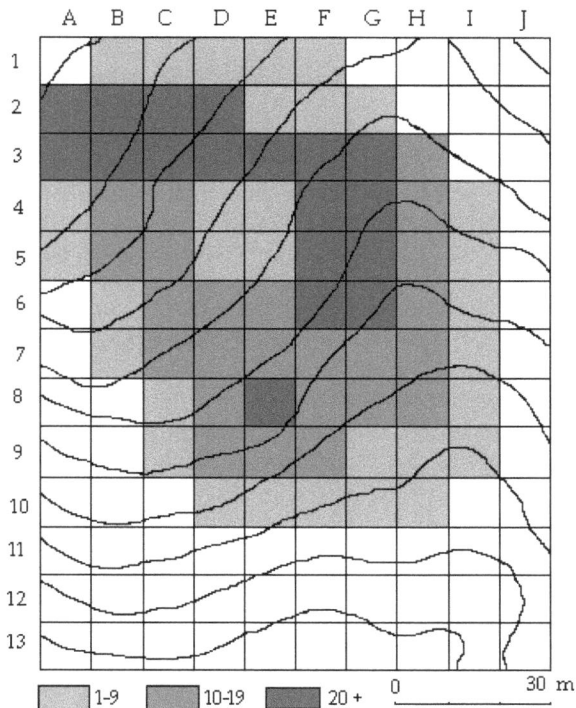

Fig. 4.2. Map showing the surface density of marble finds over the surface of the site

B. Main Marble Products of the Workshop

No complete finished artifacts were found on the surface, probably due to their burial through cultural or natural processes or their removal from the workshop for exchange. The main products of the workshop, however, can be identified on the basis of debris and unfinished pieces. Based on morphology and function, the preform fragments documented among the surface assemblage permit the identification of two major classes of artifacts: vessels and figurines (Fig. 4.3). Marble vessels are further subdivided into types as pointed beakers and bowls with pointed bases. Pieces that belong to different vessel forms, such as flat-based bowls and globular jars, also occur in very small quantities among the marble assemblage, but are not included in this classification.

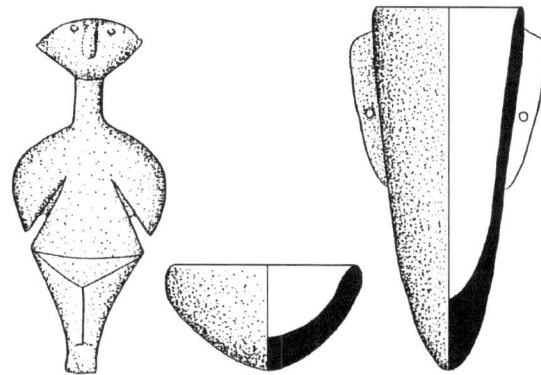

Fig. 4.3. Three major marble products of the workshop

1. Pointed Beakers

The Kulaksızlar beaker has a conical shape with two opposed vertical lugs on the upper part of the body. These vertically elongated lugs are pierced so that the vessels may be suspended. Finished examples show that the rims of pointed beakers were plain, but the majority of rim, base, and wall fragments are found in an unfinished state, confirming that this site was a manufacturing locus. This conclusion is further supported by the fact that the exteriors of many unfinished pointed beaker fragments have flaking, pecking, drilling, or rubbing marks. An examination of stylistic and productive attributes of nearly four hundred diagnostic specimens shows that almost 20 % of the manufacturing errors occurred during the flaking and pecking process before drilling began. In other words, nearly one fifth of the marble beaker fragments are represented by defective and discarded upper halves and lower ends of roughed-out pointed beakers indicative of the initial stages of production. The majority of 400 diagnostic specimens (75 %) are represented by rejected rim fragments with finely pecked exteriors and roughly shaped vertical lugs, wall fragments with downward sloping angles, and lower-end fragments with hollowed out interiors. All of these fragments have horizontal lines of rotary drilling on their interiors. The remaining 5% are represented by rim fragments with very thin walls, which belong to the final stages of refinement. Unfinished beaker fragments appear to display a pattern of clustering over the surface. Roughed-out beaker fragments concentrated in an area covered by squares A-B, 2-3. Conversely, the fragments of pointed beakers bearing traces of drilling, rubbing, and smoothing are predominantly found in squares F-G and 3-6.

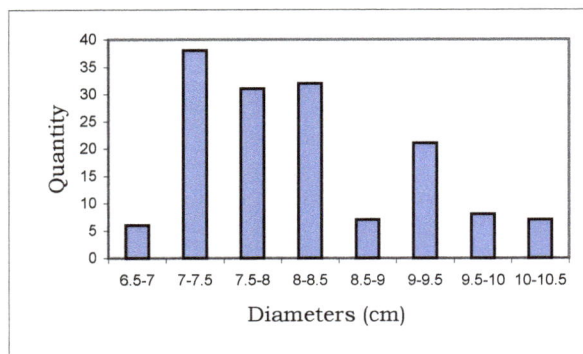

Figure 4.4. Quantitative distribution of diameters of 160 roughed-out pointed beakers

Most of the beaker fragments represent manufacturing errors that occurred either during the rough shaping of the marble (Pls. 1-2) or while the beaker preform was being drilled (Pls. 3-9). For instance, Figure 3.2 illustrates a pile of marble pointed beaker fragments that were broken during drilling. Almost all the manufacturing errors of beakers found in the squares F-G and 4-6 have the horizontal marks of rotary drilling on their interiors.The area in which these manufacturing errors were found also yielded a great amount of sandstone drill-bits with varying diameters. The coexistence of sandstone drill-bits with marble vessel fragments exhibiting drilling marks shows that an area covering squares F-G, 3-6 was the locus where the hollowing out of vessels took place. A metrical examination of the pointed beaker preforms highlights a considerable standardization in the rim diameters, with the majority falling between 7.0 and 8.5 cm. Some of the roughed-out pointed beakers appear to have been rather elongated in shape, while the others display more visually balanced proportions in terms of the ratio of rim diameter to height. Such variability was probably determined by the size of the raw marble blocks or the secondary use of manufacturing errors.

2. Pointed Bowls

Open-shaped bowls with pointed bases constitute the second major vessel form that was manufactured at the Kulaksızlar workshop. The vessel is shaped into a short cone with a conical interior that generally follows the exterior contour of the vessel. The shape is simple and the rims are always plain. 120 bowl specimens representing all stages of production from the coarse flaking to the finished product were documented during the three seasons of survey. Most of the marble fragments are found in an unfinished state and had

either flaking or pecking marks on their exteriors. It is noteworthy that the interiors of these preforms were slightly chipped out to facilitate placement of the drill-bits. These roughly-shaped bowls were concentrated in square E8 and its surrounding area. In this area alone, I noted over twenty roughed-out bowls without marks of rotary drilling. Several of the 120 roughed out bowls were longitudinally broken, whereas others were broken at the top while the interior was being chipped out (Pl. 10). In grids F5, G5, and G6, I documented a group of similar preforms with drill marks on their interiors (e.g. Pls. 11-12), associated with beaker fragments with rotary drilling marks. The small number of bowls (120 specimens) suggests that they were fashioned with lower frequency than the pointed beakers. Bowls constituted only about 20% of the marble working.

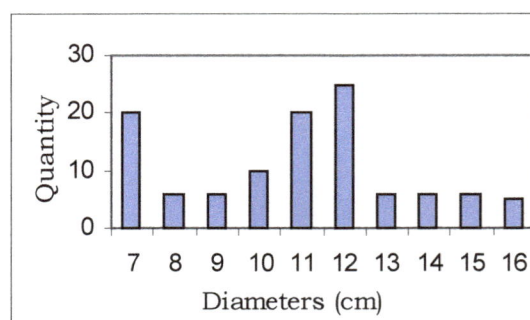

Fig. 4.5. Quantitative distribution of diameters of 120 roughed-out pointed bowls

The bowls with pointed bases do not display much stylistic variability. Metric analysis of roughed-out bowl diameters shows that the majority vary in width from 7 cm to 16 cm, although a few fragments have rim diameters as large as 40 cm. Bowls with diameters of 7, 11, and 12 cm seems to be manufactured more frequently than the other sizes. The size of the vessel was probably determined by the intended function of the final product or resulted from reworking of roughed-out bowls that were broken as the interior was chipped out. Pointed bowls with a rim diameter of 40 cm might have served a special function rather than being used in domestic settings for utilitarian purposes. This is supported by the fact that pointed bowls of such large sizes could not stand independently.

3. Kilia Figurines

This type of figurine derives its name from the site of Kilia in the Gallipoli Peninsula, where the first example was identified (Schmidt 1902; Caskey 1972). Kilia figurines demonstrate very fine craftsmanship with well balanced proportions and stylized anatomical details that show slight variations (Pls. 20-21). They are characterized by large heads, which contrast with a thin flat body. The cylindrical neck is delicate and broad shoulders slope in graceful curves ending abruptly at the elbows. The arms are sharply bent at the elbows and point upwards. These bent arms are separated from the torso by oblique incisions. The feet are also separated either by a slender cleft or by a superficial incision. Features such as eyes, nose, and ears are often indicated by raised projections. A broad pubic triangle is also emphasized by incision. The presence of the incised pubic triangle in most finished examples suggests that a female deity was embodied in the figurine. Unfinished figurine fragments such as the blanks, preforms, and manufacturing errors are primarily found in squares C-D, 2-3. The presence of countless flakes suggests that the manufacture of Kilia figurines took place in this area. The minimal number of marble artifacts representing beaker and bowl manufacture in this locus further supports the conclusion that marble figurine production occurred around squares C-D, 2-3.

A metrical study of finished figurines, based on data obtained from a comparison of fragmentary figurines with complete ones, allows the variability in height to be estimated. The height of the figurines varies from 7 cm to 23 cm. It is likely that the sizes of the figurines were determined to a large extent by the nature of demand, the cost of transportation, their function, or the skill of the craftsmen. The reworking of misformed pieces also led to variability in the height of the figurines. In order to be cost effective, the preforms broken during the sculpting of the delicate necks were reworked to produce smaller figurines. This is demonstrated by the greater quantity of head fragments, which are useless after breakage, relative to manufacturing errors representing the lower parts of figurines.

C. Stone Tools

Stone tools form an important component of the Kulaksızlar surface assemblage, emphasizing the presence of production activities and helping to reconstruct the methods of marble working. The marble working debris contains nearly three hundred stone tools used in almost all steps of manufacture, ranging from hand-hammers to polishers. The use-wear patterns observed on these stone tools indicate that they were employed in various ways for activities such as pounding, flaking, pecking, drilling, and rubbing. I provide a general description of each category of stone tool found in the manufacturing debris in relation to their morphological characteristics and the use-wear or patterns of damage found upon them. I assign names to these stone tools according to the functions that they may have served in marble working.

1. Percussors

A group of distinctive stone hand tools was identified from among the surface assemblage. These tools, used in percussive works, were made from cobbles of rocks that belong to the ophiolite sequence, such as gabbro, basalt, and serpentine. The most common rock used for percussive works at the workshop was gabbro, which is a coarse grained igneous plutonic rock that solidified under great pressure at considerable depths in the earth's crust. It is mostly composed of calcium-rich plagioclase feldspar, proxene, and olivine, all of which give gabbro a dark green to black color. Basalt, a fine-grained equivalent of gabbro, is also used for percussive works. Basalt is formed when mafic lava flows cooled at the Earth's surface. Richness in ferromagnesian minerals makes basalt and gabbro very hard and hence effective for percussive actions. Such tools can be classified as hammerstones since they range in size from 5-14 cm making them fit neatly in the palm. They can be subdivided into two groups on the basis of physical criteria. The first group comprises the percussive tools that are spherical in shape, which were most probably preferred for coarse flaking actions such as the forming of vessel and figurines blanks. These spherical tools (e.g. **135-142**) have working marks all over their surface and were located among the manufacturing debris (Pls. 22 and 39). Because gabbro and basalt do not flake off with a true conchoidal structure, the use-wears observed on these stone tools have a flat appearance.

The second group of percussive tools consists of hammerstones that are rather elongated in shape. Some of these hammerstones with pointed ends seem to have been retouched. These hand tools were probably used for finer working such as removing the flake scars and detailing the outlines of intended shapes through pecking. The pointed tool marks observed on many preforms definitely indicate the use of such tools. Working scars often occur on the narrow ends of the tools. Such tools have been identified on the surface.

2. Abrasives

Quartzitic sandstone was the predominant raw material used for abrasive work such as drilling and rubbing. Because sandstone consists of inclusions such as quartz particles, the drill-bits fashioned out of this rock are effective in pulverizing the interiors of vessels. Drill-bits found at the site can typologically be divided into two major classes: crescent-shaped and conical drill-bits (Pls. 23 and 24). The variation in the shapes of sandstone drill-bits was due the function they served. Most of the vessels manufactured at the workshop have conical outlines, requiring Kulaksızlar craftsmen to use a series of drill-bits with varying diameters and shapes to hollow out a cavity that followed the external contours of the marble vessels. As a consequence, metric and typological variations in these drill-bits were determined by the shape of the marble vessel to be hollowed out. All of these conical and crescent-shaped drill-bits have bevels on their proximal ends for attachment to the drill shaft. The tops of the drill-bits vary in diameter from 2 cm to 9.5 cm, although larger ones approaching 15 cm in diameter were also found. Those drill-bits falling into the conical category are either pointed or flat at their distal ends. Cavities are documented on the lower ends of several drill-bits. The raised projections observed on the bottom of vessel interiors (e.g. **15**, Pl. 4) were evidently created by these cavities. Besides drill-bits, sandstone was also the preferred material for the refining process, such as removing the flaking and pecking marks and thinning of the vessels' walls. Drill-bits that became useless for drilling actions were probably split into pieces and used to thin out the interiors of the vessels or to shape the anatomical details of figurines. There are several bifacial sandstone blocks of rectangular or irregular shapes that might have been used for refinement. Flat pieces of sandstone were most likely used in figurine manufacture. The figurines were evidently rubbed back and forth on these flat abrasives to create a thin body. Some of these blocks are slightly concave, suggesting their use in removing percussion marks on the roughed-out vessels.

Sandstone probably was not the only rock used for abrasive works. Several emery (corrundum) blocks of rectangular or trapezoidal shape are also attested among the surface finds (Pl. 41). These specimens, which are greenish-gray in color, may have come from the area surrounding the village of Akçaalan, where the *General Directorate of Mineral Research and Exploration* recently identified a rich deposit of emery. The minimal presence of emery (hardness 9) at the site is striking in view of the fact that it is a more effective abrasive on marble than sandstone (hardness 7). The scarcity of emery on the surface in the immediate vicinity of the workshop (e.g. in the form of cobbles) was probably the major reason for its minimal use in marble working.

3. Polishers

The final steps of figurine and vessel manufacture probably required a fine smoothing process to create a suitable finish. The use of sandstone blocks to rub vessels and figurines often leaves vertical and diagonal scratch marks on the marble, due to the presence of quartz particles in the sandstone. Marble river-pebbles collected from the banks of the Ilıcak stream nearby could have been used to smooth out these marks. Indeed, over twenty marble river-pebbles with signs of use-wear were found at the site. Most of these marble-pebble smoothers were found in squares F5 and G5-6. These archaeological finds are easily distinguished from regular river-pebbles by the use-wear marks such as a polished surface, scratch marks, and facets. The maximum lengths of these marble river-pebbles range from 6 cm to 13.5 cm. Several of these polishers are unifacial with use-wear on only one side, while several others display bifacial use-wear (Pl. 41). Among the polishing tools, two specimens possess distinctive scratching marks running in multiple directions. River pebbles were probably not the only smoothers used in the polishing of vessels and figurines. Organic materials such as leather could have also been utilized by the craftsmen, but this is difficult to document archaeologically and requires complex research involving the functional analysis of organic residues on the finished artifacts.

4. Chipped Stone

Nearly fifty chipped stone tools with diagnostic working marks were collected during the surveys. This small assemblage consists mainly of blades, flakes, awls, and cores. The most common material is flint, which occurs locally in a wide range of colors including bluish-gray, honey-brown, and creamy-white. The lack of homogeneity in their physical properties and colors shows that there was not a single flint source that craftsmen depended upon. A number of cores documented during the surface studies confirm that knapping of flint cobbles took place at the site. Blades are the predominant tools among the chipped stone artifacts. They are regular in shape and produced by direct percussion. Most of the complete blades range from 3 cm to 6 cm in length. Blades show no sign of standardization in manufacturing techniques, owing to the use of materials with different knapping properties. The maximum thickness at the bulb of percussion is usually 0.5 cm. The presence of use-wear along their cutting edges may be an indication that they were used for scraping or incision. Flint awls are poorly represented by only one complete tool and a number of fragmentary pieces. The use wear on the pointed end of the awl shows that it was used in a rotary motion, perhaps for the piercing of the vertical lugs. An examination of drilling marks on the lugs of beakers verifies the use of awls to pierce holes from both sides, because the holes produced on these lugs are slightly biconical in shape.

5. Other Grinding Tools

Twenty specimens of querns, hand-grinders, and pestles were recorded during the survey studies. Most of these implements are predominantly fashioned from the locally available reddish-yellow sandstone and reddish-brown and bluish-gray schist. Schist and sandstone occur in the seasonal stream beds that are located just north of the site. These implements are primarily found in squares D4, D5, E4, and E5 (Fig. 4.2). Querns, which are slabs of stone with at least one grinding surface, are usually concave in longitudinal profile and plano-convex in cross-section. They are the most common of the grinding implements. Kulaksızlar querns are either ovate or rectangular in outline with hemispherical sections (Pl. 42).

The working surfaces of the querns tend to be smooth and to some degree concave, with the use-wear observed on their surface resulting from a number of operations such as food processing, sharpening of tools, or flattening of the finely pecked figurines. The hand-stones found at the site are generally rectangular in outline, although complete examples were documented. Several pestles made out of schist have also been documented. They taper towards the end and is approximately round in cross section. The presence of such grinding implements is most likely an evidence of food processing on the site.

D. Pottery and the relative chronology of the site

Examining the shapes, fabric, and manufacturing techniques of the pottery is important to determine the chronological and cultural affiliations of the site within the wider framework of western Anatolian cultural history. The limitations in working with unstratified pottery become apparent as all of our archaeological knowledge about the pottery of the Akhisar region comes from surface collections, which gives only a vague idea of the cultural and chronological sequences of the region. Kulaksızlar pottery finds its closest parallels in the Troad in northwestern Anatolia and the eastern Aegean islands such as Samos, Chios, and Kalymnos. The lack of similar pottery from the sites of the Izmir region, an intermediate zone among these sub-regions, probably results from the minimal number of excavations conducted there.

The Kulaksızlar pottery appears to be relatively homogeneous in character, and is predominantly handmade and dark surfaced. The homogeneity is particularly evident in the fabric of the clay. Pottery with an olive gray-black fabric and a poor, dark burnished surface comprises the majority of the assemblage. The surface is chiefly dark faced, though the coloring ranges from full-black through shades of olive gray. The mottling observed on the surface of a number of sherds must have derived from the uncontrolled temperature of the firing and the degree of the tempering material included in the clay. There are also brownish-red and orange-brown sherds, which had no apparent differences in fabric to the other sherds. These variations may be due to uneven firing, which caused a difference in color between the core and the parts near the inner and outer surface. A total of 220 diagnostic sherds representing rims, bases, lugs, handles, and walls with decoration were collected from the site, most of which were found in area that roughly corresponds to the squares D3, E3, D4, and E4. I sorted these sherds according to the shapes to which they may have belonged. There appears a considerable homogeneity in the shapes of the vessels. The most common shapes among the pottery assemblage are wide bowls with curving sides and up-raised handles set on top of the rim and wide-mouthed or collar-necked large jars.

Most of the fragments representing wide bowls ranged in diameter from 30 to 36 cm and had flat bases. The large handles apparently stood more or less upright above the rim, while some examples show that the handles curved inwards over the rims. Handle fragments with knobs and rim fragments with handle stumps were recovered in great quantity (**182-186**, Pl. 45). Handles were probably applied to the top of the rim after the bowls were made, so that the shape of the rim was preserved at the base of the handle. Such distinctive type of bowls are evident at the periods X-VIII at Emporio on Chios, levels II-III at Tigani on Samos, and Vathy Bay Cave on Kalymnos, as well as at the recently excavated site of Gülpınar on the coastal

Troad. Handle fragment **184** has a hole through it, similar examples of which were found at period X at Emporio (Hood 1981: no. 311). A few twisted handles belonging to the same form of bowl are also evident (**187** and **188**, Pl. 45). Such twisted bowl-handles are known to us from Gülpınar, period VIII at Emporio, and level II at Tigani in the eastern Aegean islands (Hood 1981: no.321; Felsch 1988: no. 47.2,5 and 74.5).

Large globular jars constitute the second most common pottery type. Most of the wide-mouthed large jars have inward sloping sides (**195-197**, Pl. 45). The large jars with a collar-neck bodies are basically globular, while the necks are more or less differentiated from the shoulders. Some of the jars have relatively fine fabric and their surfaces are poorly burnished. Rims normally either slope inwards or stand upright (**198-200**, Pl. 45). The bases were probably flat (**191-194**, Pl. 44), since all the base fragments found on the surface were flat. Handles appear to have varied in form. Jars with upright and inward-sloping collar necks have a pair of small vertical strap handles (sometimes knobbed) joining the neck to the shoulder (**204-205**, Pl. 45). This type of jar with handles on the shoulder or belly is very prominent at Emporio (periods X-VIII), Tigani (levels II-III). Similar upright rims with clear differentiation between the neck and shoulder also occur at Saliagos in small quantities (Evans and Renfrew 1968: 37, fig. 53.4 and 8), and are also known from the Late Neolithic period sites of Thessaly (Hood 1981: 195).

Because the vertical handles were not found attached to sufficiently large pieces of vessels, it is difficult to estimate precisely how they were attached to the jars. They may belong to a collar-necked jar, rising from the shoulder to the end of the rim. Such use of vertical handles on jars is known to us from level VIII at Emporio (Hood 1981: no. 346), level II at Tigani (Felsch 1988: pl. 78), Saliagos (Evans and Renfrew 1968: fig. 44), Bağbaşı (Eslick 1992: pl. 43), and at Demircihöyük (Seeher 1988: pl. 28.9). One other form of handle associated with this type of globular jar is the vertical strap handle with pinched up ridge at top (**206**, pl. 45). Such a handle form was a common trait in this period as it is found at a number of sites such as Bağbaşı in southwest Anatolia (Eslick 1992: pl. 64.9) and Tigani and Saliagos in the eastern Aegean islands (Felsch 1988: fig. 58; Evans and Renfrew 1968: fig.45.6). There are also occasional cases where these jars are adorned with crescent lugs (**209**) and relief decorations such as knobs with rounded sections (**208**, pl. 45). Crescent lugs were common at Saliagos (Evans and Renfrew 1968: fig. 47), Emporio IX (Hood 1981: no. 128), and Demircihöyük (Seeher 1988: pl. 23.10). These projections, or special types of ledge lugs, seem to have served as handles. Vertical strap-handles were often placed on these jars, similar examples of which are documented at Tigani levels II and III (Felsch 1988: pls. 60 and 64). Some of these large jars had horizontally running parallel relief bands on their bodies as a decoration (**207**, Pl. 45). Incised patterns forming triangles filled with white paste (*pointillé*) are found on a number of wall fragments from jars (e.g. **201-202**, Pl. 45). The presence of a few fragments with *pointillé* is not surprising since it was common throughout the Chalcolithic Anatolia and has been found at several sites in the Aegean, including Tigani (levels II-IIIA) on Samos (Heidenreich 1936: pl.29.2: Felsch 1988: no. 248, 251), Aghio Gala Upper Cave (Hood 1981: no. 286), and Vathy Bay Cave on Kalymnos (Furness 1956: pl. 22.23). *Pointillé* is also found at Demircihöyük in the Eskişehir region in northwest Anatolia (Seeher 1988: pl. 21) and Karaağaçtepe on the tip of the Gallipoli Peninsula in Turkish Thrace (Demangel 1926).

Several rims with flattened tops and flat base fragments of storage jars and coarse cooking vessels have also been documented during the surface studies at the site. In addition, several sling-balls made out of red-clay have also been found at the site. Presence of such artifacts in a certain area over the surface of the site clearly indicates that the site did not merely served as a locus of manaufacture.

Hand-made dark burnished pottery comparable to that of Kulaksılzat was a common feature of this period in most parts of western Anatolia and adjacent islands during the fifth and early fourth millennia B.C., although local variations occur among the sub-regions. This pottery was represented by groups such as Kuruçay Late Chalcolithic Gray Burnished ware, Bağbaşı Ware, Kızılbel Middle Chalcolithic ware in the southeast; Kumtepe 1a in northwest Anatolia; and Emporio X-VIII pottery and Tigani Dark Burnished in the eastern Aegean islands (Yakar 1985: 122). Kulaksızlar pottery can easily be placed into the Kumtepe1a/Beşik-sivritepe/Gülpınar horizon of the Troad in northwestern Anatolia (Takaoğlu 2004). Temporal placing of the Kulaksızlar assemblage into the second quarter of the fifth millennium B.C. is possible on basis certain similarities between the assemblages of Kulaksızlar and those of Beşik-Sivritepe, Kumtepe 1a, and Gülpınar. The recent archaeological excavations carried out at the site of Gülpınar by the resent author confirmed the relative dating offered for the Kulaksızlar assemblage. Homogeneity observed in the manufacturing techniques and shapes, as well as their recovery in a single cultural level confirm that the Kulaksızlar assemblage must also be dated to a single period. Like Kulaksızlar, Gülpınar also represents a settlement with a single cultural level, yielding pottery nearly identical to that of the Kulaksızlar.

Excavations on the eastern Aegean islands also provide the cultural and chronological basis for Kulaksızlar pottery since it shares a number of similarities with ceramics from Tigani and Emporio. Period VIII at Emporio is often synchronized with the pottery of Kumtepe 1a horizon in Troad, which was characterized by hand-made plain dark burnished wares. Pattern-burnished ware has been to used to date the Kumtepe 1a horizon. It occurs at Kumtepe 1a and Beşiktepe in the Troad, Tigani on Samos, and Toptepe 1 and Hoca Çeşme in Turkish Thrace. Özdoğan (1993: 183) presents archaeological evidence from excavations at Hoca Çeşme and Toptepe in Turkish Thrace for the existence of a considerable time gap between Kumtepe 1a and 1b phases, which pushes the date of Kumtepe 1a pottery back almost a millennium before that of Kumtepe 1b pottery. Özdoğan documented pattern-burnished ware in phase I at Toptepe along with Karanovo III/IV sherds, which contradicts the traditional approaches of seeing Kumtepe 1a and 1b as successive chronological phases. This evidence indicates a date for Kumtepe 1a pottery (and hence for pottery of Emporio VIII, Tigani II, and Kulaksızlar) possibly somewhere within the second quarter of the fifth millennium B.C.

The relative date obtained for Kulaksızlar pottery through synchronization is in accord with the C^{-14} date proposed for the two marble Kilia figurine fragments from Aphrodisias and two rim fragments of marble pointed beakers from Beşik-Sivritepe. Excavations at Late Chalcolithic Aphrodisias provided three C^{-14} dates (two from level VIIIA and one from VIIIB), which can be useful for the dating of the two Kilia figurine torsos found in level VIIIA. Joukowsky (1986: 164) proposes a calibrated 4360-4100 BC date for level VIIIA, in which two Kilia figurine fragments were found. There are additional calibrated C^{-14} dates from Troad for establishing chronology. Likewise, rim fragments of marble pointed beakers found at Beşik-Sivritepe and Gülpınar also provides us with dates. A relative date can be offered for the pattern-burnished ware on the basis of radiocarbon dates obtained from Beşik-Sivritepe, which provides us with dates ranging from 4780 and 4500 B.C. (Korfmann and Krome 1993; fig. 4). Kumtepe 1a also also yielded similar radiacarbon dates ranging from 4805 and 4370 cal. B.C. (Korfmann et al. 2003: 236). Since Kulaksızlar temporally belongs to the period characterized by the Kumtepe 1a/Beşik-sivritepe/Gülpınar horizon, there is no reason not to place the site within a period that roughly corresponds to the second quarter of the fifth millennium B.C.

The similarities among the pottery assemblages of the sub-regions of western Anatolia and adjacent eastern Aegean islands are suggestive of complex cultural interactions. The interaction among the Troad in northwestern, Akhisar region in central-western Anatolia, and the eastern Aegean islands could have been at an intra- or inter-regional level, depending on whether one sees these sub-regions as part of the same cultural interaction sphere or not. Eslick (1980: 13) observed a similar cultural link between the pottery of the Elmalı plain in southwestern Anatolia and the eastern Aegean islands during this period. She does not rule out cultural interaction mechanisms involving a maritime route, which would be no surprise in view of the proximity of the eastern Aegean islands to the western Anatolian mainland. Kulaksızlar pottery adds a new dimension to the extent of these cultural contacts in the eastern Aegean. The Akhisar plain is nearly 100 km away from Izmir and could have been reached through a land route following the Gediz river. A maritime trade route was in existence in addition to the land trade that was documented through the movements of rare goods and other types of pottery.

Indeed, the most important problem that western Anatolian archaeology still faces today is the nature of the transition between the Early and the Late phases of the Chalcolithic period. This problematic transitional period is represented by sites such as Kulaksızlar, Gülpınar, Beşik-sivritepe and Kumtepe 1a. The Late Chalcolithic period reveals a new phase in the cultural history of western Anatolia, characterized by an increase in the number of settlements, changes in the building construction techniques, the development of copper-based metallurgy and its subsequent diffusion, and the replacement of existing pottery traditions such as the sophisticated red-on-cream ware of the Hacılar culture with an inferior monochrome pottery tradition (Yakar 1985: 121). The impetus behind these cultural changes may be internal, generated by factors such as population growth or technological change, or may equally be the result of external stimuli at the regional or super-regional level, such as long-distance trade or the arrival of new peoples. Whether these changes reflect local cultural development or the arrival of newcomers remains open to debate. Archaeologists have proposed a number of theories favoring both endogenous and exogenous factors to explain the changes that occurred in this period. It is difficult to substantiate arguments for a local transition from Eearly to Late Chalcolithic cultures due to the fact that the Middle Chalcolithic period of western Anatolia is poorly understood. The vagueness of this transitional stage makes it difficult for archaeologists to make explicit statements about the cultural processes that resulted in the appearance of new social and cultural traditions in Late Chalcolithic western Anatolia.

In the earlier works, the changes associated with the Late Chalcolithic period were ascribed to the gradual and continuous penetration of foreign nomad and pastoralist groups from southeastern Europe into northwestern and central Anatolia and Turkish Thrace (Yakar 1985: 28). James Mellaart (1971: 120; 1998: 62) likewise favored an explanation based on the arrival of newcomers from the Balkans. He argues that disastrous events in the Balkans resulted in a flood of refugees into Anatolia. He bases his argument on the destruction of the Gumelnitsa-Karanovo VI culture and a marked decline in the number of settlements in Bulgaria and parts of Romania. The lack of a destruction layer and the presence of a gap between the Early and Late Chalcolithic levels at both Aphrodisias and Kuruçay have been used to support the peaceful arrival of the newcomers. Conversely, Mehmet Özdoğan (1993: 176) minimized the role of

immigration as the cause of culture change. He explains these culture changes with a model of interregional interaction. Intensive archaeological research conducted in the region of the sea of Marmara has provided sufficient Middle Chalcolithic period evidence to identify similarities in the cultural assemblages of southeast Europe, Turkish Thrace, and northwest Anatolia. Özdoğan sees the Balkans, northwest and central Anatolia as part of a unified cultural formation zone that developed simultaneously under the same pressures; notwithstanding, each sub-region also undertook unique strategies to meet those pressures (Özdoğan 1993: 176). Thus, the similarities exhibited between the Balkan and northwest Anatolian assemblages must be seen as a result of interregional interaction or the regions adopting similar strategies to overcome similar pressures within a given environment prior to Late Chalcolithic period. Therefore, the appearance of a new cultural tradition in Late Chalcolithic western Anatolia was most likely due to a complex set of factors, including population movements, cultural interactions, economic changes, and social reorganization. The lack of cultural continuity from Early to Late Chalcolithic periods, lack of destruction layers at resettled sites, increase in settlement numbers, presence of Balkan elements in Anatolian pottery, and changes in building construction techniques all demonstrate that the multi-factor model plausibly explains the culture change observed between the Early and Late Chalcolithic periods. Kulaksızlar evidence fills in part the gap between these periods.

E. Summary

General description of the main marble products of the workshop and the stone tools used in their manufacture and the spatial clustering of different artifact groups over the surface of the site clearly indicates that surface assemblage belonged to a small village with an economy primarily based on marble working. In addition, artifacts representing everyday life activities such as pottery and food processing implements were also found at the site confirms the presence of small scale activities other than marble working. The ratio between the marble artifacts (90%) and other archaeological evidence (10%) demonstrates that the inhabitants of this site did not prefer to carry out intensive agricultural pursuits as other Chalcolithic cultures had done. Evaluation of the basic features of pottery enabled me to reconstruct the cultural and chronological affiliations of the site, allowing Kulaksızlar to be temporally placed within the mid-fifth millennium BC. The main marble products of the workshop were also identified from the analysis of the manufacturing debris. Use-wear patterns observed on the manufacturing errors and stone tools prepares the grounds to reconstruct the sequences of production and craftsmen's tool use. Spatial distribution of surface finds were also mapped so that the aspects of craft production and internal work division among the craftsmen could be reconstructed.

Part Five

PATTERNS OF KULAKSIZLAR MARBLE WORKING

Although marble-working was a feature of prehistoric western Anatolian and Aegean communities as early as the Neolithic period, the technological and socio-economic aspects of marble working have not been examined in detail. This is because as yet there is no direct evidence such as manufacturingd debris associated with the production of marble artifacts available. Full recovery of manufacturing debris through a systematic excavation would undoubtedly be the best way to understand the technological aspects of marble working. The potential significance of studying lithic artifacts was underestimated in western Anatolian archaeology until the last few decades. Previously, studies of lithics have often involved typology construction in order to establish the chronological and cultural affiliations. In contrast, current archaeological models place more emphasis on explaining cultural processes that are closely linked to the production system. The social context that gave meaning to technologica actions and products, and the process by which artifacts are produced, distributed and exchanged are often integrated into the study of lithics (e.g. Runnels 1985b: 100; Perlès 1992). This study of the socio-economic and technological aspects of Kulaksızlar marble working shows that lithic studies are useful in illuminating past human behavior.

Analysis of manufacturing debris from Kulaksızlar is important since it provides information on technological and socioeconomic aspects of production such as how the marble figurines and vesseis were manufactured,where the materials were acquired, what kinds of tools were used, and how they were used. Moreover, the marble working evidence can be examined to reveal patterns of exchange and consumption in western Anatolia. The patterns of Kulaksızlar marble working are analyzed with reference to processes such as the choice of raw material to be utilized, prospecting and extraction of raw materials, preparation and manufacture of goods, their distribution, and finaliy consumption of finished artifacts. For this purpose, this chapter was divided into six parts. First, the factors that affected the selection of raw materials were analyzed in relation to issues such as relative cost, workability, efficiency, and aesthetic associations of raw materials. Then, the prospecting strategies involved in the identification of suitable raw materials are discussed in order to answer the question of how prospectors recognized suitable sources. This is followed by an evaluation of the methods involved in extraction of raw materials by considering possibilities such asquarrying and collecting. After the discussion of these preliminary stages of production, the sequences of production of marble beakers, bowls, and figurines at Kulaksızlar are

reconstruct by using archaeological evidence supplemented with ethnographic data and replication studies. Because ethnoarchaeology has contributed much to our understanding of past stone-working systems, including stone-vessel making, ethnographic analogies derived from Anatolia and neighboring regions such as Iran and Egypt are also used to aid in the archaeological interpretation of Kulaksızlar evidence. Technological analyses of stone vessel making evidence from the Early Bronze Age sites of Tepe Yahya (Kohl 1974) and Shar-i Sokhta in eastern Iran (Tosi 1969; Ciarla 1981), and from Knossos on Crete (Warren 1969; Evely 1980) provide technological knowledge on ancient stone vessel making. Besides ethnographic examinations of contemporary production systems, replication studies are also carried out for a more practical understanding of the manufacturing process such as the complexity of making marble artifacts and the methods of tool use.

A. Decision Making

Any attempt to understand the technological and socio-economic aspects of production systems must start with a reconstruction of the factors involved in the selection of the materials. Considerations such as workability, the relative costs involved in extraction, and aesthetic and religious associations of materials are the main factors affecting the selection of a particular raw material (Runnels 1981: 63 and 1985: 102). The availability of raw materials is an important variable that conditions productive activities, making the study of geological resources an important component in understanding the level of complexity involved in the acquisition of raw materials. If the raw materials used were locally available, or found in abundance close to the site, then it can be assumed that the relative cost was an important consideration in raw material selection. If certain raw materials were present within a circumscribed area of a community, individuals living close to the source could have gained some advantage by beginning to experiment in products made with that resource. In such a circumstance, access to raw materials becomes essentially unlimited for the people and the simple mechanism adopted for the acquisition of raw materials becomes an incentive for independent specialization to emerge. Therefore, it is necessary to look closely at the interaction of social subsystems with their environment when working on non-agricultural production systems.

The relative cost of materials was probably one of the most important factors that led Kulaksızlar craftsmen to exploit the raw materials at hand in the immediate vicinity of the site. The geologic map of the Akhisar region prepared by Hoşgören (1983: 18) allows the identification of possible sources where marble might have been acquired. Marble is a soft rock (hardness 3) whose texture varies from coarse-grained with large calcite crystals to very fine-grained with calcite that is indistinguishable with the naked eye. Figure 6 illustrates the location of the various geological sources available in the vicinity of the workshop area. The area surrounding the villages of Kediyusu, Delibeyli, Gölmarmara to the south of Kulaksızlar and the area around the village Harmandalı to the north have rich marble resources. The marbles from each of these sources display slight differences in color, partially derived from the dissemination of the calcareous impurities (e.g. sand, clay, and iron oxides) during metamorphism or re-crystallization of limestone. For instance, iron oxides gave a yellowish or reddish color, while the substances of organic origin gave marble a grayish color. Because the aesthetic association of marble was important, the heterogeneity in color resulted in the variability in the final appearances of the marble artifacts. The crystalline form and compact structure of marble and variations in its color from creamy- to bluish-white gave the finished artifacts an attractive appearance after they were finely polished.

The simple mode adopted in acquiring marble is also evident in the types of stone tools used at the workshop. The gabbro and basalt cobbles, preferred as hammerstones for flaking and pecking at the workshop, are found in abundance within walking distance of the workshop area. Hoşgören (1983: 26) presents geological evidence that the area of Kulaksızlar in the eastern part of the Selendi plain was rich in rocks of the Ophiolite sequence, including gabbro, serpentine, and rhyolite of the Mesozoic age. The river-pebbles used for polishing could have been collected from the banks of the Ilıcak stream to the west of the workshop. This is suggested by the fact that all of the pebble-smoothers found at the workshop have water-worn surfaces. It can also be assumed that local cobbles of flint were used, which were likely to have been obtained from erosional deposits such as gravel beds and other alluvial sources within a short walking distance. A number of cores documented during the surface studies at the workshop area indicate that flint knapping took place at the site. Blades and awls were mainly manufactured from flint cores, but the color and physical properties of the flint artifacts display no homogeneity, suggesting the use of various sources.

Sandstone is another local raw material that was widely utilized in the workshop as an abrasive. A visual examination of sandstone found at the site, in terms of texture and color, indicates that the reddish-yellow sandstone used by the Kulaksızlar craftsmen was taken from a source near to the village of Sarıçalı, which is located within walking distance from the workshop. Sandstone found near the village of Sarıçalı includes small particles of quartz (Hosgören 1983: 21), and is identical to that used at the workshop. There is also a similarity in color between the sandstone from the

source near the village of Sarıçalı and that found at the workshop, both of which are reddish-yellow in color. For actions such as drilling or removing flaking and pecking marks, sandstone is a very effective material since quartz (hardness 7) particles provide a good abrasive powder for working marble.

Besides the relative cost, such factors as ease of workability is also important for the selection of raw materials. Marble can be classified a workable and moderately durable material for figurine and vessel production as it is easy to flake, peck, and polish. Pounding, pecking, or chipping actions require fine-grained or crystalline hard stones such as igneous rocks. The hardness of gabbro and basalt (hardness 6-7), caused to a large extent by their ferromagnesian contents, make them suitable for percussive actions. These rocks are nearly twice as hard as marble, which makes them appropriate materials for marble working. Flint is another material that was used for tools because it breaks with a conchoidal fracture, making it easy to knap and create blades for incision and scraping and awls for piercing vertical lugs of marble pointed beakers.

B. Prospecting

Prospecting can be defined as the search for or identification of the raw materials available (Runnels 1985: 102). Since the raw materials used for production at Kulaksızlar occur naturally in the surrounding landscapes, the ways in which prospectors recognized these useful stone sources is an important question that needs to be addressed. Runnels (1985: 102) points out that experimentation with raw materials might have resulted in the identification of the most useful geological resources. Ethnographic analogies indicate that chance discovery of geological deposits, combined with unlimited access to the source, the stone's workability, and experimentation with the raw materials, result in the recognition of suitable resources prior to their becoming a major component of any lithic production system. For example, ethnographic examination of lithic production systems in remote parts of Anatolia provides valuable information on the patterns of prospecting. Black amber bead-making at the village of Dutlu in eastern Turkey (Gündoğdu 2004) demonstrates that unlimited access to the resources, workability, durability, and aesthetic appearance made black amber a desirable material for both producers and consumers. Exploitation of black amber sources within and outside the villages in the Oltu region dramatically increased when the demand for amber products began to increase due to their aesthetic appeal, durability, and rarity.

Useful information on prospecting for lithic raw materials can also be drawn from the flint-knapping activities near the village of Çakmak in northwestern Anatolia, where the villagers manufacture flint blades for threshing sledges (Bordaz 1959; Weiner 1981). The farmer specialists originally knapped flint cobbles that they collected from ravines or stream beds in order to fulfill their requirements for threshing activities. The search for flint cobbles apparently resulted in the identification of suitable geological deposits. Subsequently, quarrying began to supercede collecting as the preferred strategy, mainly due to the relatively lower costs and enhanced access to flint. Because flint-cobbles did not occur abundantly on the landscape and their search required a great amount of time, quarrying was a more efficient means of supplying the great demand. It seems that attention to environment, the diverse and abundant presence of cobbles on the landscape, and acquaintance with the properties of marble and stone tools through experimentation resulted in the identification of suitable stone resources at Kulaksızlar. Because cost-cutting strategies shape the patterns of independent specialization, production of artifacts using locally available raw materials must have been a characteristic feature of specialization (whether home- or village-based) that occurred in non-urban societies such as Kulaksızlar. The two ethnographic examples from Anatolia mentioned above support the role of basic economic forces, as well as the aesthetic quality of the selected raw materials.

C. Extraction

Archaeological studies reconstructing sequences of production must also reconstruct patterns of extracting raw materials. Mechanisms for extraction can take a variety of forms, including collection from the surface and quarrying (Runnels 1985: 103). There are a number of valuable archaeological lithic studies that examine the quarrying of raw materials, ownership of the sources, labor organization, the tools used in quarrying, and the spatial layout of extraction activities (Bordaz 1959; Torrence 1982; Runnels 1981: 225-52; Perles 1990 and 1992). These studies focus on materials such as obsidian, flint, and milistones to of establish how raw materials were extracted before they were transformed into artifacts. The distance from the production site to the source probably determined the nature of the strategy involved in the extraction of raw materials. Because the geological sourcesited exploited at Kulaksızlar were located within walking distance from the site, craftsmen adopted a strategy of collecting marble required for vessel and figurine production. The available archaeological evidence confirmsthat marble and stone used in the various stages of production were actually collected from the immediate vicinity of the site by the craftsmen two or their subordinates. The lack of homogeneity in physical properties combined with the variability in the colors of marbles found at the site clearly shows that craftsmen did not depend on a single source.

A great quantity of large marble cobbles found during the site survey have water-worn surfaces, suggesting that craftsmen collected these pieces from stream beds. It is clear that they were originally broken off from the slopes of the marble-rich mountainside by erosion and were gradually wore down into small cobbles, and eventualiy deposited in stream beds. Cobbles naturally occurred in sizes that would have been adequate for figurine and vessel production at the workshop. The Lydian Üçtepe tumulus, which is located just 1 km west of the workshop area, contains a considerable amount of marble cobbles of various sizes with water-worn surfaces, indicating that they were surface collected. Similar marble cobbles observed at Kulaksızlar leads me to believe that the craftsmen collected marble blocks from the Selendi plain or from the banks of the Ilıcak stream in a similar manner to that of their Lydian successors who used thern in tumulus building four millennia later. Kulaksızlar craftsmen preferred to collect whole cobbles at the source rather than coarse flaking them before they were transported back to the site. It may be speculated that the craftsrnen removed some flakes from the marble to test the quality of the texture before transporting it.

Archaeologists utilize a wide range of techniques to identify the source where the marbles were obtained. The isotopic or chemical properties of the archaeological rnarble artifacts are matched with the sources or quarry from which they may have been obtained. Techniques such as trace element analysis, electron-spin resonance spectroscopy, strontium isotopic ratio, and stable isotope analysis of oxygen and carbon are the most widely used techniques in sourcing of marble (Herz 1987 and 1992). In trace element analysis, rnass spectrometry determines up to thirty minor and trace elements in white marbles with a good precision. It is a non-destructive method and a marble fragment weighing an average of 200 mg is sufficient to obtain the elernental ratios within the raw material. The values of elernents are monitored as ppb (parts per billion) and compared to those of geological sarnples from which archaeological materials were made. This is one method that I utilized to determine where Kulaksızlar craftsmen acquired the marble.

Stable isotopic analysis of oxygen and carbon is also a very useful technique in sourcing the marble. Oxygen and carbon are abundant in marble with varying isotopic ratios in different rocks, depending on their geologic histories. Measurements of their stable isotopic ratios are carried out with a mass spectrometer, an instrument that can measure proportions in very small samples. The measurement of the isotopic ratios $^{18}O/\,^{16}O$ and $^{13}C/\,^{12}C$ in marble is carried out after suitable chemical treatment separated these elements in the form of CO_2 from the calcium carbonate (Craig and Craig 1972). The ratios of carbon and oxygen are expressed on a diagram in terms of the deviation from a conventional standard. This deviation is expressed as 13C and S180 in parts per thousand or per million and the signature is presented on a diagram (Herz 1992: 38). Isotopic analysis is a non-destructive method and is requires samples as small as tens of miligrams. This method is also used to determine the homogeneity in the isotopic properties of marble used by the Kulaksızlar craftsmen.

Sample	Li	Sc	Ni	Cu	Rb	Nb	Pb	U	Mg	Zn	Sr	Ba	Rb/Sr	U/Pb	% dol.
1	13	96	1328	455	108	3	179	65	251301	12396	38979	959	0,003	0,367	0,191
2	341	187	6672	1469	1089	97	533	52	1021746	4547	45870	8670	0,024	0,097	0,775
3	145	133	2413	801	422	24	378	38	741216	4282	40140	3602	0,011	0,101	0,562
4	397	253	10068	1900	1452	135	385	62	1093797	6924	40720	10145	0,036	0,161	0,830
5	68	109	1731	529	163	6	101	64	1308501	12902	57016	2479	0,003	0,633	0,993
6	14	96	1305	533	48	4	102	31	257749	7327	30532	1473	0,002	0,302	0,196
7	5	90	1388	643	19	3	369	46	348349	7649	38081	2648	0,000	0,124	0,264
8	19	95	1180	620	161	5	148	61	372629	18602	41976	1558	0,004	0,414	0,283
Source K	106	110	2569	763	285	13	531	48	642552	20716	39086	40008	0,007	0,090	0,488

Table. 5.1. Results of the trace elements analysis of eight marble samples from archaeological materials and one geological sample taken from an area near the modern village of Kedikuyusu. Samples 1-3: beakers, 4-5: bowls, 6-8 figurines). Note the homogeneity in the values of Strontium, a diagnostic element in marble sourcing studies. All values in the table are ppb [parts per billion]

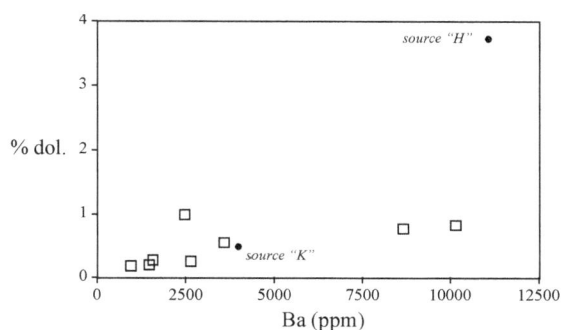

Fig. 5.1. Diagram showing the relationship in the chemical properties of marble from a source and eight samples taken from archaeological materials

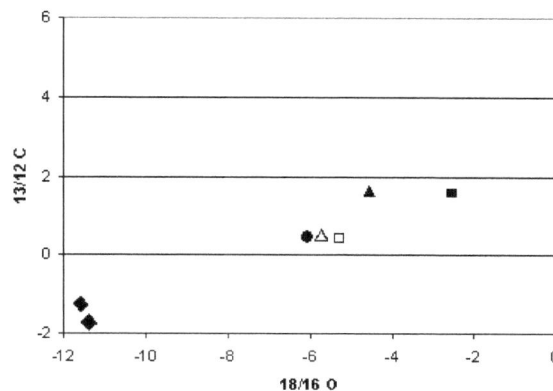

Fig. 5.3. Stable isotope analysis of four archaeological samples showing the homogeneity in carbon/oxygen isotopes

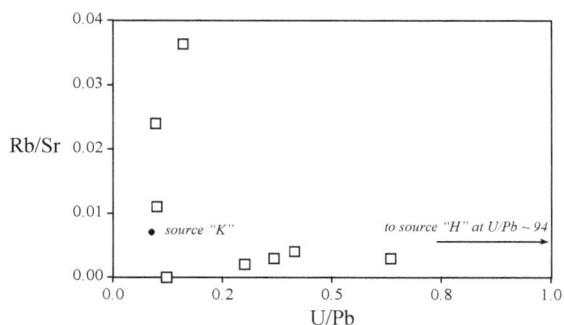

Fig. 5.2. Diagrmas showing the relationship in the chemical properties of marble from a source and eight samples taken from archaeological materials

Sample	$\delta^{18}O$	$\delta^{13}O$
△ Pointed beaker	- 5.352	+ 0.342
▲ Pointed bowl I	- 4.546	+ 1.650
□ Pointed bowl II	- 5.634	+ 0.576
● Kilia figurine	- 6.064	+ 0.465
❶ Harmandalı I	-11.392	- 1.677
❶ Harmandalı II	- 11.577	- 1.249

Table 5.2. $\delta^{18}O$ ve $\delta^{13}O$ of four archaeological and two geological samplesfromthe Harmandalı source

The determination of the Mn 2+ ion in marble by using electron spin resonance spectroscopy (ESR) is another technique that provides results useful for marble provenance studies (Cordischi et. al. 1983). This techniques is based on the measurements of the concentration of manganese and the ratio of calcite to dolomite in a marble sample. Because the spectra of calcite and dolomite are distinct and distinguishable, the measurement of the diagnostic ratio of calcite to dolomite using ESR spectroscopy helps to identify the source of marble from which archaeological materials were acquired (Cordischi et. al. 1983). This useful technique is not utilized in this dissertation due to the high cost required for the intended task.

In an attempt to demonstrate where Kulaksızlar craftsmen acquired marble, I requested from Drew Coleman at the Earth Sciences department at Boston University to carry out trace element analysis and Judit Zoeldfoldi at the Tübingen University to carry out carbon/oxygen isotopic analyses of the selected archaeological and geologic samples. In the trace element analysis by Drew Coleman, eight samples taken from marble vessel and figurines and one geological sample taken from a perennial spring bed near the village of Kedikuyusu were used. The method used for the analyses of the selected geological and archaeological samples at Boston University can briefly be described as follows: approximately 200-mg sample were dissolved in concentrated nitric acid, leaving a small amount of insoluble residue. To eliminate the residue, the samples were dried and redissolved in a sealed beaker on a hot plate (~100°C) in a mixture of hydrofluoric and nitric acid. All samples were completely dissolved at this stage. They were dried and redissolved in nitric acid and diluted to a total mass of approximately 150-g solution. Prepared solutions were analyzed using a VG PQ ExCell ICP-MS (Inductively Coupled Plasma-Mass Spectrometer) at Boston University. The ICP-MS run conditions resulted in sensitivities ~ 80 Mcps/ppm 115In. Each batch consisted of the unknowns (run products), a blank and 3 rock standards (USGS-W2, USGS-AGV, and Japanese basalt JB-3). Each unknown was analyzed twice in the run, and a solution was analyzed every 5 tubes to monitor drift. While signal drift could be large, as high as 10% per hour, it was correctable. Although a comprehensive suite of major and trace elements were monitored, only those elements that were consistently present in abundances above detection limits (generally greater than 1 ppb in the prepared solutions) are reported. Following blank-subtraction and a linear drift correction, the % RSD on the replicates was generally <2% within the run. R-values for the calibration curves, based on 2-3 standards and the origin, were > 0.99. All concentrations are reported as ppb (ng element/g sample). The ratios of trace elements listed in the Table 5. 1 clearly shows that chemical properties of analyzed geological sample from source K (kedikuyusu) was similar those of eight samples taken from Kulaksızlar

marble vessels and figurines. This is particularly evident in the values of strontium, which is a diagnostic element in marble provenance studies. Two diagrams were also created from the trace values provided for the trace elements to show the homogeneity in the chemical properties of the marbles used at the Kulaksızlar workshop. For example, the diagram based on the ratio of dolomite ta barium demonstrates that the properties of geologic and archaeological samples are very close since they occur almost in straight line. (The anomaly represented by the two samples in this diagram is probably due to the contamination). The diagram based on the ratio of rubidium/strontium to uranium/lead also displays a similar affinity in terms of chemical properties. It is also clear from the diagram illustrated in Figures 5.1 and 5.2 that nearby Harmandalı quarry (source H) was not exploited by the Kulaksızlar craftsmen or their subordinates. The reason for including this marble source into this analysis was that this quarry was extensively exploited by the classical city of Thyateira (present-day Akhisar) (Dinç 1996a). Therefore, the results obtained from the trace element analysis alone confirm that those eight samples taken from the marble vessel and figurine fragments were made from marble blocks that were collected from an area where the analyzed geological samples was taken, that is the immediate region of the site.

Carbon and oxygen isotopic analysis, on the other hand, involved four samples taken from marble figurines and vessels and three geological samples taken from the Harmandalı quarry located several kilometers northwest of Kulaksızlar. This isotopic study shows that the marble used in the figurine, bowl, and vessel manufacture at Kulaksızlar were not taken from the area surrounding the Harmandalı quarry. This isotopic analysis of carbon and oxygen also indicates that marbles used by the Kulaksızlar craftsmen were acquired from a circumscribed area near the site. Table 5.2 lists the deviation documented in the carbon and oxygen of the selected archaeological and geological samples. The difference between the values of for archaeological materials and geological ones appears to confirm that Kulaksızlar craftsmen or their subordinates did not have long trips for procuring the marble blocks.

The results of both chemical and isotopic analyses of selected archaeological and geological marble samples demonstrate that there was a homogeneity in the properties of marbles used by the Kulaksızlar craftsmen. This homogeneity was apparently due to the exploitation of the immediate vicinity of the site rather than traveling far from the site. Difficulties involved in the transportation of marble presumably prevented longer trips. Therefore, archaeological evidence pointing to an extraction pattern involving collecting is in accord with the results of archaeometric study involving the analyses of chemical and isotopic properties of the samples taken from the selected marble materials. The mechanisms used to extract marble were probably similar to those employed in acquisition of other rocks used for pounding, pecking, or chipping actions. Kulaksızlar craftsmen or their subordinates concentrated some of their time solely collecting raw materials, such as gabbro, basalt, and blocks of sandstone, that were distributed within the immediate vicinity of the site, and that may have been suitable for percussive and abrasive works. Figure 5.4 illustrates some of these sandstone blocks and gabbro cobbles with eroded surfaces. Collecting also included the acquisition of schist, granite, and fluvial-pebbles from an area within a 2-3 kilometers radius from the site. These rocks with different physical properties were used for various purposes such as grinding, abrading, and polishing.

Fig. 5.4. Cobbles of marbles with water-worn surfaces (larger pieces), sanstone block (in the front) and gabbro hammer-stones (dark stones in the center)

Archaeological evidence from Anatolia demonstrates that quarrying also occurred in addition to collecting during the Neolithic period. It seems that both methods were adopted in the extraction of obsidian at this time. Excavations of obsidian workshops at the Neolithic site of Kaletepe in central Anatolia (Balkan-Atlı et. al. 1999: 137) demonstrate that obsidian was naturally present in the form of elongated blocks in ravines that cut the plateau. Neolithic obsidian workers evidently exploited this seam, as the evidence of quarrying in the stream bed indicates. Knapping deposits excavated in this area further confirm that this ravine bed was intensiveiy exploited (Balkan-Atlı et. al.1999:140). In a similar way, Torrence (1984) also documented obsidian mining at Sta Nychia and Demenagaki on the island of Melos, where there are remains of pits and hollows excavated into the cliff following a rhyolite seam. Torrence (1984: 54) argues that the obsidian was mined from these holes with a digging implement, despite the fact that such tools were not identified among the debris. Rhyolite bifacial tools found at the

quarry area may also have been used for digging out the obsidian. The information obtained from these archaeological studies of prehistoric extracting patterns bears strong similarities to the ethnographic evidence. Contemporary flint blade-making near the village of Çakmak in northwestern Turkey (Bordaz 1959) shows that shaft mining was the primary technique for obtaining raw materials. Access to raw material in the area is not restricted, although the community as a whole has to pay rent to the state for use-rights to the source (Bordaz 1959: 74, Torrence 1985: 79). Mining is also a common extraction pattern among the black amber bead-makers in the village of Dutlu in northeast Anatolia, where the entire village community is involved in excavating horizontal tunnels. They follow the seam using simple hammer-like picks. The cubes of extracted amber are then packed in a small four-wheeled wagon. Access ta the sources is unlimited, but extraction is a seasonal activity as the long-lasting harsh winter conditions in the region prevent year-round mining (Gündoğdu 2004).

Contemporary stone vessel makers at Gurna in Upper Egypt and Mashad in eastern Iran also adopted an extraction strategy involving mining. These Egyptian and Iranian alabaster vessel making workshops show that the raw materials are mined from areas far from the workshops (Kohl 1979; Hester and Heizer 1981). To reduce the cost of transportation, raw materials are roughly shaped at the quarry area before they are carried to the workshops. The quarry that provides materials for the Gurna workshop in Upper Egypt is located almost 50 km away from the village. The miners use large pry bars or chisels ta detach large blocks of alabaster from the parent rock. Three men remain near the source ta quarry the stone and roughly shape it, while three others are responsible for the transportation of these roughed-out vesseis from the source to the workshop. Detached alabaster blocks are roughly hamrner-dressed, loaded on the pack-animals and transported to the workshops, where the final hollowing out and refinement processes take place. When a particular source is exhausted, the craftsmen open up another mine and this process continues on a year-round basis (Hester and Heizer 1981). A similar pattern is observed at the contemporary stone vessel workshops at Mashad in eastern Iran (Kohl 1974). The miners first search for an outcrop of stone and then follow the seam into the mountain and in foothilis. (This mining technology does not provide much information relevant to past extraction patterns as the miners use gun powder to split the raw material frorn the parent rock). However, modification of large blocks at the quarry area is a consistent pattern. As at the Gurna workshop in Egypt, the final stages of hollowing out of interior and refinement take place at the workshops. These ethnographic parallels demonstrate that proximity of geological resources to the workshop has led present-day craftsmen to modify the raw materials at their source in order to reduce the cost of transportation.

Kulaksızlar craftsmen or their subordinates did not need to modify the marble cobbles before transporting them to the workshop, due to the fact that raw materials occur abundantly within walking distance of the site. The evidence from Neolithic central Anatolia displays a similar pattern of extraction. Craftsmen at settlements located near obsidian sources preferred to collect unmodified raw materials and then knap them in the settlements. Core preparation and reduction debris found at Neolithic Aşıklı Höyük in central Anatolia indicates that obsidian blocks acquired from the Acıgöl area were knapped at the site rather then near the source (Balkan-Atlı 1994). This pattern of raw material procurement and their working at the site rather than near the source can also be observed archaeologically for stone vessel making at the third millennium B.C. site of Tepe Yahya in eastern Iran (Kohl 1974: 109 and 1979: 117). The stone vessel makers of Tepe Yahya seemingly collected the raw materials from the source area and then brought them to the site for further processing. The proximity of the site to the source, lack of evidence for intensive deep mining at the quarry area, the presence of large blocks with faint hammering traces, and the abundance of waste flakes at the site all confirm that raw materials were worked at the site.

These archaeological and ethnographic analogies demonstrate that a collecting strategy is preferred to quarrying when the raw materials are found locally within the environs of the site, which was the case at Kulaksızlar. Relative costs can be accepted as an important consideration for craft specialists working independently, leading Kulaksızlar craftsmen or their subordinates to adopt a less costly strategy involving collecting. Marble could have also been quarried for the large products, although I was unable to find any evidence for this pattern in the nearby stream beds.

D. Manufacture

This section reconstructs the various stages of marble working using archaeological evidence derived from the analysis of manufacturing debris. Archaeological evidence is supplemented with ethnographic evidence and replication experiments. Use-wear patterns produced experimentally are compared with those seen on archaeological materials. Archaeological evidence on stone working from the fourth and third millennium B.C. sites of neighboring areas such as Mesopotamia, Egypt, and Crete is utilized to understand how the tools found at Kulaksızlar might have been used. Ethnographic evidence derived from a study of contemporary stone vessel makers also helps reconstruct the methods of stone working. The manufacturing sequence for each marble artifact type is reconstructed separately in this section, dividing the production of marble vessels into four steps, and the production of figurines into three steps. Vessel production includes preparation of the raw material, namely outlining of the shapes on the marble (Step 1); the creation of a preform (Step 2); the hollowing out of

the vessel's interior (Step 3); and refinement and finishing (Step 4). For figurine production, the manufacturing stages include: preparation of a flat blank from the raw material (Step 1), creation of a preform of the figurine (Step 2), and refinement which involves abrasion, incision of details, and smoothing of surface (Step 3).

1. Manufacturing Pointed Beakers

After the marble has been procured, the first step involves flaking the selected piece into a shape approaching the approximate size of the beaker, using both flaking and pecking actions. From the traces left on the exterior surface of the roughly shaped beakers (Pls. 1-3), it is possible to argue that both spherical and elongated stone tools were used to roughly outline the marble into the beaker form. Working marks observed on the ovoid and narrow ends of elongated hammerstones found at Kulaksızlar are indicators of their use in direct percussive actions.

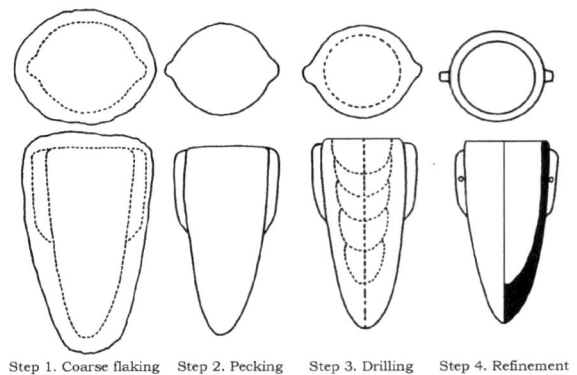

Step 1. Coarse flaking   Step 2. Pecking   Step 3. Drilling   Step 4. Refinement

Fig. 5.5. Suggested manufacture stages of beakers

During the second step of beaker manufacture, the large flaking scars are removed through pecking. A type of pointed hammer was used to gradually smooth out the large flaking marks created previously by direct percussion. At this stage, two vertical projections for lugs were roughly articulated opposite one another on the upper half of the vessel (Pl. 1). Percussive use-wear observed on many of the unfinished beaker fragments confirms the use of hammerstones with pointed ends. Following continuing use, the edges of hammerstones would become less effective, but instead of discarding them, they were probably split into pieces and retouched to obtain pointed ends. Replication experiments undertaken during the course of the study provide a more practical understanding of how stone tools were used in flaking and pecking. I utilized gabbro and basalt tools to replicate the production of a beaker. The spherical and elongated stone tools were useful for removing large flakes from a previously unworked marble block. I deliberately split the basalt and gabbro rocks into pieces to obtain pointed ends with effective working edges. These newly split stone tools helped to thin out large flaking marks created during the rough shaping of the blank. I successively employed the pointed stone tools to remove the large chipping marks and make a preform that roughly approached the size of the intended final form. I observed that small flakes were removed from the working edges of these stone tools. Similarities between the percussion marks produced experimentally on the roughed-out marble vessels and on the stone tools when compared to those observed on the archaeological materials from Kulaksızlar is quite striking.

Fig. 5.6. Replication experiments showing the preforming a pointed beaker and removing the pointed tool marks

The ratio of error is very low at this stage of beaker production. My first attempt at flaking and chipping failed due to the uncontrolled force I applied when roughly raising the vertical lugs. My second attempt to create a preform took less time. I assume that Kulaksızlar craftsmen spent less time than I did since they would have acquired a greater familiarity with each stage of manufacture, especially if an individual craftsman was responsible for only one stage of production. For example, if the preforming of a marble beaker and its subsequent drilling were carried out by two different craftsmen, then, one may argue that each craftsmen working of his or her stage achieved would achieve a certain level of expertise relating to their tasks. In turn, this means that less time would have been required for the production of the beaker as a whole. This was probably the case at Kulaksızlar since the survey data show that preforming and drilling tasks were carried out at different loci.

The third step in the manufacture of beakers is the drilling process. The implement used in drilling at the Kulaksızlar workshop was most probably a bow drill, which is a simple mechanical implement. After a cord is attached to the ends of a curved bow of wood, it is wrapped around the drill spindle and is set into osciilatory motion by moving the bow back and forth (Childe 1954: 189). Craftsman then applies his or her free hand on the top of spindle, which is usually protected by a drill-head sitting at the end of the spindle in order to obtain the necessary pressure for drilling. Unfinished beaker fragments with drilling marks show that the interior was hollowed out while the vessel was held in a vertical position. Because the pulverized marble acted as a polishing agent, the bottom of the interiors have an almost polished appearance (Pls. 3 and 5), while the horizontal lines of rotary drilling appear much clearer towards the upper part of the vessel. Since no excavations have been carried out at the site, there is no obvious archaeological evidence for actual pits used to stabilize preforms as they were being drilled. It can oniy be assumed that pointed vessels required piacement in the ground because they do not stand independentiy. Comparable archaeoiogical evidence from Hierakonpolis in Egypt shows such a placement of vessel preforms in cavities (Quibell and Green 1902: pl. 68). Ethnographic evidence derived from present-day stone vessel makers at Gurna in Egypt also shows that the craftsmen set their vessel preformss in previously dug pits in the workshop area (Hestern and Heizer 1981: 19). Whether the vessels were placed in the pits or not does not alter the conclusion that the drilling was conducted vertically using a bow-drill working in rotary motion.

The presence of drill-bits together with a great amount of use-wear observed on manufacturing errors from the site are the primary indicators of drilling activities. The drill-bits (Pls. 23, 24, 40) and a single drill-head (**156**, P1. 24) found at the workshop are so far the only physical remnants of drilling implements. The interiors of unfinished vessel fragments have an unevenly worn pattern, caused by the penetration of the drill-bit into the walls (e.g. **41**, P1. 8). it is also evident that various-sized drill-bits were successively inserted into the interior as boring progressed. The aim of this process is to shape the internal contours of the vessel in accordance with the external shape of the beaker, thereby creating a uniform thickness. A pointed vessel consequently required a conical cavity, which could have been created by the successive use of increasingly tapered drill-bits. The angle of the bevel on some rim fragments confirms that the original cavity was made with a large drill (**32**, **34**, **36**, Pl. 28).

Due to the limited number of methods that could have been used with available technology, it is unlikely that the drilling techniques adopted by the Kulaksızlar marble-workers were much different from those of ancient Egypt and Mesopotamia. There is archaeological evidence for the way the bow-drill was used in the Mesopotamian past (Moorey 1993: 58). Nonetheless it is likely that Mesopotamian craftsmen used bow-drills with figure-of-eight-shaped drill-bits. Most of our information about the hollowing out of the stone vessels in Mesopotarnia cornes frorn the drill-bits that were identified in a number of sites. Drill-heads and drill-bits recovered from Ur led Woolley to interpret thern as part of a bowdrill (1956: 14, fig. 5). His illustration (Fig. 5.7b) shows the drill-bit as a circular stone, fiat on the top and curved underneath, with an indentation on each side to attach the drill shaft. Similar figure-of-eight hard-stone drill-bits and drill-heads for bow-drills appear with the Neolithic stone vesseis at Jarmo in Iraq (Moholly-Naggy 1983: 294). Figure 5.7a illustrates one of these drill-bits from Jarmo, where head pieces for drills were also found among the stonework (Moholy-Naggy 1985: fig. 132.5). Figure-of-eight shaped hard-stone vase-borers, were common at the site of Uruk (Wartke 1979; Eichmann 1987). These drill-bits, formed into flattened spheroids with indentations, are similar to those found in Egypt much later. A schist relief of the late fourth millennium BC from Uruk depicts three squating craftsmen in the act of what appears to be hollowing out stone vessels (Amiet 1982: fig. 232; Moorey 1993: pl.6A). This relief depicts one of the possible mechanisms of drilling employed in Mesopotamia. One of these craftsmen is illustrated in Figure 6.6c. Although the surface of this distinctive relief is worn, the positioning of the body, the drill-heads at the top of the shaft, and the triangle-like object in the right hand are visible, indicating that these craftsmen are operating bowl-drills. Whether they were running a tubular metal drill or a wooden shaft with hafted drill-bits is difficult to infer from this relief, Tubular drills may have also been used in the Early Dynastic period, although it has yet to be documented archaeologically.

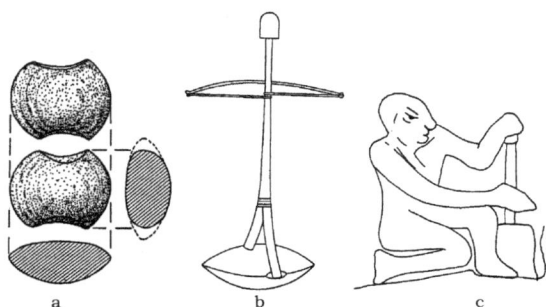

Fig. 5.7. Drilling implements in Mespotamia

In addition to the use of bow drills, the use of chisels is documented in eastern Iran, where chlorite vessels at the third millennium BC site of Tepe Yahya provided evidence for the use of chisels in hollowing out the interiors of vessels (Kohl 1974). Roughly parallel scars observed on the interiors vary in depth and angle, suggesting that metal chisels were hammered against the unfinished block. The recovery of such metal points at Tepe Yahya (Kohl 1974: fig. 16) confirms the adoption of such a methodology to hollow out stone vessels. Such chisels used to hollow out stone vessels is also documented at the third millennium BC site of Shahr-ı Sokhta in eastern Iran (Tosi 1969; Ciarla 1981). Although no direct association between tools and alabaster wasters has been identified at any of the activity areas, the traces left on the interior of several unfinished forms show that metal chisels were empioyed to hollow out large open-shaped vessels. Chisel stroke impressions, made in a downward direction, correspond to the tip of an actual chisel found during the excavations at the site (Tosi 1969: 369). The softness of chlorite apparently led Shahr-ı

Sokhta craftsmen ta adopt a strategy involving chiseling rather than rotary drilling. It is not likely that chiseling was adopted by craftsmen at Kulaksızlar, since marble is harder than chlorite, and copper tools do not provide effective results. In addition, the amount of copper needed for marble working would have been very costly.

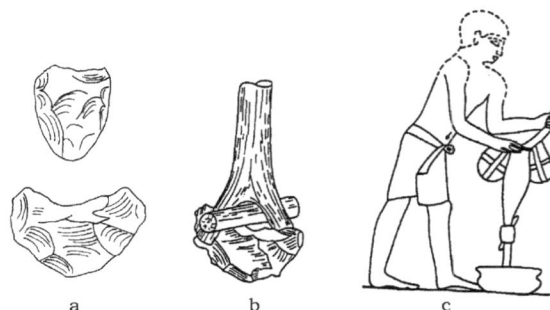

Fig. 5.8. Crank drill used in stone vessel making in Egypt

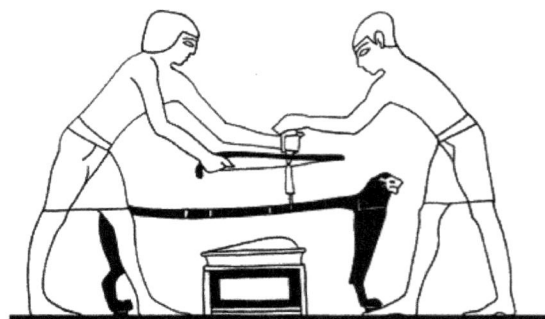

Fig. 5.9. Bow drill used in bead-making in ancient Egypt

Evidence from the Pre-Dynastic and Old Kingdom periods in Egypt, where both the bow-drill and the crank drill were used, provides useful information on ancient drilling techniques. An analysis of the ways in which the Egyptian crank- and bow-drills were used may provide useful insights into our understanding of drilling implements found at Kulaksızlar. In his study of the technology of ancient Egypt, A. Lucas (1964: 424) mentioned that stone vessels were drilled using a crank borer, on the end of which crescent-shaped drill-bits were inserted. Old Kingdom Egyptian tomb reliefs provide significant information regarding the form of drill used to hollow out stone vessels. The relief of a crank-drill being used (Fig. 5.8c) illustrates the craftsmen gripping the top of the shaft with one hand, while the other is placed just below the weight. Tying a pair of heavy stones or sacks of sand to the spindle probably provided the necessary pressure on the cutting edges of the drill-bit. The use of the weighted crank drill is pictured in a number of tombs, for example on a relief from a tomb at Saqqara, dating to the fifth dynasty (El-Khouli 1978: pl. 146).

Excavations by Caton-Thomson and Gardner (1934: pLs. 22-23) in the workshop and related areas at the Old Kingdom period site of Umm-es-Sawwan yielded considerable number of crescent-shaped flints in contexts that indicate their use for drilling in gypsum working (Fig. 5.8a-b). Whether or not these crescent-shaped drill-bits were inserted at the end of a wooden shaft remains a topic of controversy, although a considerable number of flint drill-heads were recovered in Egypt (Lauer and Debono 1950; Puglisi 1967: figs. 6-7; Caneva 1970). In addition to the use of crescent-shaped flints, figure-of-eight shaped stone borers were also used in ancient Egypt (Borchardt 1907: figs. 123-24). Remarkable similarities between the ancient and contemporary stone-vessel manufacturing techniques exist, since Egyptian craftsmen stil use the crank-drill (Hester and Heizer 1981: 19). The only difference between the modern and ancient crank-drills is the use of metal drill-bits in the former and the use of stone abrasives in the latter. It has also been elaimed that the tubular drill, which removes cylindrical blocks of material instead of pulverizing the interior, is older than the crank-drill (Hartenber and Schmidt 1981: 158).

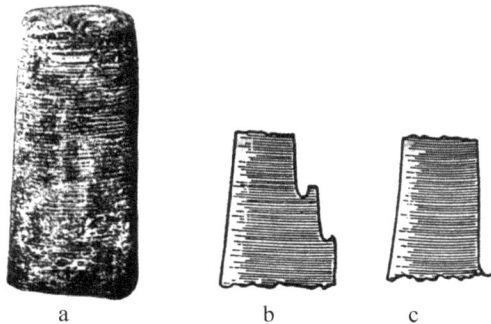

Fig. 5.9. Bore cores from Egypt (a) and Crete (b-c)

The tubular copper-drill used to hollow out stone vessels in Egypt is operated either by rolling the shaft between the palms or by means of a bow. Removing substantial volumes of stone requires less labor and effort than pulverizing the entire mass. A group of alabaster vessels found at a tomb at Saqqara demonstrates that the tubular drills were used in conjunction with abrasive powders as early as the First Dynasty in Egypt (Lucas 1960: 494). The bore core illustrated in Figure 5.9a can be accepted as evidence for the use of tubular drills in ancient Egypt (Petrie 1917: 44; Rieth 1958: 107; Roodenberg 1989: 143). This granite core was evidently produced by a tubular drill or locall available reeds fed with abrasives such as emery, sand, quartz, and corrundum. Egyptian reliefs showing the use of a bow-drill in woodworking are also useful to reconstruct the mechanics of this implement (James 1984: fig. 20). In this example (Fig. 5.9), the craftsman sets the drill into oscillatory motion, while a second person applies pressure on the drill-head. This clearly illustrates that Egyptian craftsmen often cooperated when precision required. The size of the bow is determined by the material to be drilled, since a large bow can rotate more than 360° in drilling a wooden artifact.

Third millennium B.C. Crete provides complementary evidence about the drilling techniques. According to Warren (1969) the method involving a rotating tubular drill was in use in the Early Minoan period. Warren maintains that use of a bow-drill and split reeds, fed with abrasive powder, may have been empioyed in Crete during the Early Minoan II and III periods (1969: 164). Evidence for drilling from Crete is derived from the anaiysis of over fifty stone cores that were revealed during the excavations at Knossos. The cores from Knossos, drilled out from the interior of vases, have horizontal lines produced by the drill suggesting the use of tubular drills (Warren 1969: fig. 6). All of these cores have a roughened bottom surface where they were detached from the vase (Fig. 5.9b-c). Consequently, projections were left on the interior base of the vessels after the driiled cores had been broken away. The actual cutting action of the tool could not have been done by the tubular drill itself (reed or metal), but by the abrasive powder fed into the hole in which the tubular drill ran. The abrasive powder is often found adhering to the walls of the vessel. Blue-gray powder adhering to the cores from Knossos provided evidence that the Cretan craftsmen of the third millennium B.C. drilled stone vesseis by using reed or metal tubular drills in conjunction with emery powder (Warren 1969: 164). The tubular drill apparently was set into oscillatory motion by using a bow drill.

The evidence of drilling implements used in Mesopotamia, Egypt, and Crete demonstrates that two different mechanisms were adopted to hollow out stone vessels: the tubular drill (which removes a cylindrical core from the center of the vessel) and the shaft drill (which pulverizes the interior mass of the vessel). Both drills were hand-powered by either a bow or a crank handle. The similarities in drilling techniques among the cultures of the Old World do not require any cultural connection. We know from the ethnographic record that geographically and temporally distant cultures invented similar drilling implements independently (McGuire 1882). Experimentation with different techniques and the type of artifact to be drilled probably led to the limited amount of the variation in drilling implements. The kind of drilling method used in Chalcolithic Anatolia is difficult to establish. Stone vessels are known from numerous Anatolian Neolithic and Chalcolithic sites such as Çayönü, Mezraa Teleilat, Canhasan, Körtik Tepe, Hallan Çemi, Domuztepe, and Hacılar. For instance, a fragmentary unfinished stone jar from Hacılar shows clear drilling marks in the interior, suggesting the use of a rotary drill (Mellaart 1970: 150). The high quantity of marble vessels at Late Neolithic Hacılar may be evidence of stone vessel production there. The technique used for drilling marble vessels at Hacılar might have been similar to the one used at Bouqras in northern Syria (Roodenberg 1989: fig. 82). Horizontal lines of rotary drilling observed on the interior of stone vessel fragments from Bouqras show that the implement used was most probably a bow-drill. These horizontal drilling marks share a number of similarities with those seen on Kulaksızlar artifacts, suggesting the use of similar drilling technologies in the hollowing out of stone vessels.

There is also ethnographic evidence for bow-drill use in various parts of Anatolia. Black amber bead-makers in the Erzurum region of eastern Turkey use bow-drills made out of branches of wood with dried animal entrails as cords (Fig. 5.11). Due to their precision, bow-drills are preferred to pierce the beads (Gündoğdu 2004), and are still used in lapiz lazuli bead-making in Afghanistan (Kenoyer 1992: 44) and agate bead-making in Iran (Possehl 1981: 39). Although the evidence for the use of bowdrills from Old World cultures shares similarities, there is no reason to assume that this implement was an adopted technology since it could also have been locally invented at Kulaksızlar as in most parts of the ancient and contemporary world.

Fig. 5.11. Craftsmen using bow drill in bead making in northeastern Anatolia

A replication study was also undertaken to document the amount of labor invested in the drilling stage. The drilling replication experiment provided a picture of how laborious it was to hollow out a marble pointed beaker. I made the bow from the branch of a pine tree and attached a leather cord on its both ends. I also used a sandstone drill-bit and drill-heads that I fashioned from locally available sandstone from the stream bed near the village of Sarıçalı. After I secured the beaker preform, I set the bow-drill in oscillatory motion in order to understand how the horizontal lines of rotary drilling observed on the interior of beaker fragments were formed. I confirmed that the drilling marks observed on the experimental vessel were identical to those seen on archaeological materials. Replication experiments ciarifled that sandstone drill-bits were not run wet, mainly due to the fact that sandstone dissolves when water used as a lubricant.

Once beaker preforms have been drilled, the fourth step in the production of beakers is the process of refinement, which transforms the drilled preform into a finished beaker. This step of abrading the pecking marks on the exterior of the beaker requires substantial labor input. After drilling, the vessel has a thick wall of almost 1.5 cm with horizontal lines of rotary drilling on the interior. Blocks of sandstone are then rubbed over the interior and exterior in a vertical motion to thin out the walls. Prior to refinement, the thickness of the rim fragments measures between 1.0 and 1.5 crn, while the thickness of finished rim fragrnents measures an average of 0.6 crn. This means that substantial effort was required to thin out the walls of the beakers, which could have been achieved by sandstone abrasives. The abrasive blocks were rubbed either vertically or diagonally to refine the drilling and pecking marks on the beaker exterior and the drilling marks on the interior surfaces. Example **44** (Pl. 9) shows that the scratching marks rarely follow the contour of the vessel and appear to result frorn the random motion of the craftsmen' hand. It was at this stage that the vertical lugs were also given their final shapes on the upper part of the body. This required abrasive blocks with straight edges, was a laborious process.

In the replication experirnent of the abrasion process, I used sandstone blocks by rubbing them in a vertical direction following the contour of the beaker. Quartz particles in the sandstone left deep traces on the beaker, which srnoothers could not entirely remove. The polishing process was probably carried out with marble pebbles and blocks of granite. A smoother must be fine-grained or crystalline. Some of the pebble-srnoothers found at the site possess surfaces with scratches running in various directions clearly indicating their function.

	Coarse flaking	Pecking	Drilling	Refinement
Pointed beaker	10 %	20 %	60 %	10 %
Pointed bowl	10 %	35 %	50 %	5 %
Kilia Figurine	15 %	75 %	-	10 %

Table 5.3. Estimated ratio of breakagein the marble figurine and vessel production (on the basis of entire surface finds)

Analysis of four hundred diagnostic archaeological specimens from the various stages of marble beaker manufacture demonstrates that only 30 % of this assemblage represent manufacturing errors occurring during the rough shaping of the beaker during coarse flaking and pecking. Sixty percent of the unfinished marble beaker fragments appear to have been the result of errors that occurred during the drilling process, while the remaining 10 % show breakage during the refinement and finishing steps. This analysis of four hundred beaker fragments shows that the ratio of breakage was lower during the earlier steps of manufacture such as the coarse flaking (10 %) and pecking (20 %) to create a beaker preform. This pattern was determined to a large extent by the application of uncontrolled force during percussive and drilling works, Uneven pressure applied on the drill resulted in longitudinal removal of fragment from the upper part, while the misplacement of the preform in a pit resulted in a horizontal spilt.

2. Manufacturing Bowls

In addition to the methods of beaker manufacture, I documented the techniques used in manufacturing bowls. The techniques and tools involved in fashioning bowls were nearly the same as those for beakers. A comprehensive study of the bowl fragments from coarse flaking to refinement stage suggests four manufacturing steps. The first involves the coarse flaking of a marble block into the shape that roughly approaches the size of the intended bowl. The second includes thinning out the large flaking marks on the exterior of the coarsely flaked blocks by pecking. It is at this stage that craftsmen also crudely chipped out the interiors of the bowls by using pointed tools to create emplacements for drilling.

I attempted to replicate a bowl 12 cm in height with a 12 cm rim diameter to confirm the reconstructed methodology and the tools used to manufacture a marble bowl. I used the same type of stone tools and raw materials that would have been available to Kulaksızlar craftsmen. I first reduced the size of the marble block by removing large flakes with spherical basalt cobbles that I collected from the slopes of the hills to the northeast of the site. I carried out the flaking process holding the block on my knees because working raw material on the ground raises a risk of breakage. Then, I finely pecked the exterior of the bowl to create an outline that approached the size of the future vessel. I also slightly chipped out the interior of the bowl preform to create an emplacement point for the drill-bit, which required careful attention. Errors can easily be made at this stage and I accidentally removed a small flake from the rim during the coarse flaking. Because the accidental flake removed from the rim was not very large, I decided to reduce the height of the bowl rather than discard this bowl preform, I think that this was a strategy that Kulaksızlar craftsmen also adopted. The 7 to 12 cm variation in the heights of the fifteen preform bowls with 12 cm rim diameter found at the site may have resulted from the reuse of preforms that were broken while the interior was being chipped out. In marble bowl manufacture, chipping out of the interior was the most risky stage before the drilling process began.

It was only after the rough shaping of the vessel and the crude chipping out of the interior that craftsmen began drilling (Step 3). The use of different shaped drill-bits such as crescent-shaped and conical drill-bits would explain how craftsmen hollowed out a conical cavity that followed the external contours of the vessel. To hollow out a pointed bowl with a 13 cm rim diameter, a crescent-shaped drill-bit with 9.5 cm diameter (**143**) and a tapering drill-bit with a smaller diameter (**152**) would be adequate to create a narrowing cavity that matched the exterior contours of a bowl. The drilling marks seen on the interior of several unfinished bowls (**60-62**, Pl. 11) confirm the use of at least two different drill-bits to hollow out bowls with heights ranging from 7 to 12 cm. The first

drill-bit might have had a crescent-shape, since the bevel observed around the rim (**58**, Pl. 12) has a different angle than the marks left by the second drill-bit. The projection observed near the interior center also confirms a change in the shape of the drill-bit (**60** and **61**). The replication experiment gave me an opportunity to confirm the successive use of crescent-shaped and conical drill-bits to drill the interior of a bowl with a 9 cm height and a 9 cm rim diameter. Sandstone drill-bits leave horizontal lines on the interiors of vessels, similar to those seen on the archaeological materials. When run wet, sandstone drill-bits created a very fine surface. Sandstone dissolves when used wet, forming a fine abrasive powder.

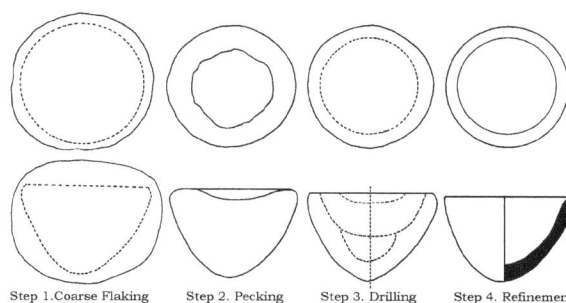

Fig. 5.12 Suggested manufacturing stages of pointed bowls

The replication experiment leads me to believe that the manufacture of a marble bowl required the cooperation of two people. It is technically difficult to simultaneously secure a 12 cm high rounded bowl, with a finely pecked exterior and a pointed base, in a previously dug pit and operate a bow-drill on such a small artifact. If one considers the fragile structure of marble, there is no reason not to assume that the hollowing out of a bowl as thin as 1 cm requires careful cooperation of at least two individuals for a successful completion. One craftsman was responsible for the running of bow-drill, while a second person probably secured the pointed bowl during drilling operation. A single craftsman could have carried out the drilling process If the vessel was not rounded or had projections on the exterior. The probable need for cooperation can be used to support the argument that Kulaksızlar production was a group-based activity. Cooperation would undoubtedly minimize the rate of error in bowl manufacture. Any individual within the household or community would have easily fulfilled this task.

The fourth step in manufacturing a pointed bowl involves removal of percussion and abrasion marks. Sandstone abrasives were rubbed over the surface to remove the pecking marks on the exterior and the drilling marks on the interior. Projections created by the use of different drill-bits on the interiors were removed by hand-held sandstone abrasive tools. Analysis of a number of unfinished marble pointed bowl fragments demonstrates that abrasive blocks were rubbed in multiple directions, depending on the size of the vessel. Sandstone provides a smooth surface, despite the fact that the quartz particles in the composition of sandstone leave small scratches on the surface. These scratches were most probably removed by fine grained rocks such as river-pebbles in conjunction with water.

Analysis of manufacturing errors related to pointed bowl manufacture shows that the ratio of error during the coarse flaking of the selected marble blocks (Step 1) was 10 %. The ratio of error appears to have increased to 35 % during the second step of the removal of the coarse flaking marks and chipping out of the vessel interior by pecking. Analysis of nearly 120 unfinished marble pointed bowls also shows that it was the drilling stage that most breakage occurred during the bowl manufacture (50 %).

3. Manufacturing Kilia Figurines

The sequences of Kilia figurine manufacture were deduced from a comprehensive study of almost 900 finished and unfinished fragments representing all stages from the rough out to discard phase. Percussion and abrasion marks observed on these fragments illustrate the methods of production adopted in their manufacture and on the craftsmen's tool use. Production of the Kilia figurines seems to have required more labor input and skill than the manufacture of marble vessels. The first step in manufacturing a Kilia figurine is to trim a marble piece to a flat blank (73-78, Pl. 13), approaching the approximate height, thickness, and width of the figurine to be made. The difficulties involved in the production of figurines must have led craftsmen to formulate a preconceived plan of the various stages involved in order to avoid time-consuming errors. It is difficult to determine whether or not the craftsmen drew the outlines of the figurine on the marble blank. The lack of any such evidence on the marble roughed-out blocks implies that drawing of the outlines of the figurine would not have been necessary after a few trials. Craftsmen may have achieved motor habits for the methods of preforming the raw material into the intended figurine form. Thinning of the notch between the head and body through pecking was the most risky stage in the first step of figurine manufacture.

The second step of manufacturing Kilia figurines was the thinning of the blank, removal of large flake scars and creation of the general anatomical details with pointed tools. Craftsmen simply started to outline the silhouette of the figurine form by removing small flakes from the previously prepared flat blank. They slightly thinned the neck-division (Pls. 14-15) and tapered the lower half of the blank to a shape in keeping with the final figurine form. A blank with a tapered end found at the site (74, Pl. 13) together with a great amount of lower end fragments of preforms (e.g. Pls. 14-15) indicate that removing small flakes from the marble blank was the main technique used in

this step. The head fragments illustrated in plates 16 and 17 clearly demonstrate the ways how the breakage may have occurred during the shaping of the necks.

Experiments to replicate the entire manufacturing process were also undertaken to understand how complex it was to make a Kilia figurine and how much skill and energy would have been necessary from the beginning to the end of the manufacturing process. Replication experiments confirmed the methods used in the first two steps of figurine manufacture. I worked on locally available marbles using stone tools that I had collected from the immediate vicinity of the site. The marble blocks that I collected allowed me to manufacture a figurine 14 cm high and 6.5 cm wide. The first step of the replication experiment involved the removal of large flakes from the marble block into a shape approaching the maximum thickness, width, and length of the figurine to be made for this step. I used stone tools with pointed ends. Due to the fragile nature of the neck, I twice failed when thinning out this part of figurine. During my third attempt, I managed to create the silhouette of the figurine. The replication experiment confirms that most breakage occurred when thinning the necks by pecking.

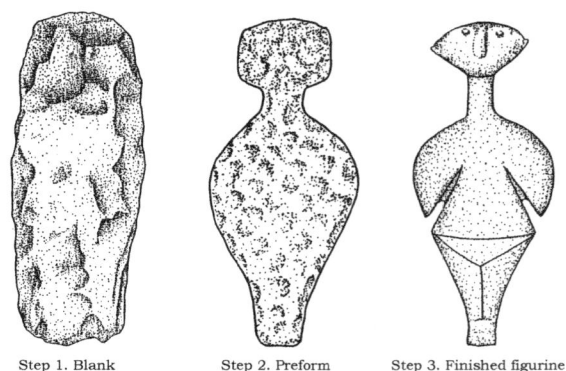

Step 1. Blank   Step 2. Preform   Step 3. Finished figurine

Fig. 5.13. Suggested three main manufacturing stages of Kilia figurine manufacture

The refinement of the marble preform into a finished figurine is the third step of production. Removal of the pecking marks was a relatively complex and arduous process since much of the fashioning of the figurine was achieved by the use of sandstone tools. The formation of a flat body and a head that was twice as thick as the body required extensive abrasive work. It is possible that the figurine preform was rubbed repeatedly over a flat abrasive such as the bifacial flat sandstone and emery blocks that were found at the site. This process could have reduced the amount of time necessary to form a flat body that contrasts with a thicker head. The flattened back of the several figurine preform fragments confirms the use of such a technique. Abrasive marks observed on one head fragment that had broken off at the neck (102, Pl. 17) demonstrate how craftsmen may have formed a circular neck. Lines of abrasion running parallel to the neck, which is elliptical in cross-section indicate that the neck was worked from both sides using an abrasive such as crushed sandstone. Replication experiments confirm how laborious it was to refine a figurine preform using abrasive tools. I used flint scrapers and blocks of sandstone to create the figurine illustrated in Figure 5. 14.

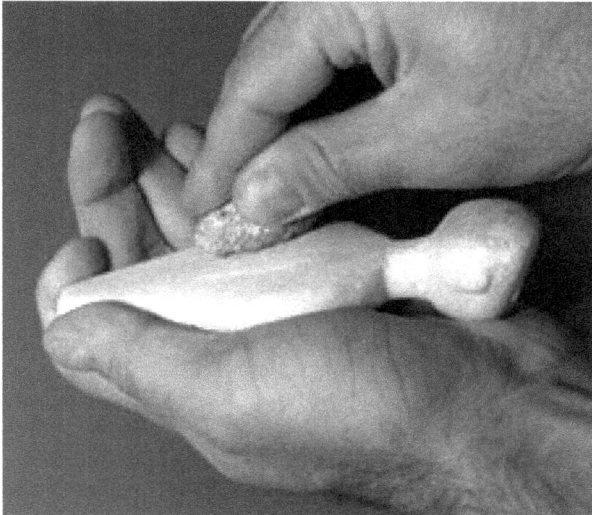

Fig. 5.14. Replicating experiment showing the refinement of a figurine by using a sandstone block

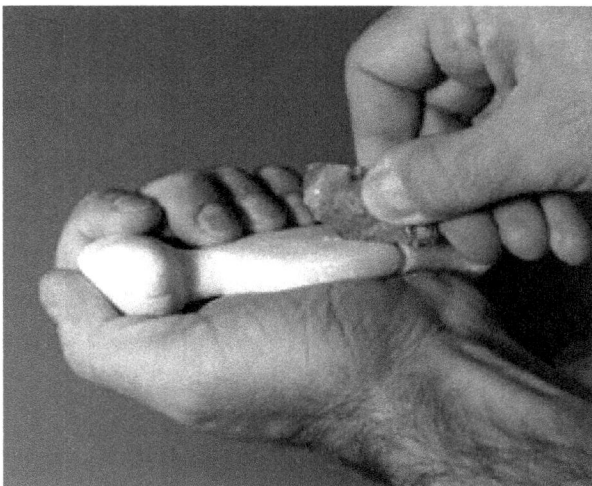

Fig. 5. 15. Replicating experiment showing the incision of the arm division of a figurine by using a flind blade

It was most likely at the stage of refinement that the nose, ears, and eyes were sculpted with the aid of crushed sandstone and flint scrappers. The diagonal breakage observed on the corners of a number of flint tools leads me to believe that division between the bent arms and body was probably created by using sharp-edged tools such as flint blades. I used flint blades to emphasize the cleft between the arms and the body incision pubic triangle (Fig. 5.15). Experimentation with a sharp-edged flint confirmed how workable was this material for incision. Archaeological evidence confirms the use of such tools in refinement process.

After the incision process was completed, the surface was finished by polishing, giving the figurines a highly reflective sheen, which might have been achieved by the use of fine-grained marble river-pebbles or organic substances such as leather and wool. The figurines illustrated in Plates 20 and 21 demonstrate the polished finish after completing such an arduous process. The intensive use of fine-grained white marble with varying shades ranging from yellow to blue gave the figurines attractive final appearances. It was probably variability in the color of the marbles and its attractive final appearance that made marble as a valuable raw material in prehistoric times. The high level of technical investment and the attractive appearance of finished figurines was most likely due to the symbolism attached in this iconography.

An examination of the artifacts representing the various stages of figurine manufacture shows that most of the breakage (75 %, Table 5.3) occurred either during the pecking or thinning of the neck or working of the waist . Because shaping of the figurine was done by abrasion after the silhouette of the figurine had been created the number of specimeris representing breakage during the refinement process is relatively small (10 %). The rate of error must have been very low for the step of refinement as the use of abrasive tools hardly requires the application of high pressure, thereby reducing the potential for breakage (10 %).

E. Distribution

Some early village societies specialized in specific crafts for the purpose of exchanging these products with other communities. This form of specialization, also called "village craft specialization" (Perlès 1992: 150), was an important aspect of prehistoric western Anatolian cultures. Exchange networks for objects of special workmanship such as prestige items and those used in cults or rituals are not well known, and the nature of their exchange networks remains to be elucidated. Movements of these specific classes of artifacts among early village societies were either direct (inter-personal or inter-societal reciprocal exchanges) or indirect (middleman trade through pastoralists or itinerant traders).

The marble Kilia figurines and pointed vessels from the Kulaksızlar workshop can be classified as valuable artifacts that were widely exchanged and highly valued. The pattern involved in their distribution can be used to demonstrate the ways in which specialist-produced marble artifacts were exchanged, which in turn highlights the motivation behind the specialized attention placed upon their production. It was argued that valuable or prestigious objects appear in the archaeological record either as a result of deliberate burial or through loss or accidental breakage (Renfrew 1972: 467). The lack of excavations of burials, combined with the minimal number of excavations of Chalcolitihic sites, leaves me with only a small number of marble Kilia figurines and vessels.

Nearly forty marble Kilia figurines and eleven pointed beakers similar to those manufactured at Kulaksızlar have been found in sites of western Anatolia, the Aegean islands, as well as Bulgaria (Appendix 2). One way to determine if these marble artifacts were actually produced at Kulaksızlar is to compare the similarities in style, manufacturing techniques, and metric details. Information derived from this sourcing study can also be used to reconstruct the patterns of cultural interactions during the Chalcolithic period. The 'down-the-line' model of exchange proposed as explanations for the distribution of valuables or prestige objects in the pre-Bronze Age Aegean world can be used to understand the patterns involved in the distribution of Kulaksızlar marble artifacts. This model is based on the argument that a certain proportion of received objects were passed down to nearby settlement, resulting in a gradual decline in the number of artifacts as ones moves away from the source (Renfrew et al. 1968). Another alternative exchange model I consider important is the 'itinerant trader model.' This model depends on the role of itinerant peoples supplying exotic goods (Perlès 1992). It is used to explain the distribution of obsidian blades in Neolithic Greece. The low density of homogeneous, high quality blades across Neolithic sites in Greece is used as evidence for the presence of itinerant traders supplying Neolithic communities with obsidian pressure-blades. Itinerant traders may sometimes take the form of 'pastoralist exchange model,' which can structurally be compared to the itinerant-trader model. It explains the spread of exotic artifacts over great distances through the activities of pastoralists. These exchange models could be relevant to the interpretation of the distribution of Kulaksızlar marble artifacts. Their application to the Kulaksızlar data can broaden our view of exchange and the distribution of special classes of artifacts. Patterns of exchange, derived from an evaluation of movements of prestige, rare, or exotic artifacts from western Anatolia, are used to determine possible mechanisms that tied the villages of this period together.

1. Sourcing of Exchanged Artifacts

Identifying the physical source of an artifact is fundamental to establishing both the presence and the extent of prehistoric exchange. The primary objective in identifying the sources of artifacts is to prove the assumed connection between the artifact and the proposed manufacturing place. Isotopic or chemical properties of the exchanged marble artifacts can be matched with probable sources. Techniques such as thin-section microscopy, electron-spin resonance spectroscopy, strontium isotopic ratio, and stable isotope analysis of oxygen and carbon are the most useful techniques that can be used in the sourcing of marble (Herz 1987 and 1992). Application of such techniques would most likely help confirm whether or not comparable marble beakers and Kilia figurines found at other sites were actually manufactured at Kulaksızlar. The current location of these comparable artifacts in nearly thirty different museums in seven

different countries made a sourcing study nearly impossible. I originally aimed to carry out sourcing studies of marble figurines and vessels found at western Anatolian sites. This was also not possible since to permission to remove small samples of marble from these specimens, which currently kept in eight different museums in western Turkey, could not be obtained because they were included in individual studies that treat the arrival of semi-precious stones into the prehistoric western Anatolia.

Stylistic analysis is the most standard and inexpensive approach adopted in sourcing studies. The basic objective of this approach is to assign an artifact to its place of manufacture by a similarity in stylistic traits. Criteria such as artifact form, and manufacturing techniques are often used to identify the place of origin for an exchanged artifact. One drawback to this approach is that local imitations of exchanged artifacts can cause confusion in detecting the manufacturing place of finished artifacts. Similarities observed in manufacturing techniques and metric details are helpful in this case. Comparisons of the manufacturing techniques, stylistic similarities, and measurements are the methods that I will use to determine whether or not comparable marble figurines and pointed vessels found at other sites were the products of the Kulaksızlar workshop. This is important because there is an unavoidable interrelationship between the nature of demand and the scale of production.

Most of the marble Kilia figurines and pointed beakers found at western Anatolian sites display strong similarities with those produced at Kulaksızlar in terms of style, metric details, and manufacturing techniques. Pointed beakers found at sites on the Aegean islands constitute a distinct group, although they display a number of similarities with those of western Anatolian examples in terms of style, measurements, and manufacturing techniques. Pointed beaker fragments are found in four different sites in western Anatolia: Kumtepe and Beşik-Sivritepe in the Troad in northwestern Anatolia and Demircihöyük in the Eskişehir region far inland in northwest Anatolia (Fig. 5.16). A lower end fragment of a pointed beaker found at Kumtepe in the Troad (**217**) may be compared to the Kulaksızlar beakers from a number of perspectives. In terms of manufacturing technique, the horizontal lines of rotary drilling observed on this lower end fragment (Sperling 1976: 322) recall a technique that was commonly employed at Kulaksızlar. In addition, the maximum diameter at the preserved height implies that it belonged to an elongated conical beaker type, similar examples of which were widely manufactured at the Kulaksızlar workshop. The elongated nature of the Kumtepe beaker, along with the use of similar manufacturing techniques, led me to the assumption that the Kumtepe beaker was a product of the Kulaksızlar marble workshop. Two rim fragments of pointed beakers (**220** and **221**) have been recovered from Beşik-Sivritepe in the Troad, which is located several kilometers south of Kumtepe. These two rim fragments are finely polished from both sides and provide little information on the drilling technique. Although they preserve no base or vertical lugs, the angle of the rim wall indicate that they belonged to conical beakers. Both have rim diameters that measure nearly 6 cm, similar sizes of which existed at Kulaksızlar. The recovery of a Kilia figurine at adjacent Beşik-Yassıtepe (Korfmann 1988: 162) supports the inference that the beakers to which these rim fragments belonged may have also been actual Kulaksızlar products. A rim fragment identical to those found at Beşiktepe has also been uncovered recently at Gülpınar on the coastal Troad (218) (Takaoğlu 2005). One rim fragment of a marble beaker (219) was also found at Demircihöyük in the Eskişehir region (Efe 1988: pl. 37; Seeher 1987: fig. 1) in a fill that was evidently brought from an earlier settlement near the Early Bronze Age mound. The pre-Bronze Age pottery with which this fragment was found suggests a similar date for this fragment (Seeher 2000 pers. comm.). This beaker can also be compared to marble pointed beakers manufactured at the Kulaksızlar workshop in terms of size and the treatment of the vertical lug. Similarities among the marble pointed beakers of western Anatolia imply that Kulaksızlar was the site that supplied the communities with these vessels during the Chalcolithic period. Although I do not want to over emphasize the similarities in the marble beaker type, the strong similarities among the pottery of Kulaksızlar, Gülpınar, Kumtepe 1a, and Beşik-Sivritepe, combined with the lack of marble sources and evidence for manufacture of pointed beakers in northwest Anatolia, leads me to consider them imports from Kulaksızlar.

Pointed vessels manufactured at Kulaksızlar also present similarities to those found in the Aegean islands such as Samos, Naxos, Lemnos, and Kephala. At first glance, one rim and a wall fragment from Tigani on Samos (214 and 215), a base fragment from Koukonesi on Lemnos (216), one complete and two fragments of pointed beakers from Kephala on Keos (211 and 213), and a complete pointed beaker from Naxos (212) all share similarities in style and manufacturing techniques with beakers manufactured at the Kulaksızlar workshop. Among these Aegean examples, it has previously been argued that one complete and two fragments of pointed beakers from the Final Neolithic level at Kephala on Keos might not habe been local products of the island (Coleman 1977: 64). There was no evidence for their local manufacture and the fine-grained and creamy white marble of the beakers differ from that of the local Kean marbles. The texture and the color of marble, the manufacturing techniques, and the artifact dimensions indicate some kind of connection with Kulaksızlar. The rim diameter of the Kephala beaker, which measures 6.8 cm, is comparable to the Kulaksızlar examples. We know from the statistical study of rim diameters at Kulaksızlar that the majority cluster around 7 cm. Lines of rotary drilling on the interior of the Kephala

beakers and the vertical and diagonal abrasive marks seen on these drilling marks, as well as the whole exterior, recall a technique that was frequently used at the Kulaksızlar workshop. The main difference between the Kulaksızlar examples and the Kephala piece is the treatment of vertical lug with horned tops, which are yet to be documented among the Kulaksızlar specimens. For this reason, it is difficult to state with certainty that the marble pointed beakers from Kephala were manufactured at the Kulaksızlar workshop. Similar problems are also involved with the beaker fragment from Tigani. Felsch (1988: 146) remarks that the marble of the fragmentary pointed beakers from Tigani can hardly have been Samian. The rim diameter measures 6.7 cm, which is almost identical to the one from Kephala. The horned ends of the vertical lugs of the Tigani beaker, as in the Kephala example, differ from the Kulaksızlar examples. The technique used in the horizontal piercing of vertical lugs on the Tigani and Kephala beakers appears to be different from the one on the Kulaksızlar fragment 44 (Pl. 9). This similarity in the treatment of vertical lugs prevents me from making an explicit statement that the marble pointed beakers from the Aegean islands were products of Kulaksızlar. In a similar way, the marble pointed beaker from Varna cemetery might have been an import from Anatolia, since the Grave 41 in which this complete beaker was found also yielded an obsidian blade originating to the central Anatolian sources (Dimitrov 2003: 32). The presence of pointed beaker type in Bulgaria seems to indicate that the cultural interaction sphere of the fifth millennium B.C. also included parts of the Balkans.

Fig. 5. 16. Map showing sites with marble pointed beakers

In *Stone Vessels of the Cyclades* (1996), Getz-Gentle briefly evaluated the western Anatolian-Aegean connection with regard to pointed beaker forms. Noting the contemporaneity of the Kilia figurine torso and the pointed beaker fragments recovered at Beşik-Sivritepe in the Troad, Getz-Gentle stated that "if, as I suspect, the beakers in these cases belong to the same cultural assemblage as the figures, then a date earlier than FN Kephala might be indicated and an Anatolian origin of the beaker type ought to be seriously considered (1996: 286, note 96)." Whether the conical vessels found in the Aegean islands were manufactured locally or in western Anatolia does not alter the fact that the cultures of the eastern Aegean islands and western Anatolia interacted with each other. The chronological priority of Kulaksızlar examples inclines me to believe that the pointed beakers from Tigani, Kephala, and Naxos were imitations of western Anatolian examples. We can argue from the overall similarities in the form of the marble pointed beakers that Kulaksızlar examples made their way into the eastern Aegean islands in the fifth millennium B.C. Being geographically adjacent, western Anatolia and the Aegean islands were part of the same cultural interaction sphere. We know from the similarities in the pottery assemblages that maritime exchange was in existence during this period. The close affinity between the pottery assemblages of Kulaksızlar and Aegean islands such as Samos, Chios, and Saliagos is evidence for this interaction. A route involving the Hermos Delta into the Bay of Izmir may have facilitated the intra-regional interaction, resulting in the presence of pointed beaker types in the Aegean world. The lack of marble pointed beakers and pottery comparable to that of Kulaksızlar and eastern Aegean islands and in the sites of the Izmir region is striking since they shared were parts of the same cultural formation zone. Therefore, I assume that marble pointed beakers found on the Aegean islands such as Samos, Naxos, and Keos, may be viewed as local imitations of Kulaksızlar marble beakers that arrived there through exchange.

Stylistic, metrical, and manufacturing techniques can also be used to detect whether or not the Kilia figurines that were widely distributed in western Anatolia were manufactured at Kulaksızlar. The figurines appear to have a more widespread distribution than the beakers. Kilia figurines were found at sites such as Beşik-Yassıtepe (**245**), Hanaytepe (**244**), Troy (**242**), and Kilia (**224**) in the northwestern; Kozağacı (**233, 235**), Aphrodosias (**336, 237**), and Karain Cave (**333**) in the southwestern; Yortan (**238**), Alaağaç (**239, 240**), Gavurtepe (**243**), Papazköy (**228**), and Selendi (**252-256**) in central-western Anatolia (Fig. 5.17). There is one complete example in the Mytilene museum on Lesbos (**230**), whose provenance is problematical. There are additional well-preserved examples of this type found in private collections, most of which reportedly came from Kırşehir in central Anatolia (**222, 223, 225, 317, 229, 249-251**). There are also several examples in private collections that are said to have come from western Anatolia, whose precise find places are unknown (**226, 227, 232, 232, 234, 246-248**).

Stylistic and metrical comparisons provide useful results in establishing a distribution pattern. Kilia figurines display distinctive anatomical characteristics that make it possible to carry out stylistic comparisons among available specimens. The bent forearms, heavy head, cylindrical neck, incisions, raised eyes, ears, and nose are characteristic features of this type. Based on these criteria, two different styles can be observed among the figurines. The first group includes figurines from Kırşehir, Kozağacı, Papazköy, Yortan, Alaağaç, and Selendi, whose heads are rather oval in shape and arms are not sculpturally distinguished (Pl. 38). It is noteworthy that, excluding those from Kozağacı and Kırşehir, most of the figurines representing this group are found at sites in central-west Anatolia. Examples were not found in excavations at Kırşehir and reports indicating finds at Kırşehir can be misleading. Purported Kırşehir examples are very similar to those of finished figurine fragments from Kulaksızlar. The torso fragments from Kulaksızlar (Pls. 19) are identical to the complete Kilia figurines (Pls. 20 and 21) which are said to have come from Kırşehir. The uniformity or standardization in style and measurements of the figurines show that the figurines ascribed to this first group were the products of Kulaksızlar craftsmen. The raising of the ears and nose, and the separation of the bent forearms from the waist are strong indicators of the use of similar manufacturing techniques among these examples. This style of depicting figurines was common at the workshop.

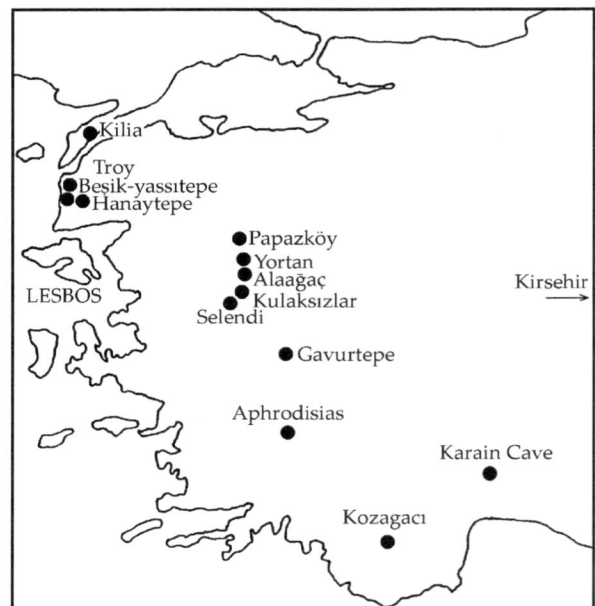

Fig. 5.17. Sites with Kilia figurines in western Anatolia

The torso from Beşik-Yassıtepe, one head from Troy (Pl. 38), one torso from Selendi (**252**), one complete figurine from Kilia (**224**), and one from the Guennol collection (**225**) (Pl. 37) belong to the second group of Kilia figurines, which offer slightly more anatomical details. Finished head fragments of such figurines are in existence at Kulaksızlar (Pl. 35). The figurine heads of this group from Kulaksızlar apparently belonged to figurines the same size as the figurine from the Kilia and the Guennol collection. It is difficult, however, to know whether or not any of these figurines found outside the Kulaksızlar workshop were local imitations, but it seems unlikely for a number of reasons. First, the similarities in manufacturing techniques, style, and measurements among the Kilia figurines point to a single production center for this type. Second, the high quantity of manufacturing debris points to a production for exchange. Third, there is no archaeological evidence for the production of similar types of artifacts in western Anatolia.

2. Reconstructing the Patterns of Exchange

In light of the relatively small quantity of marble figurines and vessels, it is not reasonable to argue for a well-organized trade during this period. However, Kulaksızlar evidence demonstrates that long-distance indirect trade including prestige items was in existence during this period. To understand how the marble artifacts were spread over great distances it is important to reconstruct the impact of exchange on the presence and maintenance of craft production at Kulaksızlar. A number of methods have been developed to test the validity of models explaining the distribution of specific craft products and to detect the processes behind their distribution in pre-urban times. These models may be tested against the Kulaksızlar data. Regression analysis has been employed to reconstruct the patterns of prehistoric exchange (Renfrew et. al. 1968). In this study, regression analysis was used to assess the relationship between distance (transport cost) and frequency (interaction). On a graph, in which frequency is represented on the y axis and distance on the x axis, all sites are plotted such that spatial variation has been collapsed to show distance as the primary determinant of interaction (Renfrew 1972: 465). In certain circumstances, the relative number of exchanged artifact types tends to decline as distance from its source increases, which is represented as a fall-off curve.

Regression analysis was used to describe the spatial patterning of exchanged Anatolian obsidian during the Neolithic (Renfrew et al. 1968: 327). The ratio of obsidian to flint in the total chipped stone industry at each site was plotted on a linear scale against the distance of the site from the relevant source. The percentage of obsidian found at sites suddenly declined between 300 and 600 kilometers from the source. The exponential decrease after 300 kilometers was explained by the argument that this area served as a supply zone, since almost 80 or 90% of the total chipped stone assemblages was comprised of obsidian. The area between 300 and 600 kilometers was viewed as a contact zone, where fall-off occurred in the percentage of obsidian. This fall-off curve ties in with the so-called "down-the-line" model, according to which village communities were keeping a proportion of the obsidian that they received before passing the given proportion to other villages. In this scheme, the quantity of obsidian drops off as one moves further away from the obsidian source. Although it is based

upon a heuristic hypothesis, Renfrew and his colleagues (1968: 329) believed that regression analysis could be useful to test models of prehistoric trade in certain circumstances. The positioning of the site in the region, recovery techniques, discard behavior, and the stage of manufacture at which the artifacts were introduced (e.g. in a roughly modified or finished state) all lead archaeologists to be cautious when applying regression analysis in interpreting the spatial distribution of artifacts. It would also appear that the down-the-line exchange of valuable artifacts can take the form of a prestige chain. Shackleton and Renfrew (1970: 1064) argued that the *Spondylus* shells of the north Aegean were traded northwards by a series of reciprocal gift-exchanges between persons of high status such as tribal leaders. *Spondylus* shells, found on the shores of the northern Aegean and used in making bracelets, were valued in the Neolithic sites of the Balkans, probably due to their exotic nature. These prestige goods are frequently handed on in subsequent exchanges, resulting in their distribution over considerable distances. They also provided a fall-off curve, suggesting a down-the-line exchange model.

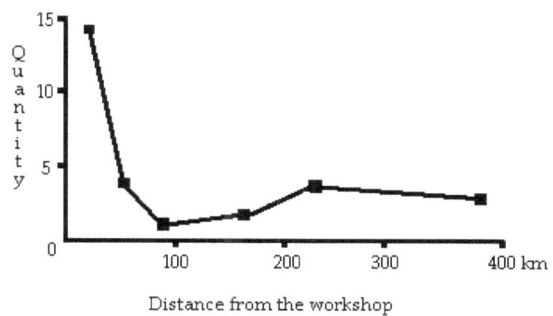

Fig.5.18. Histogram showing the distribution of Kilia figurines

Down-the-line exchange and prestige chain models can also be utilized to understand the distribution of the Kilia figurines, if one assumes that the Kulaksızlar workshop provided western Anatolian sites with these artifacts. Although the number of Kilia figurines found in western Anatolia is very small (ca. 40), regression analysis can be used to test whether or not down-the-line exchange was involved in the distribution of these figurines. The histogram illustrated in Figure 6.16 shows that the number of Kilia figurines is higher than the closer one gets to the Kulaksızlar workshop. The number of figurines found between 4 to 100 km appears to be higher than those found between 100 and 400 kilometers. Nearly fifteen fragments of Kilia figurines were found at Selendi (five of which are inventoried at the Manisa Museum and hence in the Appendix 2). When combined with two specimens from Alaağaç, one from Gavurtepe, one from Yortan, and one from Papazköy, the number of figurines approaches twenty in this region. In this context, central-western Anatolia may be viewed as the primary consumer area, since geographically and culturally this area formed a sub-region within western Anatolia. The widespread use of Kilia figurines in this area may be related to the fact that the land-based transportation costs involved in their distribution were lower there. The radius covering between 150 and 200 km from Kulaksızlar provided only two specimens, which were found in Aphrodisias in southeast Anatolia. The radius covering between 200 and 250 km from the workshop includes the Troadic sites such as Hanaytepe, Beşik-Yassıtepe, Kilia, and Troy in the northwest. Southeastern Anatolian sites such as Karain Cave and Kozağacı are located in an area that exceeds 400 km and only three examples of this type have been found there so far. The number of figurines found in the radius from 100 to 200 km is lower than one may expect for a true fall-off. The minimal number of Kilia figurines in an area covering a radius of 50 to 100 km, which appears to be an anomaly, was probably results from the lack of Chalcolithic excavations in the region .

Down-the-line exchange of these symbolic artifacts may have resulted in the observed distribution of figurines. Small portable items like Kilia figurines could have been moved along the already established trade networks through inter-personal or inter-societal exchanges. It is noteworthy that the sites with Kilia figurines are located on land-based trade routes along the major western Anatolian rivers. For example, the figurine from Gavur Tepe appears to have moved through a natural trade route following the Gediz River (ancient *Hermos*). By plotting of the Neolithic mounds on a map of western central-west Anatolia, Meriç (1993: 146) demonstrated that the concentration of settlements along the river basin during the Neolithic period was due to the importance of this route tying the coast to the hinterland. This is logical since the same route was also in use throughout the Bronze Age, Lydian period, and classical antiquity onwards. Figurines found at Aphrodisias probably arrived through this route, since it extended to the Büyük Menderes (ancient *Maender*) River basin to the south. Three specimens from Kozağacı and Karain Cave in the Antalya region in southwest Anatolia might also have been acquired via this route. The spread of Kilia figurines into the sites of Troad in northwest Anatolia was due to the use of a natural trade route. The presence of Kilia figurines at sites such as Alaağaç, Yortan, and Papazköy probably explains the arrival of similar figurines at Beşik-Yassıtepe, Hanay Tepe, and Kilia in the Troad. Affinities between the pottery of the Chalcolithic societies of the Troad and that of Kulaksızlar has already demonstrated the presence of a cultural interaction sphere during this period.

It seems that Kilia figurines moved along the main trade routes, although how they were distributed remains a question. A down-the-line exchange model is a plausible explanation for the spread of figurines over great distances, although the number of exchanged figurines is too small to make firm conclusions. Because down-the-line exchange appears to have been the main mechanism for the distribution of Kilia

figurines, we can accept the argument that inter-personal or inter-communal exchanges were taking place during this period. The distribution pattern of valuables such as the Kilia figurines was probably determined to a large extent by their intended uses. Style in this sense can be considered an important component in determining the patterns of exchange. A specific artifact may have a widespread distribution pattern if its associated symbolism is appropriate for the ideology of consumers. The exchange of artifacts that conveyed shared specific symbolic meaning could have strengthened the ties among the village communities of this period. Villages located on the natural trade routes, in which the Akhisar region had a strategic central location, seem to have passed the figurines down-the-line. This kind of mechanism could have served as a means for Kulaksızlar people to maintain relations with other communities of central-west Anatolia in addition to supplementing the village's economy.

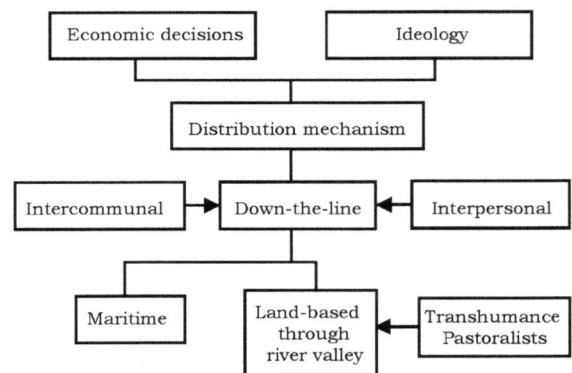

Fig. 5. 19. Simplified flow chart illustrating the patterns of exchange involving the Kulaksızlar products

Symbolically important artifacts such as marble Kilia figurines and pointed vessels could have been suitable for gift exchanges on a personal or communal basis. This is the essence of independent specialization, in which exchange between producer and consumer takes place on an inter-personal basis. In addition to land-based exchange, distribution of figurines appears to have involved maritime exchange. The figurine found at Kilia (present-day Gallipoli) across the Dardanel Strait, as well as the one found on the island of Lesbos, indicates a complex pattern of exchange involving maritime trade. Such exchange was not a casual activity, since Turkish Thrace and northwestern Anatolia were parts of the same cultural interaction sphere during this period. Arrival of Balkan elements into Chalcolithic western Anatolian assemblages confirms the presence of maritime activities that tied the cultures of this area. The recovery of most of these marble artifacts from sites located at strategically important points on natural trade routes does not necessitate a single exchange mechanism responsible for the movement of artifacts with high values over great distances. The ability to maintain long distance exchange in western Anatolia leads me to believe that nomads or pastoralists were partially involved in the distribution of Kilia figurines. Two figurines found at the site of Kozağacı in southwestern Anatolia nearly 400 km away from Kulaksızlar may well have resulted from the activities of pastoralists. The uneven pattern observed in the distribution of rare and exotic artifacts recovered in excavated western Anatolian sites seems to support the role of pastoralists. For example, obsidian from Melos and Central Anatolia, marine shell species from the Mediterranean, stone beads from Afghanistan, and carnelian from Iran might well have been introduced into Aphrodisias by nomads (Joukowsky 1986). A similar mechanism may also have been responsible for the arrival of exotic artifacts such as green-stone, obsidian, and marine shell at Bağbaşı (Eslick 1994). Therefore, I suggest that indirect exchange involving nomads or pastoralists existed alongside down-the-line exchange that took on an interpersonal or inter-communal level among the sites located on natural land-based trade routes (Fig. 5.19). Evidence for maritime trade also supports the argument that a single model alone cannot explain the distribution of Kilia figurines.

F. Consumption

Archaeologists studying prehistoric production systems often attempt to reconstruct the ways in which the finished artifacts were used. The reason for this is that production strategies were often structured by the intended function of the finished artifacts. Examination of the context in which the artifacts were found is probably the most important way to determine the ways the artifacts were used in pre-literate societies. Artifacts used in households for daily needs can be classified as utilitarian objects, characterized by low cost of production, low degree of technical investment, and the use of locally available raw materials. In contrast to these artifacts of everyday use, artifacts used in socially important contexts, brought from distant regions, or manufactured out of valuable raw materials can be classified as valuables or prestige objects. It is primarily the rarity and the specialized knowledge required in the manufacturing that differentiate prestige items from those of utilitarian character. Ownership of these valuables or prestige objects causes differentiation within the households or communities based on the visual display (e.g. status display based on wealth or specific role in rituals in household or communities). It is my belief that Kulaksızlar marble products must be viewed as valuables or prestige artifacts because of the symbolism attached them and the specialized attention placed on their manufacture. The overall uniformity of the form of Kilia figurines and pointed vessels in this sense must be significant. The symbolic meaning associated with bending the arm at the elbow in Kilia figurines was one reason why the craftsmen selected this gesture. It may have represented a particular deity that was appropriate for the circumstances in which it was used. This type of gesture appears to be a common

phenomenon of Chalcolithic figures found in most parts of western and central Anatolia, eastern Aegean islands, and the Balkans (Fig. 5.20). A small shell pendant in the form of the middle-portion of a Kilia figurine was found at Can Hasan (Fig. 5.20c) in south central Anatolia dating to 4600-4000 B.C. (French 1963: pl. 2d). Two wooden figurines found at Tigani in levels II and IV2 (Felsch 1988: pl. 85) have a similar form that recalls the middle portion of a Kilia figurine.

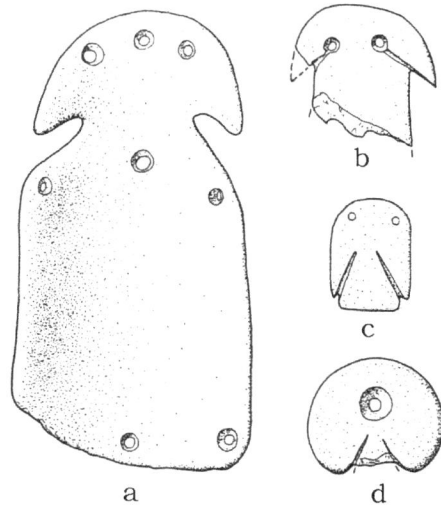

Fig. 5.20. Bent-arms figurines among the Chalcolithic cultures (a. Varna, c. Can Hasan, b,d. Tigani)

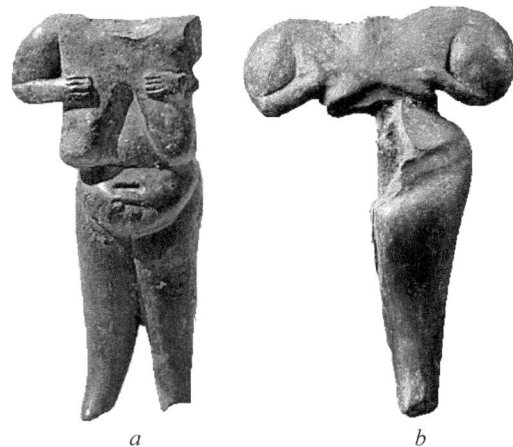

Fig. 5.21. Female figurines with bent arms found at western Anatolian sites (a. Kuruçay, b. Hacılar)

Figurines with this motif are also very common at the Chalcolithic Varna cemetery in Bulgaria (Gimbutas 1977; Ivanov 1996). Iconographic similarities among the figurines of these neighboring cultures may be a manifestation of a shared religious belief. This type of gesture evidently had its roots in the Neolithic Anatolian past, since figurines with bent-arms were found in great quantities during this period. For example, Late Neolithic baked clay female figurines found in level 11 at Kuruçay and level VI at Hacılar (Fig. 5.21a-b) display similar gestures, with bent arms holding their breasts (Mellaart 1970a: 162, Pl. II; Duru

1994: Pl. 191). Although breasts are never specifically represented in the Kilia figurines, bending of arms can be seen as a continuation of Neolithic examples (Seeher 1992: 167), since this style originated in the Late Neolithic clay figurines of the region's past. A number of scholars such as Mellaart (1970: 170) explain the Anatolian female figurines using the Mother Goddess tradition based on their presence in domestic settings (e.g. Çatal Höyük, Hacılar, Kuruçay, and Demircihöyük). Whether or not this deity was a Mother Goddess is difficult to judge, since the existence of such a goddess in the prehistoric Aegean is doubtful (Talalay 1993: 37). Basing her argument on ethnographic evidence, Talalay (1984: 262) argues that Anatolian Neolithic female figurines were used in initiation rites. This has yet to be supported by archaeological evidence. The idea that figurines served as children's toys, on the other hand, cannot be seriously considered for Kilia figurines since it is not logical to expect such costly and delicate artifacts to survive rough handling in the hands of children. Western Anatolian village communities probably did not have that wealth during this period.

In his evaluation of the use of marble figurines in the Cyclades, Renfrew (1984: 28) maintains the possibility that some of these distinctive artifacts served cultic functions. He regards the folded-arm figurines as votaries or votive offerings, in which the position of the arms has some kind of religious meaning. Kilia figurines can be viewed as objects of household ritual use, although there is no contextual evidence to prove this hypothesis at this point. A number of figurine fragments were found in household deposits in western Anatolian sites (e.g. Aphrodisias, Karain Cave, Hanaytepe). Moreover, a Kilia figurine torso was found in a burial of Early Bronze Age II date (Collignon 1901: 815), which was probably kept as an heirloom. The burial of Kilia figurines in graves was probably one aspect of cult associated with these figurines. Whether the Kilia figurines were used in household rituals or buried in graves does not alter the fact that they were highly regarded objects.

Western Anatolian pointed beaker fragments from Kumtepe and Beşik-Sivritepe in the Troad and Demircihöyük far inland in northwest Anatolia do not provide useful information on their use. The rim fragment of a marble pointed beaker from Gülpınar was found in the cemetery area within the cultural deposits overlying the pit burials for infants. Thus, it is difficult to know whether it was originally served as a burial offering or an item used in funerary ritual. However, one complete pointed beaker found in a grave facing the head of the deceased (Fig. 5.22) in a Late Neolithic level at Kephala on Keos (Coleman 1977: 64), shows that marble pointed beakers often accompanied the deceased. A similar mortuary use of marble pointed beakers is also evident in Grave 41 at the Chalcolithic cemetery at Varna in Bulgaria (Ivanov 1978: 16). Because Coleman (1993: 259) dates the site

of Kephala to ca. 4300-3500 B.C., the Varna cemetery can be viewed as roughly contemporary with the culture of Kephala, which makes the similarities in use possible. Although it is found in a geographically distant region, the mortuary use of pointed stone vessels at the Susiana cemetery in southern Iran (Morgan 1912: 8) also complements our interpretation of the use of pointed stone vessels, since it dates to ca. 4000 B.C. Pointed stone vessels were found with the female burials in the Susiana cemetery along with a number of metal valuables such as mirrors.

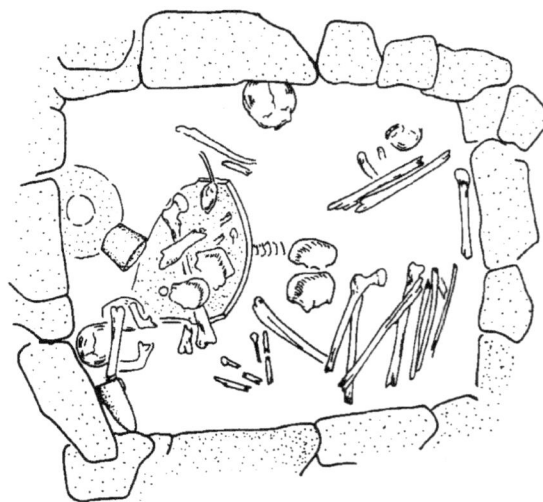

Fig. 5.22. Drawing showing the mortuary use of a pointed beaker from Kephala

Similar mortuary use of pointed beakers from the Aegean, Balkans, and from southern Iran does not necessarily imply that these artifacts were manufactured solely for mortuary uses. Pointed beakers were deposited in burials either as the valuables of the deceased, or as objects of social function, in which visual display was crucial. Their subsequent burial with their owners after death probably owes to the fact that they belonged to the deceased during their life time. This means that marble vessels served as objects of ritual drinking in household or communal rituals. Pointed beakers cannot simply be classified as utilitarian objects for everyday tasks. This kind of marble vessel with its delicate structure would not be particularly resistant to rough handling in everyday life activities. They must have been used for special occasions. If they were objects of every day tasks, then one would expect to find similar conical pots, which is not the case. Therefore, access to pointed marble beakers might have been limited to wealthy individuals or those individuals who played important roles within the communal or household rituals.

Western Anatolian evidence on the use of marble bowls from the Chalcolithic and Early Bronze Ages supports an interpretation favoring the symbolic meaning being attached to these artifacts. The prehistoric tradition of depositing personal possessions of the deceased in graves was common in Anatolia. For example, an open-shaped marble bowl was found in a grave under the chin of a skeleton at Kumtepe 1a in the Troad (Sperling 1976). This suggests a deliberate placement of the vessel for use in the afterlife. The tradition of depositing marble vessels in graves continued into the Early Bronze Age I period. A marble beaker with a flat base was found in Grave 81 in the Iasos cemetery in southwest Anatolia facing the head of the buried person (Pecorella 1984). It was perhaps intentionally placed upside down against the mouth of the dead to serve as a drinking cup for the deceased during afterlife (Getz-Gentle 1996: 62). The Early Bronze II period burials at Ovabayındır in central-west Anatolia yielded marble bowls of high craftsmanship (Mellaart 1971). Two marble bowls were also found in an Early Bronze II pithos burial at Ballıca in the Akhisar region. Recovery of marble bowls along with a metal hoard at Ballıca indicates that stone vessels were highly valued during one's lifetime, representing an accumulation of wealth. The continuity in mortuary use of stone vessels from the Chalcolithic to the Early Bronze Age may be used to interpret the ways in which the Kulaksızlar marble pointed beakers were used. The custom of depositing marble vessels in graves does not signify that they were solely manufactured for burials. They were deposited in burials because they were the possessions of the deceased during the life.

The social or symbolic roles of marble vessels may explain why a craftsman places special emphasis on marble working instead of adopting less expensive production strategies such as manufacturing same form of artifacts in clay. The costs involved in the procurement of marble and stone tools, labor input, technical investment, and time invested in stone vessel production generally far exceeds the costs incurred in shaping the same type of artifact in clay or simply pursuing a less expensive subsistence strategy. The value of marble vessels might have been increased proportionally to the distance over which they were traded, where they may have been highly regarded due to the cost of production and their exotic nature. One may infer from this discussion involving the use of marble artifacts that Kulaksızlar craftsmen were focusing on the production of symbolic artifacts, the motivation of which had non-economic components for both producers and consumers. Marble vessels can be as classified as socially important artifacts that were important in communication systems within households or communities. Their role in visual display derived from the cost of production and transportation.

G. Summary

Patterns of Kulaksızlar marble working have been reconstructed in relation to processes that were closely linked to the system of production. I attempted to reconstruct how these pre-urban craft specialists organized the production of marble artifacts. The results of the analysis show that Kulaksızlar marble working was an example of productive utilization of the environment, which is a typical feature of independent specialization. All the raw materials used at the workshop were acquired primarily in the form of cobbles from the immediate vicinity of the site. Collecting was probably an organized process that was carried out either by craftsmen or their subordinates. Unlimited access to raw materials and experimentation with different varieties of marble resulted in the identification of several geological sources suitable for marble working. I also determined the techniques used in the production of marble Kilia figurines and pointed beakers and bowls by analyzing the percussive and abrasive use-wear on the stone tools, byproducts, and manufacturing errors documented in the surface surveys. Archaeological information drawn from the cultures of Mesopotamia, northern Syria, Egypt, and the Aegean provide valuable insights into the various aspects of stone vessel making, including the drilling techniques.

The results show that Kulaksızlar craftsmen independently managed to develop successful tool-use techniques. For example, successive insertion of sandstone drill-bits to hollow out the conical vessels can be seen as an indication of the craftsmen's knowledge and technical expertise. Although recovery of finished figurine and vessel fragments at Kulaksızlar points to their use in a local village context, many of the workshop products, in particular Kilia figurines, appear to have been exchanged with other communities of western Anatolia. By carrying out a sourcing study involving comparisons of measurements, styles, and manufacturing techniques, I attempted to demonstrate that those stylistically comparable marble Kilia figurines found at other sites are likely Kulaksızlar products. The spatial distribution pattern of Kilia figurines demonstrates that the quantity of exchanged figurines was greatest within a radius of 100 km. The number of Kilia figurines drops off rapidly between 100 and 400 km from Kulaksızlar. Reciprocal exchange at the inter-personal or inter-communal levels probably resulted in the distribution of the marble artifacts in the primary consumer area. A number of marble artifacts seem to have also moved along the trade routes that had been in use since the Neolithic. Wandering pastoralists may well have been responsible for the distribution of marble artifacts found in distant regions as far away as 400 km from the workshop, since Chalcolithic western Anatolian evidence showing the distribution of other rare or exotic goods presents a similar picture.

I also attempted to demonstrate that marble Kilia figurines and pointed vessels constituted special classes of artifacts with symbolic associations. The repeated production of the same style of artifacts in a great quantity seems to show that exchange was one motivation behind their production. Desire for these symbolic artifacts was an incentive for Kulaksızlar craftsmen to economically and socially benefit from this and maintain alliances with neighboring cultures. Because inter-personal or inter-communal exchange relationships are often the norm in independent specialization, social and symbolic relations of production provided incentives for Kulaksızlar craftsmen to concentrate on marble working. The investment of a high level of craftsmanship during the production stages is a result of the intended function of artifacts and these artifacts must have served important roles in the social and symbolic realms of the communities. Because the ownership of marble artifacts helped to create differentiation within the communities through visual display, they had to display distinct features with respect to the quality of the material used and the level of craftsmanship involved in the steps of their manufacture. Ownership of a marble vessel was probably different than that of a clay one based on the criteria of material used and the cost of production.

Kulaksızlar marble working reveals a new pattern that has not been archaeologically documented in pre-Bronze Age western Anatolia: production and exchange of symbolically desired artifacts. The motivation behind the Kulaksızlar marble working appears to have been social and symbolic as much as it was economic in nature. Thus, it is reasonable to assume that Kulaksızlar marble working had non-economic components that helped to fulfill the social and symbolic requirements of both producer and consumer.

Part Six

EVIDENCE FOR CRAFT SPECIALIZATION

This part outlines the reasons for viewing Kulaksızlar marble working as a result of specialized craft activity rather than domestic production. Because craft specialization is often seen as a concomitant of urban or state societies, identifying specialized economic behavior in a non-urban environment requires further archaeological demonstration. Archaeologists identifying the presence and organization of specialized production in the archaeological record use either direct or indirect evidence (Costin 1991). Indirect evidence is used in circumstances where the place of manufacture is not known. Determination of the degree of specialization involves the use of parameters such as skill, efficiency, and standardization. In contrast, direct evidence is used where manufacturing debris showing the various stages of manufacture can be identified in the archaeological record. Parameters used in direct evidence appear to vary according to the category of the produced artifacts and the cultural context of the production system in question. Archaeological evidence identifying craft specialization in pre-urban contexts has rarely been documented, leading many archaeologists to focus on indirect evidence. Consequently, there is not a single model that can be applied cross-culturally either to reconstruct the organizational context of marble working debris from Kulaksızlar or even identify the presence of specialization. Because high concentrations of artifacts comprising blanks, waste byproducts, manufacturing errors, and stone tools were documented at Kulaksızlar, indirect evidence can be used to estimate whether this production evidence represents a specialized behavior or not. From the analysis of the surface data from Kulaksızlar, I suggest that manufacturing debris found in pre-urban contexts must display four diagnostic features in order to be considered a result of a specialized or domestic production:

a) Segregation of production: manufacturing debris must display a pattern of clustering showing that production was divided into stages and separated into different work units.

b) Volume of output: the number of finished artifacts must exceed the requirements of the people who produce them.

c) Standardization: finished products must display very little variability in the form of artifacts and manufacturing techniques.

d) Technical elaboration: finished artifacts must show that craftsmen invested considerable skill and labor in the stages of production.

Because these four parameters can be identified by using Kulaksızlar data, I employ them to understand whether or not this marble working was a result of craft specialization and to reconstruct the organization context of this production example. This, however, does not mean that these parameters are cross-culturally applicable to the analysis of all kinds of manufacturing debris found in non-urban or non-state contexts.

A. Segregation of Production

Separation of production into stages and different work units is a parameter that can be used to identify the presence and organization of specialized craft activities. A high concentration of debris scattered over the entire surface of a given site cannot simply be equated with the presence of specialization. It is fundamental to determine whether or not the manufacturing debris under study represents a primary deposit, because a given stone-working deposit can be a result of discard behavior near a locus where the actual manufacturing occurred (Lewis 1995: 381). Moreover, the spatial patterning of the surface finds must display a pattern showing the division of craft activities into stages and different spatial units in order to confirm that the debris was a primary deposit.

Cross (1993: 73) maintains that sub-specialization with specific craftsmen becoming experts in a particular stage of the production process indicates the presence of specialization. If different activity areas related to various stages of production are identified, then this information can be used to argue that each specific area served as a locus for a different stage of production. The presence of various loci reflecting the separation of production into different work units at Kulaksızlar is evidenced by patterning of the surface distribution of artifacts, which I view an evidence of village-based specialization. Analysis of the density and concentration of finds over the surface of the site revealed five major clusters. The differential distribution of production debris across the survey area suggests that production of different craft items such as Kilia figurines, beakers, and bowls was concentrated in different parts of the site. Among these clusters, the area covered by squares D-E 4-5 differs from the others since the density of marble artifacts is relatively low and the area yielded high quantities of pottery and food processing implements such as querns, hand-stones, and pestles instead of marble artifacts, suggesting that this area was not used for marble working. The high concentration of pottery together with other utilitarian artifacts seems to suggest the presence of a domestic unit in this area. The distribution of manufacturing errors and byproducts over the surface of the site shows that coarse flaking and pecking of each of the three major marble products were undertaken in different work units (Fig. 6.1). For example, square E8 contained roughly-shaped marble pointed bowls and manufacturing errors indicating their breakage during the preforming or chipping out of their interiors, whereas the area covered by the squares A-B 2-3 yielded manufacturing errors implying that coarse flaking and pecking of marble blocks into pointed beaker preforms occurred there. The area encompassed by squares C-D 2-3, on the other hand, yielded unfinished fragments that belonged to various stages of figurine production from coarse flaking to refinement. A small number of unfinished marble fragments from the production of beakers has also been found mixed with the figurine production debris, which was probably due spatial overlap of these two clusters. Because this area has long been the focus of illicit digs, the patterning of the surface finds in these squares does not provide a clear picture. Rare occurrences of unfinished marble artifacts belonging to the multiple stages of figurine production in adjacent squares confirms that Kilia figurines were manufactured there.

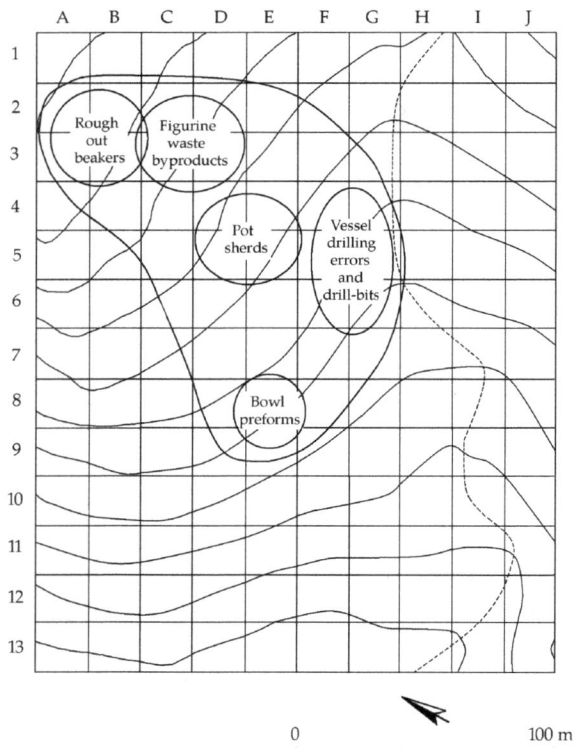

Fig. 6. 1. Approximate spatial clustering of surface finds (boundaries are approximate and some overlap exists)

The area that falls roughly into squares F4-6 and G4-6 yielded primarily marble beaker and bowl preforms with drilling marks, as well as a group of stone tools such as sandstone drill-bits and marble river-pebbles. Plate 10 illustrates the distribution of surface finds related to marble working in these squares. The beaker and bowl fragments with drilling marks on their interior represent errors that occurred during the drilling stage of vessel manufacture. The coexistence of beakers and bowls in the same area implies that the drilling of these two different vessel groups took place in the same area. This evidence can be used to argue that the manufacture of beakers was divided into stages. Whether or not different craftsmen were responsible for hollowing out the beakers or roughing out the same artifacts cannot be stated with certainty. It is reasonable to argue that a single craftsman would not carry out the entire manufacture process for the two different vessels types. The technical difficulties involved in hollowing out conical vessels with very delicate walls most likely required the collaboration of two craftsmen.

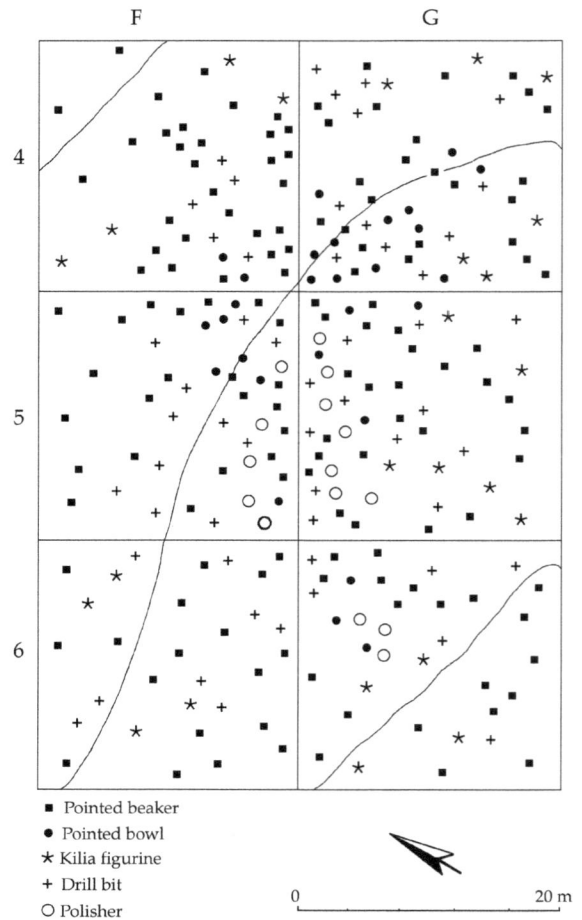

Fig. 6.2. Detailed map for grids F4-6, G4-6 (see Fig. 5.2) showing the distribution of finds related to marble working (Several overlapping symbols have been separated for clarity)

A small community comprised of several craftsmen is more likely to have been necessary for the production of marble artifacts. This assertion is supported by archaeological evidence suggesting that large numbers of vessels were produced over a short period of time. First, homogeneity observed in style, shapes, and the manufacturing techniques of surface pottery points to a short term occupation. Second, second quarter of the fifth millennium B.C. C[14] dates for the marble beakers from Beşik-Sivritepe and two Kilia figurines from

46

Aphrodisas roughly coincide with the relative date obtained of the Kulaksızlar surface pottery. Thirdly, the drilling and refinement of beakers and bowls seems to have been carried out in the same area, suggesting the simultaneous production of beakers and bowls at the site.

Archaeological and ethnographic evidence derived from stone vessel manufacture in Iran provides valuable information on how internal work division may have occurred in stone-vessel making. Kohl (1974) argues that the manufacturing of chlorite vessels was separated into work units at the third millennium BC site of Tepe Yahya in eastern Iran. Steps such as forming and drilling the chlorite vessel may have been performed by a craftsman, with another being responsible for the decoration and painting of these vessels. The present-day stone vessel workshop at Mashad, where each craftsmen specializes in his own production stage, is used as evidence to support this hypothesis on the division of work into units for Early Bronze Age chlorite vessel making in eastern Iran (Kohl 1974: 122). At the Mashad workshop, a single craftsman does not work on the vessel in a continuing sequence from the beginning to the end. Instead, each craftsman works on several vessels simultaneously and then passes them to another craftsmen for the other steps of production.

The pattern of internal work division observed both archaeologically and ethnographically for stone vessel making in Iran may be compared to that of Kulaksızlar, where clustering surface finds indicate a similar internal work division employing several craftsmen. Internal work division is one of the defining characteristics of community-based production and its archaeological documentation at Kulaksızlar confirms that pre-urban craftsmen collaborated and formed a complex production system during this period.

B. Standardization

Standardization of artifact form and the methods or technology employed in their production can be used to distinguish specialized craft activity from domestic production. According to Cross (1993: 71), "standardization means repeatedly achieving a similar value for a single variable of form or technology." Therefore, a low degree of variability in the form of artifacts and the use of similar methods in marble working are diagnostic indicators of specialized production. Two main factors generally result in the standardization of artifact forms and the techniques used in their production: intended function of finished artifact and the cost-cutting strategies. Production of a high number of standardized artifacts can be viewed as the result of basic economic forces such as cost-cutting strategies, whereby craftsmen lower their cost of production by establishing a routinized production process. This involves the use of standardized tools and manufacturing techniques in order that craftsmen may produce more artifacts per unit of energy, time and

skill invested. Ethnographic and archaeological studies confirm that the repeated production of a homogenous artifact group is a common strategy adopted in village-based specialization (Sinopoli 1988: 586; Rice 1981: 220). Such cost-cutting strategies are also a characteristic feature of independent specialization (Costin 1991: 34), if non-agricultural production forms the major part of the village economy.

The lack of variability in the form of the marble figurines and vessel and the standardized technology used in their manufacture clearly demonstrate that Kulaksızlar production was a specialized activity. Since relative cost is one of the defining characteristics of this marble workshop, use of a standard technology in the manufacture of artifacts was economically advantageous and cost-effective, a feature that defines independent specialization. Symbolic associations of the artifacts often lead to the use of standardized technology and form of the products. Although the height of the Kilia figurines ranges from 7 cm to 22.5 cm, they show little variability in form due to the adoption of the same manufacturing techniques. This standardization was also derived from the intended functions or symbolism attached to this particular form.

In a similar way, large numbers of highly standardized marble pointed beakers were manufactured with considerable uniformity in their rim diameters, the majority falling between 7.0 and 8.5 cm. Pointed marble bowls also display standardization in the manufacturing methods and rim diameters, despite the fact that the sizes of the vessels were determined by the size of the available marble blocks. Standardization in the form of artifacts, in turn, indicates the adoption of the same technology in manufacturing marble figurines and vessels. Standardization observed on the Kulaksızlar marble products was to a large extent a result of basic economic forces and intended function of artifacts.

C. Volume of Output

Volume of output is another parameter that helps identify the presence of craft specialization in the archaeological record. By definition, if the estimation of the product output well exceeds the immediate needs of the producer, production results from specialized activity (Lewis 1996: 380). This parameter cannot be documented with absolute values since the accurate dimensions of debris cannot be determine from surface remains or even from partial excavations. Because my information is derived from the surface remains, it is hard to estimate precisely the number of finished and unfinished objects manufactured by the Kulaksızlar craftsmen. We do not know the precise duration of occupation, the exact number of craftsmen, the amount of time spent in crafting per day, the number of days spent in manufacture, and who was responsible for procuring raw materials. The estimated high number of finished products seems to indicate that exchange was one motivation for Kulaksızlar craftsmen. A relative number can be proposed by quantitative analysis of available surface finds. We know that the figurine fragments constituted almost 50 % of the marble assemblage, with nearly nine hundred distinct fragments representing the various stages of figurine production. It is reasonable to assume from the available quantity that there were at least 900 attempts to manufacture a Kilia figurine. (It must be mentioned that the artifacts under study may constitute only a portion of what might have been generated by the craftsmen). How many of these 900 attempts were successful can only be ascertained if we accept the criterion established by replication experiments, which show that at least one out of every three attempts at producing a figurine may have been successfully completed. This success rate attained at the site might have been higher than the ratio I obtained from replication studies, since the technical expertise of Kulaksızlar craftsmen was probably higher due to their more intimate knowledge of the technology. The secondary use of figurines that had broken at the neck during the preforming process also causes problems in interpreting the ratio of success from the available data. It can reasonably be assumed that craftsmen manufactured at least three hundred Kilia figurines, nearly forty examples of which have already been found at other sites.

Replication experiments also show that craftsmen were able to complete at least one beaker for every two attempts. It is difficult to test the ratio of success (50 %) archaeologically since we cannot determine such aspects of production from surface study data. If we accept the error rate derived from replication experiments, then one may assume that Kulaksızlar craftsmen managed to complete more than two hundred pointed beakers. In a similar way, replication experiments show that the success rate (70 %) for pointed bowl manufacture was also high, although only one hundred and twenty fragments represent this type.

The estimated volume of production is often used to argue whether a given production system was a result of part- or full-time activity. Distinguishing manufacturing debris generated by a part-time specialist from that of full-time craft specialist presents a problem of interpretation. Archaeologists studying specialized production systems in literate urban societies also face a similar problem of interpretation. For example, the cuneiform tablets from the third millennium BC site of Ebla (Tell Mardikh) in northern Syria do not provide information on the intensity of production activities, although these Eblaite texts mention weavers, metalsmiths, and wood-carvers working for the urban center (Stein and Blackman 1993: 49).

The relative density of production debris can often illustrate whether production was carried out on a part-time or full-time basis. An unusually high concentration of manufacturing debris is said to indicate full-time production, whereas a sparse concentration indicates part-time production. Such criteria based on relative density are not useful, however, since many variables affect the amount of manufacturing debris, such as the number of workers, the percent of the time spent working, and the ratio of available debris to overall debris generated by the producers, variables that are difficult to quantify in the archaeological record. Costin (1991: 30) suggests that identifying the range of economic activities conducted at the site, such as food acquisition and processing and household maintenance, can help to determine whether production was carried out on a part- or full-time basis. According to Costin (1991: 30), households that yield evidence for both food production and craft production work only part-time at their crafts, implying that independent craft specialists work part-time at craft production to supplement their subsistence needs. Such a criterion is useful when information is derived from excavation, but it is difficult to interpret evidence derived from surface surveys.

The estimated number of finished artifacts does not seem high enough to view the manufacturing debris from Kulaksızlar as a result of full-time craft activity. What is clear from the quantity of manufacturing debris is that marble working formed the majority of the village economy, meaning that Kulaksızlar production was not domestic production. Evaluation of the surface assemblage also shows the presence of small scales activities other than marble working. The inhabitants of the site probably combined marble working with agriculture. Village population could have obtained part of their basic subsistence needs by cultivating the lower ends of the slopes of the hills. The occurrence of grinding implements such as querns, hand-stones, pestles, and sickle-blades indicate food processing on the site, while cooking pot and storage-vessel fragments also confirm the presence of subsistence activities. Presence of non-agricultural specialization does not mean that small-scale subsistence practices were not pursued at all. What I suggest is that agriculture was supplemental to marble working.

D. Technical Elaboration

Technical elaboration observed in each step of marble figurine and vessel manufacture is an important parameter that distinguishes specialized production from domestic production. The level of technical investment in the production of utilitarian and prestige artifacts varies. The role of artifacts within society determines the level of energy invested in their production, with artifacts falling into wealth or ritual categories often receiving greater attention in terms of labor, time, and skill. Objects of wealth were important for visual display, eventually leading to the rise of inequality within the household or community. One may expect the objects used in household or communal rituals to be more distinctive than artifacts used in every day tasks.

The high level of technical investment can particularly be seen in the steps followed in the hollowing of the conical vessels' interiors. The wall thickness of the upper and lower ends of the pointed beaker rim fragments is nearly identical in most examples. Craftsmen's success in using various crescent-shaped and conical drill-bits in order to hollow out an interior that matches the exterior contour of the vessel best indicates the high level of technical investment. There is very little archaeological evidence showing off-centered drilling, confirming that a very careful attention was paid in drilling step of marble pointed beaker and bowl manufacture. This high level of technical elaboration was probably due to the intended function of these conical vessels. The lack of similar conical pottery in Anatolian archaeological evidence implies that marble pointed vessels were indented to have served special social events involving visual display. Therefore, there might have been a direct relationship between the function of pointed vessels and the level of technique invested in their production. Such was also the case in the manufacture of Kilia figurines. Creation of a very thin and delicate neck in a raw material with a fragile structure requires high level of technical investment and keen decision making procedures in tool-use techniques. Very little stylistic variability observed in the anatomical details and ratios clearly points that craftsmen invested high level of skill, time, and labor in Kilia figurine manufacture. Because the iconography associated with this type of figurines had symbolic connotations, their production received special attention.

The non-economic components of production probably explain the presence of technically elaborated artifacts among the neighboring pre-urban Mesopotamian and Aegean cultures. Alabaster figurines and vessels found in burials at the Samarrian period site of Tel-es-Sawwan in northern Mesopotamia (Abu al-Soof and El-Wailly 1965) display a high level of technical elaboration, labor input, time investment, and standardization. The symbolic meaning attached to these distinctive alabaster artifacts might have been an important factor for prehistoric Mesopotamian craftsmen to create such technically elaborated artifacts. A similar pattern has also been documented in the Early Neolithic levels of Franchthi Cave in the Argolid region in Greece, where ceramic pots are thought to have been produced for special functions. Because their production required high levels of technical expertise and labor investment, it has been argued that pot-making was guided by non-utilitarian concerns. The pots were produced in a wide range of sizes and shapes, finished with different surface treatment, and fired differently that those used for utilitarian purposes (Vitelli 1989: 27). The Aegean and Mesopotamian evidence demonstrates that social factors shaped the strategies involved in the production of non-utilitarian artifacts. Similar factors probably motivated the pre-urban Kulaksızlar craftsmen. The technical quality and the elegance of the finished

Kulaksızlar marble figurines and vessels speak of the time, labor, and energy invested in each piece. In addition, the repeated production of marble Kilia figurines and vessels with little stylistic variability helps to classify these artifacts requiring high technical investment as special classes of artifacts. The level of technical investment must be viewed as an important criterion in distinguishing a specialist-produced craft from utilitarian one used in daily tasks. It was the high level of technical investment that separated highly skilled craftsman from ordinary people. In this sense, technical elaboration can be accepted as a diagnostic feature of pre-urban craft specialization.

E. Summary

Kulaksızlar marble working appears to be an example of village-based craft specialization. Organizational and technological indicators such as separation of production into stages and different work units, standardization of forms of artifacts and methods adopted in their manufacture, high volume of production, and the level of technical investment suggests that Kulaksızlar marble working was far more complex than domestic production. Surface concentrations of different types of artifact at different loci provide an indication of labor division within the site. Processes such as the acquisition of raw materials, flaking and pecking, and refinement were apparently carried out by different members of this social group. The level of standardization achieved in the methods of marble vessel and figurine manufacture either reflects cost-cutting strategies or relates to the intended function of the artifacts.

Adoption of cost-cutting strategies such as exploitation of raw material found in abundance in the immediate region of the site result from basic economic forces and is a characteristic feature of independent specialization. Another factor that resulted in the standardization of the forms of produced artifacts is the function that these marble figurines and vessels served. The quality and elegance of finished figurines and vessels show the high level of technical investment, which classified them as prestige or symbolic artifacts that helped to differentiate their owners on the basis of wealth. It is difficult to estimate with precision whether marble working was a part- or full-time activity, although the estimated number of finished artifacts seems to be very high to view them as domestic production oriented towards local consumption. This is a characteristic feature that differentiates specialized craft activity from domestic production carried out to fulfill the requirements of the local population.

The location of the site in or close to the woods leads me to believe that it was the abundance of marble that led these people to settle at this locality rather than agricultural land. In other words, agriculture played a secondary role in the economy of the village. If we accept the idea that agriculture formed the major part of economy instead of marble working, then we must explain why the Kulaksızlar people did not settle in the alluvial plain that was much more suitable for farming activities. Because the exchange of finished marble artifacts formed the major part of the Kulaksızlar economy, basic subsistence goods were primarily obtained in return for exchanging the products of their special skills. This picture argues against the view that specialization in pre-urban times is a simple or casual activity. Agricultural production was probably complementary to marble working, rather than other way around. The evidence from Kulaksızlar contributes significantly to the study of specialized production systems, since it shows that pre-urban craft specialization could be highly complex.

Part Seven

CONCLUSIONS

This study represents a modest attempt to reconstruct the socio-economic and technological aspects of a marble workshop from the Chalcolithic site of Kulaksızlar in western Anatolia. A comprehensive analysis of material remains from the surface surveys carried out at this site has been utilized, along with the results of replication experiments and ethnographic evidence, to deal with several archaeological and theoretical considerations. First, I attempted to determine how Kulaksızlar marble working was organized and what th eeconomic, social, and symbolic relations of production were. Second, I discussed what this specialized craft activity implies for our understanding of the Chalcolithic western Anatolian culture and society. Third, I demonstrated one way in an implicit way that specialized craft activity may have developed independently in pre-urban times, using information derived from the analysis of marble working at Kulaksızlar. I belive that these perspectives could enhance our understanding of the aspects of production, exchange, and consumption of specialist produced artifacts. It must be mentioned that minimal archaeological evidence and reliance on data derived from surface surveys prevents one from going far to provide a comprehensive picture. Available archaeological evidence presented an opportunity to outline a model of how pre-urban specialization occurred at Kulaksızlar in western Anatolia.

A. Model of pre-Urban Craft Specialization at Kulaksızlar

The archaeological record reveals only limited information about Chalcolithic western Anatolian culture and society and is hampered by minimal number of excavations and the problems involved in explaining the nature of transitional Middle Chalcolithic period, to which the cultural assemblage from Kulaksızlar belonged to. The cultural, social, and economic changes observed in the fabric of this transitional period's societies were most probably resulted from multiple factors such as cultural interactions, social reorganization and population movements. Although subsistence activities occupied a central place in the economy of this period's societies, most villagers had their own part-time craftsmen, including potters, knappers, and weavers. Such small-scale domestic production activities often involved the use of locally available raw materials and simple technologies, primarily due to the fact that production was oriented towards the fullfillment of the requirements of local population. Casual exchange of locally manufactured artifacts with neighboring communities resulted in the spread of artifacts or ideas related to specific technologies. Kulaksızlar marble working evidence illuminates one of the unknown aspects of the production systems of this period, that is

a specialized craft production. Kulaksızlar evidence sheds new light on the question of how a specialized craft activity occurred in the village contexts and how the specialist-produced products were exchanged and used by the Chalcolithic western Anatolians. Kulaksızlar marble working was village-based specialization carried out by a small social group that collaborated and carried out production in different spatial units within the site. They concentrated their attention on the production of Kilia figurines, pointed beakers, and bowls manufactured out of local marble. The availability of marble, basalt, gabbro, and sandstone was an important variable that structured the Kulaksızlar production, since these raw materials used in stone tool making were found in abundance close to the site. Because relative cost was an important consideration for independent specialists in raw material selection, unlimited access to raw material and the simple mechanisrn adopted for their acquisition led craftsmen living close to these sources to experiment in products made with them. This feedback relationship between raw material availability and the adopted technological behavior can be seen as a characteristic feature of home- or village-based craft production systems. The distance from the production site to the source also determined the nature of the strategy involved in the extraction of raw materials. Available archaeological evidence confirms that marble and stone tools used in the various stages of production were primarily collected in the shape of cobbles from the immediate vicinity of the site by the craftsmen or their subordinates. The lack of homogeneity in physical properties and the variability in the colors of marbles found at the site clearly shows that craftsmen acquired raw materials from a circumscribed area. Provenance studies of the selected archaeological and geological samples confirmed the use of surface collected marbles found within the immediate region of the site.

These patterns of selecting, identifying, and extracting raw materials are defining features of independent specialization, which were determined in part by basic economic forces. It must taken into the account that these patterns alone do not indicate the presence of specialized behavior since they also characterize dornestic production. The surface patterning of the manufacturing debris allowed me to make a distinction between specialized craft activity and domestic production. Craftsmen were specialized in the production of different artifacts in different work units, since the surface concentration of different types of artifact at different work units is an indication of labor division among the craftsmen. Due to the cost-cutting strategies and the intended function of marble artifacts, Kulaksızlar craftsmen repeatedly produced the same style of artifacts using standardized technology. The technical quality and the elegance of finished marble figurines and vessels classify them as a special class of artifacts. Another feature that differentiates this marble working from domestic production is the high volume of production. The site level attention placed on the production of marble artifacts suggests that exchange formed the major part of the village economy. Because similar artifacts are found outside the place of manufacture in most parts of western Anatolia, I view this marble working evidence as an example of a regional facility, that is production for exchange. This criterion alone differentiates specialized craft Kulaksızlar marble working from domestic craft production.

The main reason behind pursuing laborious, time-consuming, and risky marble working instead of adopting a less complex production strategy were both economic and non-economic. Because marble working formed the major part of Kulaksızlar economy and products conveyed symbolic meanings within the belief system of the Chalcolithic western Anatolian communities, marble figurines and vessels of the workshop were exchanged. The widespread presence of Kilia figurines within a radius of 100km from the site in central-west Anatolia can be related to the geographical positioning of the site in the region. Down-the-line exchange carried on in an inter-personal or inter-communal basis seems to be a plausible explanation for the spread of figurines within central-west Anatolia. A specific artifact may have a widespread distribution pattern if its associated symbolism is appropriate for the ideology of consumers. Marble Kilia figurines and pointed vessels could have been exchanged to fulfill the subsistence needs or to maintain relationships with the neighboring settlements through gift exchanges. The idea that exchange between the producer and consumer takes place on an interpersonal basis is the essence of independent specialization in the ethnographic record.

The presence of Kulaksızlar marble artifacts at the sites located on the main natural land-based trade routes imply the movement of these artifacts through inter-individual or inter-communal exchange. I also believe that middlemen such as pastoralists were also played some roles in the distribution of marble artifacts over great distances. This can be supported by the presence of two Kilia figurines in the village of Kozağacı in southwestern Anatolia, which is located nearly 400 km away from the workshop. The low amount and uneven distribution of rare or exotic artifacts recovered at excavated Chalcolithic westernAnatolian sites points to the presence of long-distance exchange mechanism showing the spread of valuable goods over great distances. In addition to land-based trade, presence of a figurine at the site of Kilia (modern Gallipoli) on the coast of Turkish Thrace across the Troad and one example on the adjacent eastern Aegean island of Lesbos points to the presence of maritime trade during this period. These land-based and maritime exchange involved in the distribution of valuable marble artifacts can be accepted as an evidence for the presence of complex exchange relationships and a reliance on specialist-produced artifacts during this period.

Non-economic factors also played an important role for the development and maintenance of Kulaksızlar specialization. The location of the site away from the best arable land induced me to believe that it was the abundance of marble that led these people to settle at this locality. This suggests that Kulaksızlar people chose a non-agricultural motivation from the outset and settled at this locality. The theory, according to which pre-urban specialists worked only during the times left over from subsistence production and supported from this agricultural surplus must be reconsidered. If agriculture was the main source of income, then one must answer the question of why Kulaksızlar people did not settle in the alluvial plain that was much more suitable for agricultural pursuits. I do not suggest that activities such as farming and stock-raising were never carried out by the Kulaksızlar people, but rather I argue that the exchange of marble artifacts for subsistence needs could have formed the majority of the village economy or provided other requirements of the village population. Basic subsistence was probably obtained in exchange for the marble products from their workshop. This means that pre-urban villages can adopt non-agricultural production strategies even in environments that are highly suitable for basic subsistence activities. It is also likely that exchange of symbolic marble artifacts heiped to maintain social relationships between the Kulaksızlar people and their neighbors. Therefore, it is not only the economic motivation but also the social and symbolic relations of production that shape the patterns of specialized behavior at this pre-urban setting in western Anatolia. Because marble artifacts appear to have conveyed a symbolic meaning to their consumers, technological behavior was dependent on non-economic processes. This is probably one of the most important contributions of the analysis of Kulaksızlar archaeological evidence to the theories of prehistoric craft specialization as well as to the study of Chalcolithic Anatolian culture and society. Recovery of evidence for the presence of specialized craft activity at Kulaksızlar is also important since it provides evidence that Chalcolithic western Anatolian production and exchange systems were not as simple as it has often been thought. The accumulation of wealth and the elaboration in ritual behavior are important factors for the rise and development of specialized craft activities in pre-urban times. Increased desire for specialist-produced artifacts during this period was probably due to the increasing role of artifacts in communication systems. What I mean by communication system is twofold. First, specialist-produced artifacts were perceived as prestige items that helped to transmit messages to segments of of the society and the ownership of prestige artifacts helped to differentiate their owners from the rest of the society on the basis of wealth. Second, specialist-produced artifacts conveyed symbolic meanings that were important in household or communal rituals. The visual display of symbolic artifacts in ritualistic contexts created a class of individuals based on the social roles that played in the households or communities. The cost of production and transportation involved in the acquisition of marble artifacts probably made them accessible to wealthy individuals or those who played important roles in the household or communal rituals. Craft specialization in this sense helped to create interpersonal ties and redefined differences in status.

The rise of village-based craft specialization at Kulaksızlar is in accord with the social, cultural, and technological changes observed during prior to the rise of the Late Chalcolithic cultural tradition in western Anatolia. Evidence from Kulaksızlar points to a short-lived flat settlement with a single cultural level lasting approximately a century or so. Thus, Kulaksızlar evidence is of great archaeological significance. This is because the sites of this period are difficult to detect archaeologically on the surface, as they are primarily represented by flat settlements with short-term occupations. Because of its chronological position, Kulaksızlar with evidence for specialized craft production helps us to estimate the level of cultural interactions that took place within the eastern Aegean world and beyond during this period. Close parallels for the Kulaksızlar pottery are to be found among the remains of the sites of the eastern Aegean islands, including the periods X-VIII at Emporio and the Upper Cave at Aghio Gala on Chios, levels II-III at Tigani on Samos, and the Vathy Bay Cave on Kalymnos. Presence of elements comparable to that of Gülpınar have also been found at Gülpınar, Beşik-Sivritepe, and Kumtepe 1a in northwestern, as well as Kuruçay, Lower Bağbaşı, and Karain Cave in southwestern Anatolia. The yearly increasing field studies carried out in Turkish Thrace, Greek mainland, the Aegean islands, and the Balkans continue to reveal parallels with the cultural assemblages of the second quarter of the fifth millennium B.C. These similarities must not be over emphasized since there are also important differences between these cultures. Why most of the sites of this period were represented only by short-term occupations, however, remains an important question that remains unanswered. Sudden appearance of these flat sites or single-period occupations with no apparent predecessors in the Troad, combined with the emergence of new elements in pottery and construction techniques in the cultural assemblages of these sites, seem to indicate that the sudden rise of cultures such as Kulaksızlar, Gülpınar, Kumtepe 1a, and Beşik-Sivritepe does not represent a cultural upheaval that occurred in western Anatolia during the second quarter of the fifth millennium B.C. There must be other factors to explain this phenomenon. I accept the theory that the large geographic area encompassing southeastern Europe, western Anatolia, and the eastern Aegean islands formed a cultural interaction sphere during this period, notwithstanding each of these sub-regions developed simultaneously under similar constraints. This theory requires to be cautious against the approaches that favor an explanation based on the gradual and continuous penetration of foreign nomad and pastoralist groups from southeastern Europe into northwestern Anatolia during a period between the Early and Late periods of western Anatolian Chalcolithic. In this context, marble working evidence at Kulaksızlar presents a rare opportunity to demonstrate the extent to which the similarities observed between the assemblages of the sites of southeastern Europe, western Anatolia, and the eastern Aegean islands reflect cultural interactions during this poorly understood cultural stage of the Aegean history.

Future Prospects

The Kulaksızlar evidence provides valuable insights into some of the least understood subsistems of western Anatolian Chalcolithic: production, exchange, and use of specialist-produced artifacts. This study of lithic production reveals that the small number of excavation in western Anatolia prevents the formation of a view of the importance of the lithic studies. Contextual evidence showing the production and use of lithic artifacts can enhance our understanding of the economic, social, and symbolic realms of the cultures with which they were associated. Therefore, more attention must be paid to the lithic artifacts in reconstructing the behavioral patterns of past Anatolian societies. Studies dealing with production of lithic artifacts in western Anatolia must be integrated within a framework that embraces not only economic motives, but also the social and symbolic components that shape the patterns of production. Excavations and new surface surveys must be carried out in the Akhisar region to provide a better picture of Chalcolithic culture and society. Survey studies must pay attention to the discovery of short period occupations located on higher grounds such as the foothills that encircle the alluvial plains of the region. A survey strategy concentrated on the higher grounds can reveal information the transitional Middle Chalcolithic period and enable one to identify the origin of the Kulaksızlar culture. Moreover, excavations in one those long-occupied mounds of the region can be very important in clarifying chronological and cultural questions in the Akhisar region and in western Anatolia as a whole. There are several settlements in the region that provide evidence from both earlier and later stages of the Chalcolithic period (e.g. Kayışlar, Alibeyli). Excavations at these sites canreveal information on the use of Kulaksızlar lithic artifacts and demonstrate their cultural and chronological affiliations. Available surface evidence from the Akhisar region clearly demonstrate the importance of the area in reconstructing the cultural history of pre-Bronze Age western Anatolia. In light of the minimal number of studies dealing with the production, exchange, and consumption of lithic artifacts, it is hoped that this study will encourage further archaeological works in this part of the Aegean world.

Appendix 1: Catalogue of Selected finds

This appendix catalogues 209 representative artifacts (45 pointed beakers, 27 pointed bowls, 62 Kilia figurines, 47 stone tools, and 28 pot sherds) collected during the 1994, 1995, and 1999 surveys at the site. I selected the most diagnostic marble specimens that were helpfull in reconstructing the multiple sequences of marble vessel and figurine production. In a similar way, use-wear (e.g. abrasion or rubbing) was the main criterion in the identification and selection of stone tools. The surface finds are arranged under different headings such as pointed beakers, bowls, figurines, percussive tools, abrasives, polishers, chipped-stone, and pottery. The order of abbreviations used in the description of these artifacts is as follows: artifact number (1-299), survey catalogue number (Kul.: Kulaksızlar; the year of discovery (e.g. 94, 95, or 99); survey catalogue number); the square in which the artifact is found (if available); the museum in which the artifact is currently kept (Ma.M.: Manisa Museum, Mi. M.: Milet Museum), and reference to illustrations within text. The artifacts are described in terms of the morphological aracteristics, state of preservation, texture, color, and use-wear. The entries also includes available measurements. The abbreviations used for the measurements (in meters) are: D.R.: Diameter at Rim, D.B.: Diameter at Base, H.: Height, W.: Width, Th.: Thickness; L.: Lenght, Pres.: Preserved dimensions of broken pieces).

Pointed beakers

1. Kul. 99.29, Square B3, Ma.M.　　　　Pls. 1 and 25
D.R. 0.083, Pres. H. 0.16
Preform fragment, lower half is missing; medium-grained, creamy-white marble; the exterior has pointed tool marks; two vertical lugs are roughly-shaped; the top is slightly drilled to about 0.006.

2. Kul. 95.150, Square B4, Ma.M.　　　　Pls. 1 and 25
D.R. 0.098, Pres. H. 0.142
Preform fragment, lower half is missing; medium-grained, creamy-white marble; the exterior has pointed tool marks; the vertical lugs are roughly-shaped.

3. Kul. 95.149, Square B4, Ma,M.　　　　Pls. 2 and 25
D.R. 0.103, Pres. H. 0.104
Preform fragment, lower half is missing; fine-grained, creamy-white marble: the exterior has peck marks.

4. Kul. 94.148, Ma.M.　　　　Pls. 2 and 25
Pres. H. 0.102
Lower end fragment of a preform; fine-grained, grayish-white marbie; surface is covered with pointed tool marks.

5. Kul. 95.36, Ma.M.　　　　Pls. 2 and 25
Pres. H. 0.103
Lower end fragment of a preform; fine-grained, grayish-white marble; surface is covered with pointed tool marks.

6. Kul. 94.146, Ma.M　　　　Pl. 2
Pres. H. 0.148
Lower end fragment of a preform; fine-grained, grayish-white marble; the surface has pointed tool marks.

7. Kul. 95.101, Ma.M.　　　　Pl. 2
Pres. H. 0.098
Lower end fragment of a preform; fine-grained, grayish-white marble; the surface is covered with pointed tool marks.

8. Kul. 95.216, Ma.M.　　　　Pl. 2
Pres. H. 0.082, Bottom solid for a height of 0.065
Lower end fragment of a drilled-preform; medium-grained, creamy. marble; the exterior is finely pecked, the interior has horizontal lines of rotary drilling.

9. Kul. 99.38, Square G4, Ma.M.　　　　Pl. 2
Pres. H. 0.085, bottom solid for a height of 0.027
Lower end fragment of a preform, split longitudinally; medium-grained, greenish-white marble; the exterior has pecking marks; the drilling is off centered.

10. Kul. 99.37, Ma.M.　　　　Pl. 25
Pres. H. 0.082
Lower end fragment of a preform; fine-grained grayish-white marble; the exterior has calcareous incrustation.

11. Kul. 99.3 1, Square G6, Ma.M.　　　　Pl. 25
Pres. H. 0.098
Lower end fragment of a preform; fine-grained, grayish-white marble; exterior has pointed tool marks.

12. Kul. 95.216, Square B2, Ma.M.　　　　Pls. 7 and 26
D.R. 0.104, H. 0.078
Preform, lower half is missing; medium-grained, creamy-white marble; the exterior has pointed tool marks, the interior is drilled to a depth of about 0.015 and has horizontal lines of rotary drilling.

13. Kul. 95.214, Ma.M.　　　　Pls. 3 and 26
D.R. 0.074, Pres. H. 0.11, H. of Lug 0.064
Preform, lower half is missing; medium-grained grayish-white marble; the vertical lug is slightly-shaped; the exterior has pointed tool marks, the interior is drilled to a depth of about 0.014.

14. Kul. 95.213, Ma.M.　　　　Pl. 4
Pres. H. 0. 134
Lower end fragment of a preform; medium-grained grayish-white marble; the exterior is finely pecked; the drilling is off-centered.

15. Kul. 95.219, Ma.M.　　　　Pl. 4
Pres. H. 0.114
Lower end fragment of a drilled preform; medium-grained grayish-white marble; the exterior is finely pecked, a projection is left on the base of the bottom interior.

16. Kul. 99.32, Square G5, Ma.M.　　　　Pls. 5 and 26
Pres. H. 0.095, bottom solid for a height of 0.068
Lower end fragment of a preform; fine-grained, grayish-white marble; the exterior is finely pecked, horizontal lines of rotary drilling are barely visible on the bottom interior.

17. Kul. 99.35, Square G5, Ma.M.　　　　Pls. 5 and 26
Pres. H. 0.075, bottom solid for a height of 0.053
Lower end fragment of a preform; fine-grained, creamy-white marble; the exterior has peck marks, horizontal lines of rotary drilling are barely visible on the interior.

18. Kul. 94.229, Ma.M.　　　　Pl. 26
Pres. H. 0.081, bottom solid for a height of 0.017
Lower end fragment of a drilled-preform; medium-grained, bluish-white marble the exterior has peck marks, the interior has horizontal lines of rotary drilling.

19. Kul. 94.222, Ma.M.　　　　Pl. 26
Pres. H. 0.0076, bottom solid for a height of 0.0621

Lower end fragment of drilled-preform; medium-grained, creamy-white marble the exterior has peck marks, the interior has horizontal lines of rotary drilling; a projection is left on the base of the bottom interior.

20. Kul. 95.218, Ma.M.   Pl. 26
Pres. H. 0.105, Bottom solid for a height of 0.076
Lower end fragment of a drilled-preform; medium-grained, creamy-white marble; the exterior is finely pecked, drilling is off centered.

21. Kul. 94.225, Ma.M.   Pl. 26
Pres. H. 0.05 1, W. 0.07, bottom solid for a height of 0.056
Lower end fragment; medium-grained, creamy-white marble; the exterior has peck marks, the interior has horizontal lines of rotary drilling.

22. Kul. 94.223, Ma.M.   Pl. 26
Pres. H. 0.095, bottom solid for a height of 0.068
Lower end fragment of a preform; medium-grained, white marble; the exterior is finely pecked, the interior has lines of rotary drilling; a projection is left on the base of the interior bottom.

23. Kul. 95.217, Ma.M.   Pl. 26
Pres. H. 0.069, bottom solid for a height of 0.057
Lower end fragment of a drilled-preform; medium-grained, creamy-white marble; the peck marks on the exterior are smoothed, the interior has horizontal lines of drilling.

24. Kul. 94.228, Ma.M.   Pl. 26
Pres. H. 0.065, bottom solid for a height of 0.029
Lower end fragment of a drilled-preform; fine-grained, grayish-white marble exterior is finely pecked, the interior has horizontal lines of rotary drilling.

25. Kul. 99.3, Square F5, Ma.M.   Pl. 27
D.R. 0.076, Pres. H. 0.125, W. 0,057, H. of lug 0.102
Rim fragment of a drilled-preform; fine-grained, greenish-white marble; exterior surface has pointed tool marks; the vertical lug is roughly-shaped; the unevenly worn interior has lines of rotary drilling.

26. Kul. 99.14, Square F4, Ma.M   Pl. 27
D.R. 0.086, Pres. H. 0.096, Pres. W. 0.082
Rim fragment of a drilled-preform; medium-grained, grayish-white marble vertical lug is roughly-shaped; the exterior surface has pointed tool marks, the interior has lines of rotary drilling.

27. Kul. 99.9, Square F4, Ma.M.   Pl. 27
D.R. 0.084, Pres. H. 0,104; Pres. W. 0.055, H. of Lug 0.102
Rim fragment of a drilled-preform; fine-grained, grayish-white marble; exterior has peck marks; the vertical lug is roughly-shaped; the interior is unevenly worn and has horizontal lines of rotary drilling.

28. Kul. 99.25, Square F5, Ma.M.   Pl. 27
D.R. 0.075, Pres. H. 0.096, Pres. W. 0.036, H. of Lug 0.098
Rim fragment of a drilled-preform; fine-grained, grayish-white marble; the vertical lug is roughly-shaped; the exterior has pointed tool marks and calcareous incrustation, the evenly-worn interior has horizontal lines of rotary drilling.

29. Kul. 94.242, Ma.M.   Pl. 27
D.R. 0.092, H. 0.054, W. 0.055
Rim fragment of a drilled-preform; fine-grained, greenish-white masble; the exterior has peck marks, the interior has

lines of rotary drilling; the vertical lug was broken during piercing.

30. Kul. 99.7, Square G4, Ma.M.   Pls. 6 and 27
D.R. 0.085, Pres. H. 0.099, H. of Lug 0.097
Rim fragment of a drilled-preform; fine-grained, creamy-white marble; the exterior surface has pointed tool marks, the interior is unevenly worn and has lines of rotary drilling.

31. Kul. 99.27, Square F5, Ma.M.   Pl. 6
D.R. 0.095, Pres. H. 0.086, Pres. W. 0.054
Rim fragment of a drilled-preform; fine-grained, creamy-white marble; the vertical lug is roughly-shaped; the exterior surface has pointed tool marks, the interior has horizontal lines of rotary drilling.

32. Kul. 99.26, Square F4, Ma.M.   Pls. 7 and 28
D.R. 0.094, Pres. H. 0.074, Pres.W. 0.044
Rim fragment of a drilled-preform; medium-grained, grayish-white marble; the exterior has pointed tool marks, the interior has horizontal lines of drilling.

33. Kul. 95.143, Ma.M.   Pls. 7 and 28
D.R. 0.089, Pres. H. 0.063, Pres. W. 0.062
Rim fragment of a drilled-preform; fine-grained, greenish-white marble; the exterior has pointed tool marks, the interior has horizontal lines of rotary drilling.

34. Kul. 99.34, Square 05, Ma.M.   Pl. 28
D.R. 0.082, Pres. H. 0.065, Pres.W. 0.055
Rim fragment of a drilled-preform; fine-grained, grayish-white marble; the exterior has pointed tool marks and calcerous incrustation, the interior has horizontal lines of rotary drilling.

35. Kul. 99.28, Square F4, Ma.M   Pl. 28
D.R. 0.083, Pres. H. 0.059, Pres. W. 0.062
Rim fragment of a drilled-preform; fine-grained, grayish-white marble, the exterior has pointed tool marks, the interior has horizontal lines of drilling.

36. Kul. 99.17, Square F4, Ma.M.   Pl. 28
D.R. 0.094, Pres. H. 0.075, Pres. W. 0.051
Rim fragment of a drilled-preform; fine-grained, grayish-white marble; the exterior has pointed tool marks, the interior has horizontal lines of rotary drilling; both surfaces are partially incrustated.

37. Kul. 95.126, Ma.M.   Pls. 8 and 28
D.R. 0.089, Pres. H. 0.091, Pres. W. 0.058
Rim fragment, broken during refinement; fine-grained, yellowish-greenish marble; the interior has finely polished surfaces; the exterior has scratching marks running in multiple directions.

38. Kul. 99.24, Square F4, Ma.M.   Pl. 28
D.R. 0.08 1, Pres. H. 0.04, Pres. W. 0.09
Rim fragment, broken during the refinement; fine-grained, grayish-marble; the exterior has lines from abrasive tools; the interior has calcareous incrustation.

39. Kul. 94.205, Ma.M.   Pl. 28
D.R. 0.103, Pres. H. 0.055, Pres. W. 0.035
Rim fragment, broken during refinement; fine-grained creamy-white marble, the exterior is finely polished, the horizontal lines of rotary drilling on the interior are partially smoothed.

40. Kul. 99.2, Square F14, Ma.M.   Pl. 29
D.R. 0.071, Pres. H. 0.134; Pres. W. 0.061
Rim fragment of a drilled-preform; fine-grained, grayish-white marble; the vertical lug is roughly-shaped; the exterior has pointed tools marks, the interior has lines of rotary drilling.

41. Kul. 95.132, Ma.M.   Pls. 8 and 29
D.R. 0.087, Pres. H. 0.135, Pres. W. 0.061
Rim fragment of a drilled-preform; medium-grained, bluish-white marble; the exterior is finely pecked and has vertical and diagonal scratching, the interior has horizontal lines of rotary drilling.

42. Kul. 99.11, Square F5, Ma.M.   Pl. 29
Pres. H. 0.103, W. 0.045
Wall fragment of a drilled-preform; medium-grained, grayish-white marble; the exterior has calcerous incrustation, the interior has horizontal lines of rotary drilling.

43. Kul. 95.113, Ma.M.   Pls. 9 and 29
Pres. H. 0.06 1, Pres. W. 0.049
Wall fragment fo a drilled-preform; fine-grained, grayish-white marble; the exterior is finely pecked, the interior has horizontal lines of rotary drilling.

44. Kul. 99.5, Square E4, Ma.M.   Pls. 9 and 29
D.R. 0.084, Pres. H. 0.108, Pres. W. 0.058
Rim fragment, broken during the refinement; fine-grained, creamy-marble; exterior has vertical and diagonal scratches, interior has calcareous incrustation.

45. Kul. 95.154, Ma.M.   Pls. 9 and 29
D.R. 0.072, Pres. H. 0.089
Rim fragment of a finished beaker; medium grained, greenish-white marble; both surfaces are finely polished; the vertical lug is horizontally pierced both sides, the piercing is slightly biconical in shape.

Pointed bowls

46. Kul. 99.29, Square E8, Ma.M.   Pls. 10 and 31
D.R. 0.185, H. 0.115
Preform, broken during the chipping out of the interior; medium-grained, grayish-white marble; the exterior is unevenly pecked.

47. Kul. 99.39, Square E8, Ma.M.   Pl. 31
D.R. 0.086, H. 0.089
Preform, split longitudinally; fine-grained, creamy white marble; the exterior has pointed tools marks, the interior is slightly chipped-out to a depth of 0.007.

48. Kul. 99.4 1, Square E8, Ma.M.   Pl. 31
D.R. 0.096, H. 0.089
Preforın; fine-grained, creamy-white marble; the exterior has pecking marks, the top is unevenly pecked.

49. Kul. 99.40, Square E8, Ma.M   Pl. 31
D.R. 0.102, H. 0. 086
Preform; fine-grained, grayish-white marble; the exterior has pointed tool marks; the top was broken off while being chipped out.

50. Kul. 95.110, Ma.M.   Pls. 10 and 31
D.R. 0.086, H. 0.075
Preform, split longitudinally; medium-grained, grayish-white marble; exterior is covered with pointed tool marks, the interior is chipped-out to a depth of 0.0 11.

51. Kul. 99.42, Square 04, Ma.M.   Pl. 31
D.R. 0.094, Pres. H. 0.059
Rim fragment of a preform, split diagonally during the chipping out of interior; fine-grained, creamy-white marble; the exterior has pointed tool marks, the interior is chipped-out to a depth of 0.007.

52. Kul. 95.111, Ma.M.   Pl. 31
D.R. 0.056, H. 0.053
Preform; almost half is missing; fine-grained, greenish-white marble; the exterior has peck marks, the interior is slightly chipped-out to a depth of 0.005

53. Kul. 95.136, Ma.M.   Pl. 31
D.R. 0.064, H. 0.043
Drilled-preform; medium-grained, greenish-white marble; the exterior has peck marks, the interior is drilled to the depth of 0.064.

54. Kul. 99.54, Square E8, Ma.M.   Pl. 31
D.R. 0.068, H. 0.044
Preform; medium-grained, greenish-yellowish marble; the interior is slightly chipped-out to a depth of 0.006.

55. Kul. 99.45, Square E8, Ma.M.   Pl. 31
D.R. 0.065, H. 0.041
Preform; fine-grained, grayish-white marble; the exterior is finely pecked, the interior is chipped-out to a depth of 0.009.

56. Kul. 99.47, Square E8, Ma.M.   Pl. 31
D.R. 0.074, H. 0.038
Preform; fine-grained, grayish-white marble; the exterior has pecking marks; the interior is chipped-out to a depth of 0.004.

57. Kul. 99.50, Square E8, Ma.M.   Pl. 31
D.R .0.066, H. 0. 036
Preform; fine-grained, grayish-white marble; the exterior has pointed tool marks; the interior is slightly chipped out to a depth of 0.004.

58. Kul. 95.176, Ma.M.   Pls. 12 and 32
D.R. 0.084, Pres. H. 0.044
Rim fragment of a drilled-preform; medium-grained, greenish-white marble; interior has lines of rotary drilling, bevel of the rim suggests the use of two different sizes and diameters of drill-bits.

59. Kul. 99.59, Square F8, Ma.M.   Pl. 32
D.R. 0.116, Pres. H. 0.089
Rim fragment of a preform, the pointed base is missing; fine-grained, grayish- white marble; the exterior has peck marks, the interior has horizontal lines of rotary drilling.

60. Kul. 95.111, Ma.M.   Pls. 11 and 32
D.R. 0.094, H. 0.043
Lower end of a drilled-preform; fine-grained, creamy white marble; the exterior has pointed tool marks, the interior has horizontal lines of rotary drilling, the projection on the inner side suggests the use of two different drill-bits.

61. Kul. 95.110, Ma.M.   Pls. 11 and 32
D.R. 0.92, H. 0.045
Lower end of a drilled-preform; almost half is missing, medium-grained, creamy white marble; the exterior is finely pecked, the interior has horizontal lines of rotary drilling.

62. Kul. 95.94, Ma.M.   Pls. 11 and 32

D. at Rim 0.72, H. 0.059
Drilled-preform; fine-grained, creamy-white marble; the exterior is finely pecked, the interior has horizontal lines of rotary drilling.

63. Kul. 95.113, Square E8, Ma.M.   Pl. 32
D. at Rim 0.2 1, Pres. H. 0.061
Preform; medium-grained, creamy-white marble; the interior is slightly chipped out to a depth of 0.015.

64. Kul. 99.53, Square E8, Ma.M.   Pl. 32
D.R. 0.128, Pres. H. 0.037
Rim fragment of a drilled-preform; medium-grained, creamy-white marble; the exterior has pointed tool marks and calcareous incrustation; the interior is slightly chipped-out to the depth of is 0.007.

65. Kul. 99.55, Square E8, Ma.M.   Pl. 32
D.R. 0.144, H. 0.034
Preform; fine-grained, greenish-white marble; the exterior has pointed tool marks, the interior is chipped-out to a depth of 0.008.

66. Kul. 99.57, Square E8, Ma.M.   Pl. 32
D.R. 0.142, Pres. H. 0.036
Rim fragment of a drilled-preform; medium-grained, greenish-white marble; the exterior has pointed tool marks, the interior is slightly chipped-out to a depth of 0.011.

67. Kul. 99.49, Square G5, Ma.M.   Pl. 32
D.R. 0.154, Pres. H. 0.064
Drilled-preform, fine-grained, greenish-white marble; the exterior has pecking marks and incrustation, the interior is unevenly worn and has horizontal lines of rotary drilling.

68. Kul. 99.5 1, Square G4, Ma.M.   Pl. 32
D.R. 0.108, Pres. H. 0.042, Pres. W. 0.072
Rim fragment of a drilled bowl preform; fine-grained, creamy-white marble; the exterior has peck marks, the interior is finely smoothed.

69. Kul. 99.25, Square F4, Ma.M.   Pl. 32
D.R. 0.092, Pres. H. 0.049, Pres. W. 0.048
Rim fragment of a drilled-preform; fine-grained, creamy-white marble; the exterior has pointed tool marks and incrustation, the interior has lines of rotary drilling.

70. Kul. 99.52, Square F5, Ma.M.   Pl. 12
D.R. 0. 103, Pres. H. 0.046, Pres. W. 0.083
Rim fragment of a drilled-preform; fine-grained, creamy-white marble; the exterior is finely pecked, the interior has horizontal lines of rotary drilling.

71. Kul. 99.1, Ma.M.   Pl. 12
Pres. H. 0.086, Pres. W. 0.0971
Rim fragment of a drilled-preform; fine-grained, grayish-white marble; the exterior is finely pecked, the interior has horizontal lines of rotary drilling.

72. Kul. 94.155, Ma.M.   Pl. 12
D.R. 0.242, Pres. H. 0.064
Rim fragment of a drilled-preform; medium-grained, grayish-white marble; the exterior is finely pecked, the interior has horizontal lines of rotary drilling.

Kilia figurines

73. Kul. 93. Et.1, Ma.M.   Pls. 13 and 33
H. 0.12, W. 0.083

Blank of a figurine, elongated and rectangular in shape; fine-grained, grayish white marble; the surface has flaking scars.

74. Kul. 94.145, Square C3, Ma.M.   Pls. 13 and 33
H. 0.256, W. 0.093, Th. 0.043
Blank a figurine, elongated and rectangular in shape with tapering upper medium-grained, grayish-white marble; the surface has both pecking flaking scars.

75. Kul. 94.3, Square C4, Ma.M.   Pl. 13
H. 0.112, W. 0.048, Th. 0.0211
Blank of a figurine, elongated and rectangular in shape; fine-grained, grayish white marble; the surface has flaking scars

76. Kul. 94.9, Square C4, Ma.M.   Pl. 13
H. 0.089, W. 0.036, Th. 0.027
Blank of a figurine, elongated and rectangular in shape; fine-grained, greenish marble; the surface has flaking scars

77. Kul. 94.1, Square C3, Ma.M.   Pl. 13
H. 0 W. 0.05 1, Th. 0.039
Blank of a figurine, elongated rectangular in shape with tapering lower end; fine-grained, greenish-white marble; the surface has flaking scars.

78. Kul. 95.1, Square C3, Ma.M.   Pl. 13
H. 0.128, W. 0.042, Th. 0.025
Blank of a figurine, elongated rectangular in shape; fine-grained, grayish-white marble; the surface has flaking scars.

79. Kul. 94.70, Square D2, Ma.M.   Pls. 14 and 33
H. 0.142, W. 0.071, Th. 0.031
Blank of a figurine, rectangular in shape; fine-grained, greenish-white marble; the surface has pointed tool marks.

80 Kul. 95.98, Square D3, Ma.M.   Pls. 14 and 33
H. 0.0 137, W. 0.028, Th. 0.021
Preform of a figurine; fine-grained, grayish-white marble; the surface has flaking scars, a notch occurs at the upper half.

81. Kul. 93.4, Ma.M   Pl. 14
H. 0.091, W. 0.046
Head fragment of a preform, broken off during working of the neck; fine-grained, grayish-white marble; back of the head is missing; the surface has small flaking scars.

82. Kul. 93.93, Ma.M.   Pl. 14
Pres. H. 0.056, W. 0.03 1
Upper part of a preform, fine-grained, grayish-white marble; the surface is finely pecked, the neck is slightly thinned.

83. Kul. 99.67, Square C3, Ma.M.   Pls. 15 and 34
Pres. H. 0.115, W. 0.084, Th. 0.042
Lower end fragment of a preform, broken off at waist; fine-grained, creamy-white marble; the surface has pointed tool marks.

84. Kul. 99.64, Square D4, Ma.M.   Pls. 15 and 34
Pres. H. 0.099, W. 0.054, Th. 0.021
Lower end fragment of a preform, broken at waist; fine-grained, creamy-white marble, the surface has flaking scars.

85. Kul. 99.69, Square C3, Ma.M.   Pls. 15 and 34
Pres. H. 0.079, W. 0.059
Lower end fragment of a preform, broken off at waist; fine-grained, greenish-white marble; the surface has flaking scars.

86. Kul. 99.68, Square D4, Ma.M.   Pl. 34
Pres. H. 0.084, W. 0.059
Lower end fragment of a preform, broken off at waist; fine-grained, creamy-white marble; the surface has flaking scars.

87. Kul. 99.66, Square D4, Ma.M.   Pl. 15
Pres. H. 0.10, W. 0.064
Lower end fragment of a preform, broken off at waist; fine-grained, creamy-white marble; the surface has flaking scars.

88. Kul. 95.31, Ma.M.   Pl. 34
Pres. H. 0.66, W. 0.036, Th. 0.021
Lower end fragment of a preform, broken off at waist; fine-grained, grayish-white marble; the surface has flaking scars.

89. Kul. 95.41, Ma.M.   Pl. 34
Pres. H. 0.056, W. 0.043, Th. 0.021
Lower end fragment of a preform, broken off at waist; fine-grained, grayish -white marble; the surface flaking scars.

90. Kul. 95.35, Ma.M.   Pl. 34
Pres. H. 0.066, W. 0.033
Lower end fragment of a preform, broken off at waist; fine-grained, grayish-white marble; the surface has flaking scars.

91. Kul. 95.39, Ma.M.   Pl. 34
Pres. H. 0.059, W. 0.042
Lower end fragment of a preform, broken off at waist; fine-grained, grayish-white marble; the surface has flaking scars.

92. Kul. 95.36, Ma.M.   Pl. 34
Pres. H. 0.052, W. 0.032
Lower end fragment of a preform, broken off at waist; fine-grained, grayish-white marble; the surface has flaking scars.

93. Kul. 95.32, Ma.M.   Pl. 34
Pres. H. 0.54, W. 0.033, Th. 0.018
Lower end fragment of a preform, broken off at waist; fine-grained, grayish-white marble; the surface has flaking scars.

94. Kul. 94.106, Ma.M.   Pls. 16 and 35
H. 0.083, W. 0.052, Th. 0.062
Head fragment of a preform, broken off during the thinning of neck; fine-grained, green marble; the surface has small flaking marks.

95. Kul. 99.73, Ma.M.   Pls. 16 and 35
H. 0.051, W. 0.046, Th. 0.056
Head fragment of a preform, broken off at neck; medium-grained, creamy-white marble.

96 Kul. 95.74, Square D4, Ma.M.   Pl. 16
H. 0.062; W. 0.049, Th. 0.04 1, Pres. Th. 0.041
Head fragment of a preform, broken off during the working of neck; fine-grained, grayish-white marble; the surface has small chipping scars.

97. Kul. 94.106, Ma.M.   Pl. 35
H. 0.096, W. 0.07 1, Th. 0.054
Head fragment of a preform; medium-grained, white marble; the surface is covered with pecking marks.

98. Kul. 95.85, Square D4, Ma.M.   Pl. 17
Pres. H. 0.032, W. 0.032
Head fragment of a preform; broken off at neck; fine-grained, grayish-white marble, the surface has small flaking scars.

99. Kul. 93.5, Ma.M.   Pl. 17

H. 0.074, W. 0.079, Th. 0.049
Head fragment of a preform; broken off during the working of neck; fine-grained, grayish-white marble; the surface has flaking scars.

100. Kul. 93.8, Ma.M.   Pl. 17
H. 0.064, W. 0.069
Head fragment of a preform; broken off during the thinning of neck; fine-grained, grayish-white marble; surface has flaking scars.

101. Kul. 95.4, Mi.M.   Pls. 17 and 35
H. 0.059, W. 0.07 1, Th. 0.049
Head fragment, broken off at the neck; medium-grained, bluish-white marble; the surface has small flaking scars.

102. Kul. 99.7 1, Ma.M.   Pl. 17
H. 0.05 1, W. 0.046, Th. 0.042
Head fragment of a preform, broken off at neck; medium-grained, greenish-white marble; the surface has small flaking scars, abrasion marks show the thinning out of the neck.

103. Kul. 95.11, Mi.M.   Pl. 35
H. 0.059, W. 0.059, Th. 0.049
Head fragment, broken off at neck; fine-grained, white marble; abrasion marks over the pointed tool marks.

104. Kul. 93.30, Ma.M.   Pls. 18 and 35
H. 0.064, W. 0.043
Head fragment of a figurine with upper part of torso; fine-grained, grayish-white marble; the surface has lines of abrasion, calcareous incrustation occurs on part of the head.

105. Kul. 95.5, Mi.M.   Pl. 18
H. 0.053, W. 0.06, Th. 0.048
Head fragment, broken off at the neck; fine-grained, bluish-white marble; abrasion marks over pointed tool marks, the surface has small chipping scars.

106. Kul. 95.14, Mi.M.   Pl. 18
H. 0.042, W. 0.042, Th. 0.042
Head fragment, broken off at the neck; fine-grained, white-marble; lines of abrasion over pecking marks.

107. Kul. 95.8, Mi.M.   Pl. 35
H. 0.036, W. 0.044, Th. 0.033
Head fragment, broken off at the neck; fine-grained, greenish-white marble; the surface is finely smoothed.

108. Kul. 95.9, Mi.M.   Pl. 35
H. 0.04 1, W. 0.045, Th. 0.039
Head fragment, broken off at the neck; fine-grained, grayish-white marble; the surface is finely smoothed.

109. Kul. 95.16, Mi.M.   Pl. 35
H. 0.051, W. 0.046, Pres. Th. 0.026
Head fragment, broken off at the neck; fine-grained, greenish-white marble; back of head is missing, nose is raised; the surface is finely smoothed.

110. Kul. 95.18, Mi.M.   Pl. 35
H. 0.051, W. 0.046, Th. 0.029
Head fragment, broken off at the neck; fine-grained, creamy-white marble; marks of flint-blade use around the raised nose and ears; the surface is finely smoothed, calcareous incrustation occurs on parts of the head.

111. Kul. 93.17, Mi.M.   Pl. 18

H. 0.033, W. 0.0321
Head fragment of finished figurine, broken off at the neck; the back of the head is missing, nose is raised.

112. Kul. 95.19, Mi.M.   Pl. 18
H. 0.04 1, W. 0.042
Head fragment, broken off at the neck; fine-grained, grayish-white marble; the nose and ears raised, the surface is finely smoothed; incrustation occurs on parts of the head.

113. Kul. 95.29, Mi.M.   Pl. 19
H. 0.056, W. 0.039, Th. 0.009
Torso fragment, broken during refinement; fine-grained, grayish-white marble; left arm division is incised; the surface has lines of abrasion.

114. Kul. 95.28, Mi.M.   Pls. 19 and 36
H. 0.069, W. 0.065, Th.0.021
Torso fragment, broken during, refinement fine-granied, creamy-white marble; the left arm division is incised; the surface is finely smoothed.

115. Kul. 95.27, Mi.M.   Pls. 19 and 36
H. 0.047, W. 0.052, Th. 0.013
Torso fragment, broken during refinement; fine-grained, bluish-white marble; the arm divisions are incised.

116. Kul. 95.26, Mi.M.   Pl. 19
H. 0.021, W.0.033
Torso fragment, broken during refinement; fine-grained, greenish-white marble; arm divisions are incised; the surface is finely smoothed.

117 Kul. 93.101, Ma.M.   Pl. 36
H. 0.031, W. 0.021
Torso fragment, broken during refinement; fine-grained, grayish-white marble; the surface has lines of abrasion, left arm is incised.

118. Kul. 93.113, Ma.M.   Pl. 36
H. 0.039, W. 0.034, Th. 0.009
Torso fragment, broken during refinement; fine-grained, grayish-white marble; the surface has lines of abrasion; arm divisions are emphasized with incision.

119. Kul. 93.114, Ma.M.   Pl. 36
H. 0.035, W.0.025
Torso fragment, broken during the refinement; fine-grained, grayish-white marble; the surface is finely smoothed, left arm division is incised.

120. Kul. 93.112, Ma.M.   Pl. 36
H. 0.035, W. 0.21
Torso fragment, broken during refinement; fine-grained, grayish-white marble; the surface has lines of abrasive; left arm is division incised.

121. Kul. 95.32, Mi.M.   Pl. 36
Pres. H.0.036, W. 0.029, Th. 0.011
Waist fragment, broken during refinement; fine-grained, greenish-white marble; pubic triangle and leg division are incised; the surface is finely smoothed.

122. Kul. 93.107, Ma.M.   Pl. 36
Pres. H. 0.058, W. 0.033, Th. 0.008
Waist fragment, broken during refinement; fine-grained, grayish-white marble; the surface is finely smoothed.

123. Kul. 95.38, Mi.M.   Pl. 36
Pres. H. 0.039, W. 0.033, Th. 0.013
Waist fragment, broken during refinement; fine-grained, creamy-white marble; the surface is finely smoothed.

124. Kul. 95.24, Mi.M.   Pl. 36
Pres. H. 0.047, W. 0.029, Th. 0.011
Waist fragment, broken during refinement; fine-grained, grayish-white-marble; the leg division is incised.

125. Kul. 95.39, Mi.M.
Pres. H. 0.057, W. 0.034, Th. 0.011   Pl. 36
Waist fragment, broken during refinement; fine-grained, white marble; the surface is finely smoothed.

126. Kul. 95.35, Mi.M.   Pl. 36
Pres. H. 0.054, W. 0.043
Lower end fragment, broken during refinement; fine-grained, grayish-white marble; the surface is finely smoothed.

127. Kul. 93.129, Ma.M.   Pls. 19 and 36
Pres. H. 0.037, W.0.026
Lower end fragment, broken off at the waist during refinement; fine-grained, grayish-white marble; the surface is finely smoothed.

128. Kul. 93.117, Ma.M.   Pl. 36
Pres. H. 0.046, W. 0.024
Lower end fragment of a finished figurine, broken off at waist; fine-grained, grayish-white marble; the surface is finely smoothed.

129. Kul. 93.115, Ma.M.   Pl. 36
Pres. H. 0.04 1, W. 0.022
Lower end fragment, broken off at the waist during refinement; fine-grained, grayish-white marble; the surface is finely smoothed.

130. Kul. 93.133, Ma.M.   Pls. 19 and 36
Pres. H. 0.054, W.0.0035
Lower end fragment, broken off at the waist during refinement; fine-grained, grayish-white marble; the surface is finely smoothed.

131. Kul. 93.126, Ma.M.   Pl. 36
Pres. H. 0.052, W. 0.038
Lower end fragment, broken off at the waist during refinement; fine-grained, grayish-white marble; the surface is finely smoothed.

132. Kul. 93.130, Ma.M.   Pl. 36
Pres. H. 0.048, W.0.042
Lower end fragment, broken off at the waist during refinement; fine-grained, greenish-white marble; the surface is finely smoothed.

133. Kul. 93.131, Ma.M.   Pl. 36
Pres. H. 0.04 1, W.0.024
Lower end fragment, broken off at the waist during refinement; fine-grained, creamy-white marbie; the surface is fineiy smoothed.

134. Kul. 93.125, Mi.M.   Pl. 19
Pres. H. 0.021, W. 0.028
Lower end fragment, broken off at the knees during refinement; fine-grained, grayish-white marble; the surface is finely smoothed.

Tools

135. Kul. 95.224, Ma.M.   Pls. 22 and 39
H. 0.09, W. 0.053, Th. 0.037
Hammerstone, spherical in shape; dark-green to black gabbro; it has heavy-percussion use-wear.

136. Kul. 95.231, Ma.M.   Pls. 22 and 39
H. 0.063, W. 0.031, Th. 0.022
Hammerstone, elongated in shape with pointed ends; dark-green to black gabbro; the narrow ends have percussive use-wear.

137. Kul. 95.226, Ma.M.   Pl. 39
H. 0.111, W. 0.075, Th. 0.055
Hammerstone, spherical in shape; dark-green to black gabbro; it has heavy- percussion use-wear.

138. Kul. 99.75, Ma.M.   Pls. 22 and 39
H. 0.061, W. 0.032
Basalt hammerstone, elongated in shape and tapers towards bottom; dark-gray to black basalt; it is broken on one end, the narrow end have percussive usewear.

139. Kul. 95.227, Ma.M.   Pl. 39
H. 0.069, W. 0.076, Th. 0.042
Hammerstone, dark-green to black gabbro; spherical in shape with original work marks.

140. Kul. 95.228, Ma.M.   Pl. 39
H. 0.049, W. 0.045, Th. 0.031
Hammerstone, spherical in shape; dark-green to black gabbro; it has heavypercussion use-wear.

141. Kul. 95.225, Ma.M.   Pls. 22 and 39
H. 0.06, W. 0.065, Th. 0.053
Gabbro hammerstone, elongated in shape; dark-green to black gabbro; the pointed end has percussive use-wear.

142. Kul. 95.230, Ma.M.   Pl. 39
H. 0.05 1, W. 0.043, Th. 0.024
Hammer-stone; dark-green to black gabbro; elongated in shape, the narrow ends have percussive use-wear.

143. Kul. 93.182, Ma.M.   Pls. 23 and 40
H. 0.058, W. 0.095
Drill-bit, crescent in shape; reddish-yellow sandstone; it is beveled at the proximal end.

144. Kul. 99.83, Grid G5, Ma.M.   Pl. 40
H. 0.046, W. 0.078
Drill-bit, crescent in shape; reddish-yellow sandstone; it is beveled at the proximal end and flat at the distal end.

145. Kul. 99.82, Grid F4, Ma.M.   Pls. 24 and 40
H. 0.046, W. 0.089
Drill-bit, crescent in shape; reddish-yellow sandstone; it is beveled at the proximal end and flat at the distal end.

146. Kul. 95.206, Ma.M.   Pl. 40
H. 0.044, W. 0.077
Drill-bit, crescent-shaped; reddish-yellow sandstone; it is beveled at the proximal end and flat at the distal end.

147. Kul. 95.195, Ma.M.   Pls. 24 and 40
H. 0.099, W. 0.058
Drill-bit, crescent in shape; reddish-yellow sandstone; it is beveled at the proximal end and flat at the distal end; the tip has a cavity.

148. Kul. 99.86, Ma.M.   Pls. 23 and 40
H. 0.079, W. 0.059
Drill-bit, conical in shape; reddish-yellow sandstone, longitudinaliy split; it beveled at the proximal end and flat at the distal end.

149. Kul. 95. 200, Ma.M.   Pls. 23 and 40
H. 0.056, W. 0.051
Drill-bit, conical in shape; reddish-yellow sandstone, it is beveled at the proximal end, the rounded distal end has a conical cavity.

150. Kul. 95.184, Ma.M.   Pl. 40
H. 0.054, W. 0.058
Drill-bit, conical in shape; sandstone; it is beveled at the proximal and flat at the distal end.

151. Kul. 95.180, Ma.M.   Pl. 40
H. 0.036, W. 0.046
Drill-bit, conical in shape; reddish-yellow sandstone, it is beveled at the proximal and rounded at the distal end.

152. Kul. 95.176, Ma.M.   Pls. 23 and 40
H. 0.045, W. 0.038
Drill-bit, conical in shape; reddish-yeilow sandstone, it is beveled at the proximal and rounded at the distal end.

153. Kul. 95.169, Ma.M.   Pl. 40
H. 0.041, 0.044
Drill-bit, conical in shape; reddish-yellow sandstone, it is beveled at the proximal end, the rounded distal end has a cavity on its tip.

154. Kul. 99.89, Ma.M.   Pl. 23
H. 0.059, W. 0.026
Drill-bit, conical in shape; reddish-yellow sandstone, it is beveled at the proximal and rounded at the distal end.

155. Kul. 95.171, Ma.M.   Pl. 24
H. 0.044, W. 0.052
Drill-bit, conical in shape; reddish-yellow sandstone, it is beveled at the proximal end and rounded at the distal end, the tip has a cavity.

156. Kul. 93.173, Ma.M.   Pl. 24
H. 0.044, W. 0.033
Drill-head, conical in shape; reddish-yellow sandstone; a cavity occurs at its wider end.

157. Kul. 95.233, Ma.M.   Pl. 41
L. 0.09, W. 0.053, Th. 0.037
Bifacial abrasive, emery; rectangular in shape and flat in section; one corner is broken off.

158. Kul. 94.299, Ma.M.   Pl. 41
L. 0.082, W. 0.077, Th. 0.028
Bifacial abrasive, gray granite; roughly rectangular in outline and flat in section.

159. Kul. 95.232, Ma.M.   Pl. 41
L. 0.06, W. 0.065, Th. 0.053
Bifacal abrasive, greenish-gray emery (?); trapezoidal in shape; broken off at both ends.

160. Kul. 99.76, Ma.M.   Pl. 41
L. 0.093, W. 0.059, Th. 0.026

Unifacial marble polishing-pebble, ovate in shape with hemispherical section; it has a water-worn surface.

161. Kul. 99.74, Ma.M.   Pl. 41
L. 0.112, W. 0.057, Th. 0.027
Unifacial marble polishing-pebble, ovate in shape with hemispherical section; it has a water-worn surface, one side has scratches running in multiple directions.

162. Kul. 95.235, Ma.M.   Pl. 41
L. 0.111, W. 0.075, Th. 0.055
Unifacial marble polishing-pebble, ovate in shape with hemispherical section; it has a water-worn surface.

163. Kul. 99.125, Square E4, Ma.M.   Pl. 42
L. 0.129, W. 0.149, Th. 0.054
Quern, ovate in shape with hemispherical section; reddish-yellow sandstone; almost half is missing.

164. Kul. 95.239, Square D4, Ma.M.   Pl. 42
L. 0.168, W. 0.165, Th. 0.068
Quern, ovate in shape with hemispherical section; bluish-gray schist; almost half is missing.

165. Kul. 95.238, Square D4, Ma.M.   Pl. 42
L. 0.265, W. 0.135, Th. 0.051
Quern, nearly rectangular in shape with hemispherical section; reddish-yellow schist.

166. Kul. 99.126, Square E4, Ma.M.   Pl. 42
L. 0.124, W. 0.121, Th. 0.042
Quern rectangular in shape with hemispherical section; reddish-yellow sandstone; nearly half is missing.

167. Kul. 99. 95, Square D4, Ma.M.   Pl. 43
L. 0.0068, W. 0.034, Th. 0.009
Blade, bluish-gray flint; slight use-wear along the cutting edges.

168. Kul. 99.99, Square E4, Ma.M.   Pl. 43
L. 0.046, W. 0.024, Th. 0.005
Blade, creamy-white flint; broken off at one end, use-wear occurs only along one edge; one corner is broken off.

169. Kul. 95.253, Ma.M.   Pl. 43
L. 0.046, W. 0.039, Th. 0.007
Blade, creamy-white flint; broken off at both ends, use-wear on both edges.

170. Kul. 95.248, Ma.M.   Pl. 43
L. 0.042, W. 0.023, Th. 0.007
Blade, light brown flint; broken off at both ends, both cutting edges have use-wear.

171. Kul. 95.247, Ma.M.   Pl. 43
L. 0.036, W. 0.019, Th. 0.009
Blade, brownish-black flint; broken off at both ends, both cutting edges have use-wear.

172. Kul. 99.97, Square E4, Ma.M.   Pl. 43
L. 0.039, W. 0.0 14, Th. 0.005
Blade, light-brown flint; broken off at one end, both cutting edges have use-wear.

173. Kul. 94.305, Ma.M.   Pl. 43
L. 0.052, W. 0.021, Th. 0.008
Blade, light brown flint; both cutting edges have use-wear.

174. Kul. 93.179, Ma.M.   Pl. 43
L. 0.042, W. 0.021
Blade, light brownish-white flint; use-wear along both edges; one corner of the blade is broken off.

175. Kul. 94.312, Square E4, Ma.M.   Pl. 43
L. 0.046, W. 0.022, Th. 0.06
Blade, light brown flint; both cutting edges have use-wear.

176. Kul. 94.303, Ma.M.   Pl. 43
L. 0.05, W. 0.022, Th. 0.006
Blade, white flint; broken off at both ends, both cutting edges have use-wear; one corner of the blade is broken off.

177. Kul. 94.308, Ma.M.   Pl. 43
L. 0.039, Th. 0.008
Blade, creamy white flint; broken off at end, both cutting edges have use-wear.

178. Kul. 94.310, Square D4, Ma.M.   Pl. 43
L.0.042, W. 0.023, Th. 0.007
Awl, light brown flint; use-wear derived from revolving on the pointed end.

179. Kul. 95.251, Ma.M.   Pl. 43
L. 0.032, W. 0.002 1, Th. 0.006
Blade, creamy-white flint; broken off at both ends, both cutting edges have use-wear; one corner of the blade is broken off.

180. Kul. 94.306, Ma.M.   Pl. 43
L. 0.028, W. 0.0 17, Th. 0.004
Blade, creamy white flint; broken off at both ends, both cutting edges have use-wear.

181. Kul. 95.250, Ma.M.   Pl. 43
L. 0.028, W. 0.0 13, Th. 0.005
Blade, creamy-white flint; broken off at both ends, both cutting edges have usewear; one corner is broken off.

Pottery

182. Kul. 99.108, Square D4, Ma.M.   Pl. 44
H. 0.087, W. 0.064
Stump of a bowl handle with a knob-like projection, circular in section; medium-fired, gray-brown to black clay with inclusions.

183. Kul. 94.368, Ma.M.   Pl. 44
H. 0.088, W. 0.049
Fragment of a large bowl handle with a knob-like projection; medium-fired, gray-black clay with incuisions, the exterior has mottling.

184. Kul. 99.112, Square D4, Ma.M.   Pl. 44
H. 0.091
Bowl handle with a projection, circular in section with a hole through it; medium-fired, gray-brown to black clay; surface is poorly burnished.

185. Kul. 95.37, Ma.M.   Pl. 44
D.R. 0.306, H. 0.046, W. 0.066
Stump of a bowl handle; medium-fired, gray-brown to black clay with poorly burnished exterior.

186. Kul. 99.109, Ma.M.   Pl. 44
H. 0.073, W. 0.081

Stump of a bowl handle with a projection, elliptical in section; gray-brown to black clay, the exterior is poorly burnished in black.

187. Kul. 99.115, Square E4, Ma.M.　　　　Pl. 44
H. 0.07 1, W. 0.053
Stump of a bowl handle with a projection at base, circular in section; gray-brown to black clay with inclusions.

188. Kul. 99.123, Square D4, Ma.M.　　　　Pl. 44
H. 0.073
Twisted bowl handle with circular section; medium-fired, gray-black clay; the exterior is poorly burnished.

189. Kul. 99.116, Square E4, Ma.M.　　　　Pl. 44
H. 0.083
Twisted bowl handle with circular section; medium-fired, gray-black clay; the exterior is poorly burnished.

190. Kul. 94.373, Ma.M.　　　　Pl. 44
H. 0.082
Stump of a bowl handle, circular in section; medium-fired, gray-brown to black clay with inclusions; the exterior is poorly burnished.

191. Kul. 94.369, Ma.M.　　　　Pl. 44
H. 0.037, D.B. 0.088
Flat base fragment of a jar; medium fired, brown-black clay with inclusions, medium-fired, poorly burnished exterior.

192. Kul. 94.357, Ma.M.　　　　Pl. 44
H. 0.044, D.B. 0.084
Flat base fragment of a jar; poorly-fired brown-red clay with inclusions; unburnished exterior, interior has mottling.

193. Kul. 94.360, Ma.M.　　　　Pl. 44
H. 0.024, D.B. 0.14
Flat base fragment of a jar; medium-fired, gray-black clay with inclusions; poorly burnished exterior with mottling.

194. Kul.94.356, Ma.M.　　　　Pl. 44
H. 0.027, D.B. 0.09
Flat base fragment of a bowl; medium-fired, brown-black clay with inclusions; both surfaces have mottling.

195. Kul. 95.3, Ma.M.　　　　Pl. 45
D.R. 0.33, H. 0,077, W. 0.075
Rim fragment of a necked large jar; medium-fired, brown-black clay with inclusions.

196. Kul. 95.2, Ma.M.　　　　Pl. 45
D.R. 0.32, H. 0.07 1, W. 0.063
Rim fragment of a necked large jar; medium-fired, brown-black clay with inclusions.

197. Kul. 95.1, Ma.M.　　　　Pl. 45
D.R. 0.36, H. 0.062, W. 0.078
Rim fragment of a necked large jar; medium-fired, brown-black clay with inclusions.

198. Kul. 99. 107, Square E4, Ma.M.　　　　Pl. 45
D.R. 0.058, W. 0.067
Rim fragment of a jar with straight collar-neck; medium-fired, gray-brown to black clay with inclusions; the exterior is finely burnished.

199. Kul. 99.105, Square E4, Ma.M.　　　　Pl. 45
H. 0.063, W. 0.074

Rim fragment of a jar with straight collar-neck; medium-fired, gray-brown to black clay with inclusions, the exterior is finely burnished.

200. Kul. 99.111, Square E4, Ma.M.　　　　Pl. 45
H. 0.043, W. 0.053
Rim fragment of a jar with straight collar-neck; medium-fired, gray-brown to black clay with inclusions; the exterior is finely burnished.

201. Kul. 99.100, Square E4, Ma.M.　　　　Pl. 45
H. 0.094, W. 0.083
Wall fragment of a jar; medium-fired, gray-black clay with inclusions; finely burnished black exterior has incised chevrons filled with white-paste-filled punctuated dots.

202. Kul. 95. 46, Ma.M.　　　　Pl. 45
H. 0.043, W. 0.023
Wall fragment of a jar; medium-fired, gray-black clay; black burnished exterior has punctuated dots.

203. Kul. 99.101, Square E4, Ma.M.　　　　Pl. 45
H. 0.068, W. 0.054
Wall fragment of a jar with pouring spout; brownish-red clay with inclusions; the exterior is left unburnished, both surfaces have mottling.

204. Kul. 99.117, Square D4, Ma.M.　　　　Pl. 45
H. 0.084, W. 0.057
Strap handle of necked jar, oval-thin in section; medium-fired, grayish-brown to black clay; the exterior is poorly burnished in gray-black.

205. Kul. 94.380, Ma.M.　　　　Pl. 45
H. 0.046, W. 0.037
Knobbed handle of a necked jar; medium-fired, grayish-brown to biack clay; the exterior is poorly burnished in gray-black.

206. Kul. 95.47, Ma.M.　　　　Pl. 45
H. 0.062, W. 0.063
Jar fragment with vertical handle with pitched upright ridge, thin-oval in section; gray-black clay; the exterior is poorly burnished.

207. Kul. 99. 102, Ma.M.　　　　Pl. 45
H. 0.043, W. 0.047
Wall fragment with relief decoration; medium-fired, gray-black clay with fine burnished exterior.

208. Kul. 95.49, Ma.M.　　　　Pl. 45
H. 0.056, W. 0.047
Wall fragment of a bowl with crescent lug; medium-fired, gray-black clay; the exterior is poorly burnished.

209. Kul. 99.104, Square E5, Ma.M.　　　　Pl. 45
H. 0.057, W. 0.077
Wall fragment with rounded relief decoration; medium-fired, gray-black clay; the exterior is finely bumished.

Appendix 2: Catalogue of Comparable Artifacts

This section catalogues 12 pointed beakers and 35 Kilia figurines that were found outside the site of Kulaksızlar. The reason for their inclusion in this section is that they share close stylistic and metric similarities to marble Kilia figurines and beakers manufactured at Kulaksızlar. Information such as the texture and color of the marbles, use-wear, and measurements of these marble artifacts are presented. This forms a basis for sourcing the exchanged artifacts described in the Chapter six. The order of catalogue is the same as that adopted in Appendix 1. Relevant published works are cited at the end of each entry.

Pointed beakers

210. Varna   Pl. 30
Historical Museum at Varna, inv. no. VEN 683
H. 0.156, D.R. 0.056
Complete finished beaker; white marble with traces of red paint on its exterior; it bears no vertical lugs.
Reference: Ivanov 1996: fig. 34; Höckman 1987: 73; Weishaar 1982: 324

211. Kephala   Pl. 30
Kea Archaeological Museum, inv. no. Kph. 1.1
D.R. 0.068, H. 0.168
Complete finished beaker; fine grained, yellowish-white marble; lines of rotary drilling are visible on the interior bottom; vertical lines of abrasion on upper part of interior and the entire exterior; two verticaliy elongated .Lugs are pierced, the holes are drilled near the top of the vertical lug.
Reference: Coleman 1977: pls. 23 and 67

212. Naxos   Pl. 30
Copenhagen, 4762, The National Museum of Denmark
D.R. 0.038, H. 0.113, H. of Lug 0.048
Complete finished beaker; downward sloping vertical lugs are horizontally pierced; the exterior has lines of abrasion.
Reference: Renfrew 1972: pl. 1.2; Weishaar 1982: fig. 2.1

213. Kephala   Pl. 30
Kea Archaeological Museum, inv. no. Kph. 1.7,
H. 0.037, W. 0.03, Th. 0.009
Wall fragment from the lower part of a finished beaker; fine-grained, white marble; the exterior has diagonal marks of abrasion, the interior has vertical lines of abrasion on its upper part and lines of rotary drilling on the lower part.
Reference: Coleman 1977: pls. 23 and 67

214. Tigani   Pl. 30
Samos Museum, fragment V23
Pres. H. 0.061
Wall fragment of a finished beaker; the downward sloping angle suggests that it belongs to the lower part; fine-grained white marble; the exterior is finely polished.
Refererıce: Felsch 1988: Pis. 48 and 75

215. Tigani   Pl. 30
Samos Museum, fragment V.26
D.R. 0.067, H. 0.067
Rim fragment of a finished beaker; white marble; the vertical lug is pierced.
Reference: Felsch 1988: Pls. 48 and 75

216. Koukonesi, Lemnos
No measurements available
Lower end of a marble pointed beaker
Reference: Devetze 1997, fig.1

217. Kumtepe   Pl. 30
Istanbul Museum, inv. no. K-50
H. 0.085, W.0.041
Lower end of a finished beaker; white-marble; the exterior is unevenly worn, the interior has horizontal lines of rotary drilling.
Reference: Sperling 1976: 322; Weishaar 1982: fig. 2

218. Gülpınar   Pl. 30
Excavation storage, inv.no. GLP.04.C4.Q3.69
D. at Rim 9.3 cm, Pres. H. 4.4, Pres.W. 6.8
Rim fragment of a pointed beaker, fine grained creamy-white marble, slight traces of pointed tool marks on the exterior

219. Demircihöyük   Pl. 30
D.R. 0.11, H. 0.072, W. 0.0729
Rim fragment of a finished beaker; fine-grained white marble; the pierced vertical lug is partially preserved.
Reference: Seeher 1987: fig. 1; Efe 1988: 79, pl. 37

220. Beşik-Sivritepe
Excavation storage, inv. no. KK 83.95
D.R. 0.06 (?), H. 0.037
Rim fragment of a finished beaker, no lug is preserved.
Reference: Getz-Gentle 1996: 52, note 96; Seeher 2000, Pers. Communication, Utta Gabriel 2002, Pers. Communication.

221. Beşik-Sivritepe
Excavation storage, inv. no. KK 83.43
D.R. 0.06 *(?)*, H. 0.032, W. 0.036
Rim fragment of a finished beaker, no lug is preserved.
Reference: Getz-Gentle 1996: 52, note 96; Seeher 2000, Pers. Communication, Utta Gabriel 2002, Pers. Communication.

Kilia figurines

222. Kırşehir (?)   Pls. 20 and 37
Leon Levy Collection, New York
H. 0.174, W. 0.077
Finished figurine; fine-grained, creamy-white marble; the arms are set off from the body by oblique cuts; the forearms are sharply bent at the elbows; the pubic triangie and the leg division are incised.
Reference. VonBothmer 1990: no. 4; Seeher 1992: no. 22

223. Kırşehir (?)   Pl. 37
Museum of Primitive Art, New York
H.0.172, W. 0.064
Finished figurine; the pubic triangle and the leg division are incised; the nose and the ears are sculpturally raised.
Reference: Farkas 1964: no. 118; Seeher 1992: no. 25, fig. 3a

224. Kilia   Pl. 37
American School of Archaeology at Athens
H. 0.145, W. 0.0721
Finished figurine; the leg division is incised, no pubic triangle is incised; eyes, nose, and ears are sculpturally raised
Reference: Calvert 190 1:329; Caskey 1972: pl. 44

225. Kırşehir (?)   Pls. 20 and 37
Guennol Collection, New York
H. 0.225
Finished figurine, the lower end is missing; the leg division and the pubic triangle are incised; eyes, nose, and ears are sculpturally raised; the bent forearms are sculpturally distinguished from the upper arms.
Reference: Joukowsky 1986:2 02; Seeher 1992: no. 28, fig. 1

226. Anatolia/unproveneinced   Pl. 38
D. and J. De Menil Collection, Houston, inv. no. X155
H. 0.108
Finished figurine, lower end is missing; white marble; surface is fineiy smoothed and has ancient abrasive tool marks; eyes, nose, and ears are sculpturally raised; the back is heavily incrusted.
Reference: Thimme 1978: no. 563; Seeher 1992: fig. 4d, no. 17.

227. Anatolia/unproveneinced   Pl. 38
Ruth Lax Collection, New York
Finished figurine, lower end is missing; white marble; original polished surface; pubic triangle is incised; nose and ears are sculpturally raised; abrasive tool marks are visible around the bent forearms.
Reference: Thimme 1978: no. 560; Seeher 1992: no. 18

228. Papazköy   Pl. 38
H. 0.098; W. 0.038
Berlin Museum, inv. no. 31457
Finished figurine, left foot is partially missing; the pubic triangle and the leg division are incised; eyes, nose, and ears are sculpturally raised.
Reference: Thimme 1978: no. 561; Rohde 1974: 149; Seeher 1992: no. 6, fig. 2c

229. Kırşehir (?)   Pl. 38
Norbert Schimmel Collection, New York
H. 0.108; W. 0.035
Finished figurine; white marble; the pubic triangle and the ieg division are incised; eyes, nose, and ears are sculpturally raised.
Reference: Muscarella 1974: no. 8; Thimme 1978: no. 562; Seeher 1992: no. 23

230. Thermi   Pl. 38
Mytilene Museum
No measurements available
Finished figurine, broken off at the neck; upper body has heavy incrustation.
Reference: Seeher 1992: no. 13; Evangelides 1930: fig. 10

231. Anatolia/unproveneinced   Pls. 21 and 38
Private Collection in Germany
H. 0.067
Finished figurine, the head with part of the neck, the lower part of the left arm, and the feet are missing; gray marble, the surface is finely smoothed; back part has heavy incrustations.
Reference: Seeher 1992: no. 15; Thimme 1978: no. 565

232. Anatolia/unproveneinced   Pls. 21 and 38
Private Collection in Germany
H 0.074
Finished figurine, head, neck, and feet are missing; yellowish-white marble; surface is finely smoothed with partial incrustation and abrasive tool marks
Reference: Thimme 1978: no. 566; Seeher 1992: no. 16

233. Kozağacı   Pl. 38
Ashmolean Museum, Oxford
No measurenents available
Finished figurine, the head is missing; white marble
Reference: Woodward and Ormerod 1910: p1. 7.19; Seeher 1992: no. 11

234. Anatolia/unproveneinced   Pl. 38
Solothum Private Collection

H. 0.082
Finished figurine, the head and feet are missing; gray marble; surface is finely smoothed.
Reference: Thimme 1978: no. 562; Seeher 1992: no. 6

235. Kozağacı   Pl. 38
Ashmolean Museum, Oxford
No measurements available
Finished figurine, the head is missing; white marble; pubic triangle is incised,
Reference: Woodward and Ormerod 1910: p1. 7.18; Seeher 1992: no. 10

236. Aphrodisias   Pl. 38
Aphrodisias Museum, cat. no. 1598a.3
H. 0.052, W. 0.045, Th. 0.011
Torso fragment of a finished figurine, the head, upper part of the neck, lower part of the body, legs and feet and the tip of the right arm are missing; a diagonal incision sculpturally distinguishes the bent forearms; surface is smoothed and has abrasive tool marks.
Reference: Joukowsky 1986; fig. 208; 1988; fig. 4; Seeher 1992: 110. 9, fig. 4e

237. Aphrodisias   Pl. 38
Aphrodisias Museum, cat. no. 1598e.2.5
H. 0.049, W. 0.043, Th. 0.0 12
Torso fragment of a finished figurine, the head, neck, lower part of the body, feet and the end of the left arm projection are missing; fine-grained, white marble; surface has traces of abrasive tool marks; there is slight encrustation on the back.
Reference. Joukowsky 1986: fig. 207; 1988: fig. 4; Seeher 1992: no. 8, lig. 4b

238. Yortan   Pl. 38
H. 0. 037, W. 0.019
Torso fragment of a finished figurine; the head, the feet and the ends of arms are missing.
Refererıce: Collignon 1901: 815; Kamu 1982: fig. 84; Seeher 1992: no. 5, fig. 6d

239. Alaağaç   Pl. 38
Ma.M. inv. no. 7769
H. 0.031, W. 0.042
Head fragment, broken off at the neck; fine-grained, white marble; ears, nose and eyes are sculpturally raised, finely polished surface.
Reference. Dinç 1995: p1. 6b

240. Alaağaç   Pl. 38
Ma.M. inv. no. 7768
H. 0.032, W.0.026
Head fragment of a finished figurine, broken off at the neck; fine-grained, white marble; ears, nose and eyes are sculpturally raised, finely polished surface.
Reference. Dinç 1995: p1. 6a

241. Karain Cave   Pl. 38
Antalya Museum
H. 0.02, W. 0.0 12
Head fragment of a finished figurine, the top of the head is missing; the nose is sculpturally raised.
Reference. Seeher 1988: fig. 13.2; 1992: no. 12; fig. 4a

242. Troy   Pl. 38
H. 0.039, W. 0.04
Head fragment of a finished marble figurine, broken off at the neck; nose and ears are sculpturally raised.

Reference. Schmidt 1902: no. 7643; Seeher 1992: no. 2; fig. 3c

243. Gavurtepe   Pl. 38
Selçuk Museum
H. 0.036, W. 0.04
Head fragment of a marble finished figurine, broken off at the neck; eyes, nose and ears are sculpturally raised.
Reference. Meriç 1987: fig. 6; Seeher 1992: no. 7; fıg. 3b

244. Hanay Tepe
Berlin Museum, inv. no. 10047
H. 0.072; W. 0.053
Finished figurine; the head and lower part are missing
Refererıce: Virchow 1882: pl. 12.7; Calvert 1881: no. 1551; Seeher 1992: no. 3; Scahachner 1999: fig. 31.7.

245. Beşik-Yassıtepe
Çanakkale Museum, inv. no. LL83.23
H. 0.072; W. 0.053
Torso of a finished figurine; the bent forearms are sculpturally distinguished.
Reference: Korfmann 1985: fig. 8; Seeher 1992: no. 4; fig. 4c

246. Anatolia/unproveneinced   Pl. 21
Paul Getty Museum, Los Angeles
H. 0.142
Complete figurine; the ears and the nose are sculpturally raised; the division between the feet and the arm and body is completely separated; the pubic triangle is incised
Reference. Master Pieces of the J. P. Getty Museum 1997: 13

247. Anatolia/unproveneinced
Rubin Symes Collection, London
H. 0.19 1; W. 0.078
Figurine fragment
Reference. Seeher 1992: no. 19, lig. 5

248. Western Anatolia/unproveneinced
H. 0.04; W. 0.044
Figurine fragment; head fragment of a finished figurine, broken off at the neck.
Reference. Seeher 1992: no. 21

249. Kırşehir (?)
No measurements available
Figurine fragment

Reference. Muscarella 1961: no. 8; Seeher 1992: no. 24

250. Kırşehir (?)
Gustave and F.Schindler Collection, New York
H. 0.159
Figurine fragment
Reference: Muscarella 1966: no. 111; Seeher 1992: n. 26

251. Kırşehir (?)
Gustave and F.Schindler Collection, New York H. 0.159
Figurine fragment
Reference: Muscarella 1966: no. 112; Seeher 1992: no. 27

252. Selendi
Ma. M, Inv. no. 8537
H. 0.075, W. 0.072
Torso of a finished figurine; fine grained creamy-white marble; the bent forearms are sculpturally distinguished.
Reference: Not published

253. Selendi
Ma. M, Inv. no. 8068
H. 0.04, W. 0.049
Head fragment of a finished figurine, broken off at neck; fine grained creamy-white marble; the ears are sculpturally raised.
Reference: Not published

254. Selendi
Ma. M, Inv. no. 8247
H. 0.035, W. 0.043
Head fragment of a finished figurine, broken off at neck; fine grained creamy-white marble; the ears are sculpturally raised.
Reference: Not published

255. Selendi
Ma. M, Inv. no. 8248
H. 0.035, W. 0.031
Head fragment of a finished figurine, broken off at neck; fine grained creamy-white marble; the ears are sculpturally raised.
Reference: Not published

256. Selendi
Ma. M, inv. no. 8259.
H. 0.022, W. 0.028
Head fragment of a finished figurine, broken off at neck; fine grained creamy-white marble; the ears are sculpturally raised.
Reference: Not published

References

Amiet, P.
1980 *Die Kunst des Alten Orient.* Basel: Herder.

Bakır, T.
2004 "Domestic pot making at Yiğittaşı village in northeast Anatolia," *Ethnoarchaeological Investigations in Rural Anatolia,* vol. I, edited by T. Takaoğlu. Istanbul: Ege Yayinlari, pp. 67-76.

Balkan-Atlı, N. and M-C. Cauvin
1997 "Obsidian in the Neolithic in central Anatolia. From raw materials to workshops and settlements: A case study," in *Anatolian Prehistory: At the Crossroads of two Worlds,* edited by M. Otte, Liege: Universite de Liege, Liege, pp. 625-630.

Balkan-Atlı, N., G. Binder, and M.-C. Cauvin
1999 "Obsidian: sources, workshops and trade in central Anatolia," in *Neolithic Turkey,* edited by M. Özdoğan and N. Başgelen, Istanbul: Arkeoloji ve Sanat Yayınları, pp. 133-45.

Barber, R. L. N.
1984 "Early Cycladic marble figures: some thoughts on function," in *Cycladica: Studies in Memory of N.P. Goulandris,* edited by J.L. Fitton. London: British Museum, pp. 10-14.

Benac, A.
1972 "Some aspects of the migrations of cultures in northwestern Balkan," *Balcanica* 3: 1-10.

Borchardt, L.
1907 *Das Grabdenkmal des Königs Ne-User-Ré.* Leipzig: Hinrichs.

Bordaz, J.
1959 "Flint flaking in Turkey," *Natural History* 78: 73-79.

Brumfiel, E.M. and T.K. Earle
1987 "Specialization, exchange, and complex societies: an introduction,' in *Specialization, Exchange, and Complex Societies,* edited by E. Brumfiel and T.K. Earle. Cambridge: Cambridge University, pp. 1-9.

Calvert, F.
1881 "Thymbra, Hanay Tepe," in *Ilios. Stadt und Land der Trojaner,* edited by H. Schliemann. Leipzig: Brockhaus, pp. 782-797.

1901 'Ein Idol von Thracischen Chersones," *Zeitschifte für Ethnologie* 33: 329-334.

Caneva, I.
1970 "I crescenti Litici dei Fayum," *Origini* 4: 161-203.

Caskey, J.
1972 "The figurines in the Roll-top desk," *American Journal of Archaeology* 76: 192-93.

Caton-Thompson, G. and E.W. Gardner
1934 *The Desert Fayum.* London: The Royal Anthropological Institute of Great Britain and Ireland.

Childe, V.G.
1936 *Man Makes Himself.* New York: Mentor Books.

1942 *What Happened in History.* Harmondsworth: Penguin Books.

1950 "The urban revolution," *Town Planning Review* 21: 3-17.

1951 *Social Evolution.* New York: Schuman Press.

1954 "Rotary motion," in *A History of Technology,* edited by C. Singer, E.J. Holmyard, and A.K. Hall, vol. 1. Oxford: Clarendon Press, pp. 187-215.

1957 *New light on the Most Ancient Near East.* London: Evergreen.

1958 *The Prehistory of European Society.* Harmondsworth: Penguin.

Ciarla, R.
1981 A preliminary analysis of the manufacture of alabaster vessels at Shahr-i Sokhta and Mundigak in the 3rd millennium BC," in *South Asian Archaeology,* edited by H. Hartel, Berlin: D. Reimer, pp. 45-63.

Clark, J.E.
1986 "From mountains to molehills. A critical review of Teotihuacan's obsidian industry," *Research in Economic Anthropology,* Supplement 2, pp. 23-74.

1995 "Craft specialization as an archaeological category," *Research in Economic Anthropology* 16: 267-294.

Clark, J.E. and W.J. Parry
1990 "Craft specialization and cultural complexity," *Research in Economic Anthropology* 12: 289-346.

Cobb, C.R.
1993 "Archaeological approaches to the political economy of non-stratified societies," *Archaeological Method and Theory* 5: 43-100.

1996 Specialization, exchange, and power in small-scale societies and chiefdoms," *Research in Economic Anthropology* 17:25 1-94.

Coleman, J.E.
1977 *Keos 1. Kephala. A Late Neolithic Settlement and Cemetery.* Princeton: American School of Classical Studies at Athens.

Collignon, M.M.
1901 "Fouilles dans la nécropole de Yortan en Mysie," *Comptes Rendus des Séances de l'Académie des Inscriptions et belles-letres,* pp. 810-840.

Conolly, J.
1999 *The Çatal Höyük Flint and Obsidian Industry.* BAR - Inetrnational Series 787.

Cordischi, D., D. Monna, and A.L. Segre

1983 "ESR analysis of marble samples from Mediterranean quarries of archaeological interest," *Archaeometry* 25: 68-76.

Costin, C.L.
1991 "Craft specialization: issues in defining, documenting, and explaining the organization of Production," *Archaeological Method and Theory* 3: 1-56.

Craig, H. and V. Craig
1972 "Greek marbles: Determination of provenance by isotopic analysis," *Science* 176: 401-403.

Crane, H.
1988 Traditional pottery making in the Sardis region of western Anatolia," *Muqarnas* 5: 9-20.

Cross, J.R.
1993 Craft specialization in non-stratified societies," *Research in Economic Anthropology* 14: 61-84.

Demangel, R.
1926 *Le Tumulus dit de Protésilas.* Paris: De Boccard.

Devetze, A.
1997 "E parousia ton lithinon angeion os endiexeton scheseon ton nesion tou voreiou Aigaiou me ton ypoloipo aigaiako choro," in *E Poliochne kai e Proïme Epoche tou Chalkou sto Boreio Aigaio,* edited by Chr. Doumas and V. La Rosa. Athens, pp. 556-568.

Dimitrov, I.
2003 "Marble rhyta from the late prehistory of southeastern Europe," *Bulletin of the Museum of History Khaskovo* 2: 25-32.

Dinç, R.
1994 "Yortan'da bulunan Kilia tipi iki mermer heykelcik başı," in *In Memoriam I. Metin Akyurt and Bahattin Devam.* Istanbul: Arkeoloji ve Sanat Yayınları, pp. 91-94.

1996a "1994 yılı Akhisar-Kulaksızlar Mermer Atölyesi yüzey araştırması," *XIII. Araştınna Sonuçlan Toplantısı* 1: 11-41.

1996b "Kulaksızlar Mermer idöl atölyesi ve çevre araştırmaları," *XIV. Araştırma Sonuçları Toplantısı* Il: 255-82.

Drenkhahn, R.
1976 *Die Handwerker und ihre Tatigkeiten im Alten Agypten.* Wiesbaden: Harrassowitz.

Duru, R.
1994 *Kuruçay I. Results of the Excavations 1978-1988. The Neolithic and Early Chalcolithic Periods.* Ankara: Türk Tarih Kurumu

1999 "The Neolithic of the Lakes District," in *Neolithic in Turkey,* edited by M. Özdoğan and N. Başgelen. Istanbul: Arkeoloji Sanat, pp. 165-191.

Earle, T.K.
1981 "Comment on evolution of specialized pottery production: a trial model, by P.M. Rice," *Current Anthropology* 22: 23-3 1.

1982 "Prehistoric economics and the archaeology of exchange," in *Context of Prehistoric Exchange,* edited by J. Ericson and T.K. Earle, New York: Academic Press, pp. 1-12.

Efe, T.
1988 *Demircihöyük 111, 2. C. Die frühbronzezeitliche Keramik der jüngeren Phasen.* Mainz: Rudolph Habelt.

El-Khouli, Ali Abdel-rahman H.
1978 *Egyptian Stone Vessels from Predynastic period to Dynasty 111: Typology and Analysis.* Mainz: Philip von Zabern.

El-Wailly, F. and B. Abu al-Soof
1964 "The Excavations at Tell-es-Sawwan: first preliminary report (1964)," *Sumer 20:* 17-32.

Erdoğu, B.
2000 "The problems of dating prehistoric axe factories and Neolithisation in Turkish Thrace," *Documenta Praehistorica* 27: 155-166.

Erinç, S.
1978 "Changes in the physical environment in Turkey since the end of the Last Glacial," in *The Environmental History of the Near East and Middle East since the Last Ice Age,* edited by W.C. Brice, New York Academic Press, pp. 87-110.

Eslick, C.
1980 "Middle Chalcolithic pottery from southwestern Anatolia," *Ameican Journal of Archaeology* 84: 5-14.

1992 *Elmalı-Karataş 1. The Neolithic and Chalcolithic Periods: Bağbaşı and the Other Sites.* Bryn Mawr: Bryn Mawr College Archaeological Monographs.

Evangelides, D.
1930 "Ανασχαφαι και αρχαια εκ Μυτιληνησ," *Arkaiologikon Deltion* 11: 14-22

Evans, J.D. and C. Renfrew
1968 *Excavations at Saliagos near Antiparos.* London: The British Institute of Archaeology at Athens.

Evans, R.K.
1978 "Early craft specialization: an example from the Balkan Chalcolithic," in *Social Archaeology,* edited by C.L. Redman. New York: Academic Press, pp. 113-30.

Evely, R.D.G.
1980 "Some manufacturing process in a Knossian stone vase workshop," *Bulletin of the American School at Athens* 75: 127-137.

1993 *Minoan Crafts: Tools and Techniques.* Göteborg: Paul Åströms Förlag.

Farkas, A.
1964 *Thou Shalt Have No Other Gods Before Me.* New York: The Jewish Museum

Felsch, R.C.S.
1988 *Das Kastro Tigani. Die spatneolithische und chalkolithische siedlung. Samos II.* Mainz: R. Habelt.

French, D.
1961 "Late Chalcolithic pottery from north-west Turkey and the Aegean," *Anatolian Studies* 11: 99-141.

1963 "Excavations at Can Hasan," *Anatolian Studies* 13: 29-42.

1965 "Early pottery sites from western Anatolia," *Bulletin of the Institute of Archaeology at London* 5: 15-24

1969 "Prehistoric sites in north-west Anatolia, II. The Balıkesir and Akhisar/Manisa areas," *Anatolian Studies* 19: 4 1-98

Furness, A.
1956 "Some early pottery of Samos, Kalimnos, and Chios," *Proceedings of the Prehistoric Society* 22: 173-212

Gabriel, U.
2000 "Mitteilung zum stand der Neolithikums-forchung in der umgebung von Troia (Kumtepe 1993-1995; Beşik-Sivritepe 1983-1984, 1987, 1998-1999)," *Studia Troica* 10: 233-238.

Gabriel, U., R. Aslan, S.W. Blum
2004 "Alacalıgöl: eine neuendeckte siedlung des 5. jahrtausends V. Chr. In der Troas," *Studia Troica* 14: 121-133.

Gallis, K.
1987 "Die stratigraphische Einordnung der Larissa-Kultur: eine Richtstellung," *Prähistorische Zeitzchrift* 62: 147-163.

Garfinkel, Y.
1999 *Neolithic and Chalcolithic Pottery of the Southem Levant.* Jerusalem: The Hebrew University of Jerusalem.

Getz-Gentle, P.
1996 *Stone Vessels of the Cyclades in the Early Bronze Age.* Pennsylvania: Pennsylvania University.

Getz-Preziosi, P.
1977 "Cycladic sculptors and their methods,' in *Art and Culture of the Cyclades in the third Millennium BC,* edited by J. Thimme, Chicago: The University of Chicago, pp. 7l-82.

Gimbutas, M.
1977 "Varna: a sensationaliy rich cemetery of the Karanovo civilization, about 4500 BC," *Expedition* 19: 39-47.

Günal, N.
1987 "Gediz ve Büyük Menderes arasındaki bitki örtüsü özellikleri," *Bülten* 4: 93-104.

Gündoğdu, H.
2004 "Black amber bead making in northeast Anatolia," *Ethnoarchaeological Investigations in Rural Anatolia,* vol. I, edited by T. Takaoğlu. Istanbul: Ege Yayinlari, pp. 115-126.

Haggett, P.
1965 *Locational Analysis in Human Geography.*

London: Arnold.

Harmankaya, S. and B. Erdogu
2003 "The prehistoric sites of Gökçeada, Turkey," in *From Village to Cities. Early Villages in the Near East,* edited by M. Özdoğan, H. Hauptman, N. Başgelen. Istanbul: Arkeoloji ve Sanat, pp. 459-479.

Hartenberg, S.
1969 "The Egyptian drill and the origin of crank," *Technology and Culture* 10: 155-165.

Hayden, B.
1994 "Village Approaches to complex societies," in *Archaeological Views from the Countryside. Village Communities in Early Complex Societies,* edited by G.Schwartz and S. Falconer, Washington, DC: Smithsonian Institution Press, pp. 198-206.

Heidenreich, R.
1935/36 "Vorgeschichtliches in der statd Samos," *Athenische Mitteilungen* 60/61: 125-183.

Helms, M.W.
1993 *Craft and Kingly Ideal: Art, Trade, and Power.* Austin: University of Texas Press.

Herz, N.
1987 "Carbon and oxygen isotopic ratios: a data base for classical Greek ad Roman marbles," *Archaeometry* 29: 35-43.

1992 "Provenance determination of Neolithic to Classical Mediterranean marbles by stable isotopes," *Archaeometry* 34:185-94.

Hester, T.R. and Heizer, R.F.
1981 *Making Stone Vases: Ethnological Studies at an Alabaster Workshop in Upper Egypt.* Occasional Papers on the Near East, edited by G. Buccellati, vol. 1, Malibu: Undena, pp. 1-66

Hodder, I.
1982 "Toward a contextual approach to prehistoric exchange," in *Context of Prehistonc Exchange,* edited by J. Ericson and T.K. Earle, New York: Academic Press, pp. 199-211.

Hood, S.
1981 *Chios. Prehistoric Emporio and Ayio Gala,* Vol. 1. Oxford, British Institute of Archaeology at Athens, Supplementary vol. 15.

Hoşgören, Y.M.
1983 *Akhisar Havzası. Jeomorfolojik ve tatbiki Jeomorfolojik Etüd.* Istanbul: Istanbul Üniversitesi Edebiyat Fakültesi, no. 3088

Höckman, 0.
1977 "The Neolithic and Early Bronze Age idols of Anatolia," in *Art and Culture of the Cyclades in the third millennium BC,* edited by J. Thimme, Chicago: The University of Chicago Press, pp. 373-403.

1987 "Frühbronzezeitliche kulturbeziehungen im Mittelmeerbebiet unter Berücksichtigung der Kykladen," in *Ägaische Bronzezeit,* edited by A.-G. Bucholz, Darmstadt, pp. 53-120.

68

Ivanov, I.
1978 "Les fouilles archáologiques de la nécropole Chalcolithique à Varna (1972-1975)," *Studia Praehistorica* 1-2:13-26.

1996 "Das gräberfeld von Varna. Katalog," in *Macht, Herrschaft und Gold. Das gräberfeld von Vama (Bulgarien) und die Anfänge einer neuen europaischen zivilization.* Sarrbrucken: Saarland Museum Publication, pp. 183-208

Izdem, E.
1944 *Dünkü Bugünkü Akhisar.* İzmir: Ükü Basımevi

James, T.G.H.
1984 *Pharaoh's People. Scenes from Life in Imperial Egypt.* Chicago: The University of Chicago Press.

Joukowsky, M.J.
1982 "Late Chalcolithic Figurines from Aphrodisas in southwest Turkey," in *Archéologie au Levant, Recueil a la mémoire de Roger Saidah,* Paris: Diffusion de Boccard, pp. 87-94.

1986 *Prehistoric Aphrodisias. An Account of the Excavations and Artifact Studies.* Archaeologia Translantica III

Kalogirou, A.
1995 "Pottrey production and craft specialization in Neolithic Greece," in *Craftsman, Craftswoman, and Craftsmanship in the Aegean Bronze Age.* Proceedings of the Sixth International aegean Conference, edited by R. Laffieur and P.P. Betancourt, Philadelphia: Temple University, Aegaeum 16, pp. 11-16.

Kamil, T.
1982 *Yortan Cemetery in the Early Bronze Age Western Anatolia.* BAR - International Series 145.

Kayan, I.
1998 "Geomorphological outlines of Turkey," in *Archaeometry 94. The Proceedings of the 29th International symposium on Archaeometry, Ankara 9-14 May 1994,* edited by S. Demirci, A.M. Özer and G.D. Summers. Ankara, pp. 365-374.

Kenoyer, J.M., M. Vidale, and K.K. Bhan
1991 "Contemporary stone bead making in Khambahat, India." *World Archaeology* 23: 44-65.

Kenoyer, J.M.
1991 "Lapiz lazuli bead making in Afghanistan and Iran," *Ornament* 15: 71-73.

Kohl, P.C.
1974 *Seeds of Upheaval. The Production of chlorite at Tepe Yahya and an analysis of commodity production and trade in southeast Asia in the third millennium.* Ph. Dissertation, Harvard University.

1975 "A note on chlorite artifacts from Shar-i Sokhta," *East and West* 27: 111-27.

Korfmann, M. and B. Kromer
1992 "Demircihöyük, Beşiktepe, Troia-Eine Zwischenblanz zur chronologie dreier orte in westanatolien," *Studia Troica* 3: 135-172.

Kromer, B., M. Korfmann, P. Jablonka.
2003 "Heidelberg Radiocarbon dates for Troia I to VIII and Kumtepe," in *Troia and the Troad. Scientific Approaches,* edited by G.A. Wagner, E. Pernicka, and H.-P. Uerpman. Berlin, pp. 43-54.

Lamb, W.
1932 "Schliemanns Prehistoric Sites in the Troad," *Prehistorische Zeitschrifte* 23: 111-131.

Lauer, J. Ph. and F. Debono
1950 "Technique de façonnage croisssants de silex," *Annales du service des Antiquitiés de L'Égypte* 50: 1-18.

Lewis, B.S.
1996 "The role of attached and independent civilization in the development of sociopolitical complexity," *Research in Economic Anthropology* 17: 357-388.

Lloyd, S. and J. Mellaart
1962 *Beycesultan I. The Chalcolithic and Early Bronze Age Levels.* London: British Institute of Archaeology at Ankara.

Lucas, A.
1962 *Ancient Egyptian Materials and Industries.* London: E. Arnold.

McGuire, J. D.
1896 *A Study of Primitive Methods of Drilling.* Washington: Government Printing Office

Mellaart, J.
1964 "Excavations at Çatal Höyük 1963," *Anatolian Studies* 14: 39-120.

1970 *Excavations at Hacılar.* Edinburg: Edinburg University Press.

1971 "Anatolia, c. 3000-2300 BC," *The Cambridge Ancient History*, vol. 1, Part. 2, 363-416

1978 "Prehistory of Anatolia and its relations with the Balkans," *Symposium International sur l'ethnogenese des peuple balkaniques, Plovdiv, 23-28 avr. 1969,* edited by V.I. Giorgiev, Studia Balcanica 5, Sofia: Academie Bulgare des Sciences, pp. 120-123.

1999 "Beycesultan," in *Ancient Anatolia*, edited by R. Matthews. London: British Institute of Archaeology at Ankara.

Meriç, R.
1989 1987 yılı Alaşehir kazısı," *Kazı Sonuçları Toplantısı* I: 165-75

1993 "Pre-Bronze Age settlements of west-central Anatolia," *Anatolica* 19: 143-50

Miller, M.A.
1996 "The manufacture of cockle shell beads at Early Neolithic Franchthi Cave, Greece: A case of craft specialization," *Journal of Mediterranean Archaeology* 9: 7-37.

Moholy-Nagy, H.
1983 "The Jarmo artifacts of pecked and ground stone and of shell," in *Prehistoric Archaeology along the Zagros Flanks,* edited by L.S. Braidwood, Chicago: The Oriental Institute, pp. 289-346.

Moorey, P.R.S.
1994 *Ancient Mesopotamian Materials and Industries. The Archaeological Evidence.* Oxford: Clarendon Press.

Morgan, J. de,
1912 "Observations sur les couches profondes de l'Acropole à Suse," *Memoires de la Délégation en Perse* 13: 12-25.

Muscarella, Q.W.
1974 *Ancient Art. The Norbert Schimmel Collection.* New York: Metropolitan Museum.

Müller, V.
1929 *Frühe plastik Griechenland und bordereasien. Ihre typenbildung von der neolithischen bis in die griechisch-archaische zeit (rund 3000 bis 600 v. Chr.) von Valentin Muller.* Augsburg: B. Filser.

Nikolov, V.
1993 "Die Neolithischen Kulturen Karanovo I, II und III im Kontext ihrer Beziehungen zu Anatolien," *Anatolica* 19: 167-171.

2004 "The Neolithic and the Chalcolithic periods in northern Thrace," *Journal of the Turkish Academy of Sciences* 7: ?

Oustinoff, E.
1984 "The manufacture of Cycladic figurines. A practical approach," in *Cycladica. Studies in Memory of N.P. Goulandris,* edited by J.L. Fitton. London: British Museum Publications, pp. 38-47.

Özdoğan, M.
1993 "Vinca and Anatolia. A new look at a very old problem," *Anatolica* 19: 173-93.

1999 "Northwestern Turkey: Neolithic cultures in between the Balkans and Anatolia," in *Neolithic in Turkey,* edited by M. Özdoğan and N. Başgelen. Istanbul: Arkeoloji Sanat, pp. 203-224.

Peacock, D.
1982 *Pottery in the Roman World. An Ethno-archaeological Approach.* London: Longman.

Pecorella, P.E.
1984 *la cultura Preistorica di lasos in Caria.* Rome: G. Bretschneider.

Peregrine, P.
1991 "Some political aspects of craft specialization," *World Archaeology* 23: 1-11.

Perlès, C.
1992 "Systems of Exchange and Organization of production in Neolithic Greece," *Journal of Mediterranean Archaeology* 5: 115-64.

Perlès, C. and K.D. Vitelli
1995 "Craft specialization in the Neolithic of Greece," in *Neolithic Society in Greece,* edited by P. Halstead. Sheffield: Sheffield University Press, pp. 96-107.

Petrie, W.F.
1917 *Tools and Weapons.* Werminster: Aris and Philiphs.

Possehl, C.
1981 "Cambay bead making," *Expedition* 23: 39-47.

Puglisi, S.M.
1967 "Missione Per richerche preistoriche im Egitto," *Origini* 1:308-311.

Quibell, T.J.E. and F.W. Green
1902 *Hierakonpolis.* London: B. Quaritch.

Renfrew, C.
1972 *The Emergence of Civilization. The Cyclades and the Aegean in the third Millenium BC.* London: Methuen and Co. Ltd.

1984 "Speculations on the use of Early Cycladic sculpture," in *Cycladica. Studies in Memory of N.P. Goulandris,* edited by J.L. Fitton. London: British Museum. Publications, pp. 24-30.

Renfrew, C., J.E. Dixon, and J.R. Cann
1968 "Further Analysis of Near Eastern Obsidians," *Proceedings of Prehistoric Society* 34: 3 19-331.

Rice, P.M.
1981 "Evolution of specialized pottery production: a trial model," *Current Anthropology* 22: 219-240.

1987 *Pottery Analysis. a Sourcebook.* Chicago: University of Chicago.

Rieth, A.
1958 "Zur technik des Steinbohiens im neolithikum," *Zeitschift für Schweizerische Archologie und Kunstgeschichte* 20: 1-43.

Roodenberg, J.
1986 *Le Mobilier en pierre de Bouqras: utilisation de la pine dans un site Neolithique sur le moyen Euphrate (Syrie).* Istanbul: Nederland Historisch-Archaeologisch Instituut te Istanbul.

Rohde, E.
1973 "Die Frühbronzezeitliche Kykladenfiguren der Berliner. Antiken Sammlung. Staatliche Museen zu Berlin," *Forschungen und Berichte* 16: 149-167.

Runnels, C.
1981 *A Diachronic Study and Economic Analysis of Millstones from the Argolid, Greece.* University Microfilms, Ann Arbor, Unpublished Ph.D. Dissertation.

1985 "Lithic studies: some theoretical considerations," *Lithic Technology* 14: 100-106.

Sahlins, M.D.
1972 *Stone Age Economics.* Chicago: Aldine-Atherton.

Satış, B.
1994 *İlk Çağdan Günümüze Akhisar*. İzmir: Ege Üniversitesi

Schachner, A.
1999 "Der Hanay Tepe und seine Bedeutung für dies Bronzezeitliche Topographie der Troas: Die Prähistorischen funde der Grabungen von Frank Calvert im Berliner Museum für vor- und früh-geschichte,"*Acta Praehistorica et Archaeologica* 31: 7-47

Schliemann, H.
1880 *Ilios. The Country and city of the Trojans.* London: J. Murray.

Schmidt, H.
1902 *Heinrich Schliemann's Sammlung Trojanischer Altertumer.* Berlin: 0. Reimer.

Seeher, J.
1987a *Demircihöyük. Die Ergebnisse der Ausgrabungen 1975-78. 111.1: Die Keramik lA: Die neolithische und chalkolithische Keramik,* edited by M. Korfmann, Mainz: P. von Zabern.

1987b "Early Cycladic marble beakers in the Aegean and Anatolia: some considerations," *Paper Presented at the Sixth International Congress on Aegean Prehistory, Athens 1987.*

1989 "Antalya yakınlarındaki Karain mağarasında Kalkolithik Çağ buluntuları,"*Araştırma Sonuçlan Toplantısı* 11: 221-238.

1991 "Coşkuntepe-Anatolisches Neolithikum am Nordostufer der Ägäis," *Istanbuler Mitteilungen* 40: 9-15.

1992 "Die kleinasiatischen marmorstauetten vom Typ Kilia," *ArchäologischerAnzeiger,* heft 2, pp. 153-70.

Shackleton, J. and C. Renfrew
1970 "Neolithic trade routes realigned by oxygen isotope analysis," *Nature* 228: 1062-1064.

Sinopoli, C.
1988 "The organization of production at Vijayanagara, south India," *American Anthropology* 90: 580-597.

Sperling, J.R.
1976 "Kumtepe in the Troad. Trial Excavations," *Hesperia 45:* 15-64.

Stark, M.T.
1991 "Ceramic production and community specialization: A Kalinga ethnoarchaeological study," *World Archaeology* 23: 64-78.

Steele, C.N.
1971 *The Potters of Sorkun Village in northwest Anatolia: the study of a Present Day Primitive Pottery Industry and its Relevance to archaeology.* Ph. D. Dissertation, Oxford University.

Stein, G.J.
1992 "Producers, patrons, and prestige: craft specialization and emergent elites Mesopotamia from 5000 BC-3100 BC," in *Craft Specialization and SocialEvolution: In Memory of V. Gordon Childe,* edited by B. Wailes, Philadelphia University Museum of Archaeology and Anthropology, pp. 25-38.

Stein, G. and J. Blackman
1993 "The organizational context of specialized craft production in early Mesopotamian states,*"Research in Economic Anthropology* 14: 29-60.

Stocks, D.A.
1993 "Making stone vessels in Ancient Mesopotamia and Egypt," *Antiquity*

Takaoğlu, T.
2002 "Chalcolithic marble working at Kulaksızlar in western Anatolia," *Journal of the Turkish Academy of Sciences* 5: 71-93.

2004a "Cultural interactions in the eastern Aegean: new evidence," *Anatolia Antiqua* 12: 1-6.

2004 "Moralı: a neolithic mound in central western Anatolia," in *Anadolu'da Doğdu. 60. Yaşında Fahri Işık'a Armağan,* edited by T. Korkut. İstanbul: Ege Yayınları, pp. 743-751.

2005 "Prehistoric excavations at Gülpınar on the coastal Troad," *forthcoming.*

Talalay, L. E.
1984 "Neolithic initiation rites: a new interpretation of Anatolian figurines," *American Joumal of Archaeology* 88: 262.

1993 *Deities, Dolls, and Devices: Neolithic Figurines from Franchthi Cave, Greece.* Bloomington: Indiana University Press. Excavations at Franchthi Cave, Greece; fasc 9.

Thissen, L.
2000 "Thessaly, Franchthi and western Turkey: clues to the Neolithisation in Turkish Thrace," *Documenta Praehistorica* 27: 141-154.

Torrence, R.
1984 "Monopoly or direct access? industrial organization at the Melos obsidian quarry," in *Prehistoric Quarries and Lithic Production,* edited by J. E. Ericson and B.A. Purdy, Cambridge: Cambridge University Press, pp. 49-64.

1986 *Production and Exchange of Stone Tools. Prehistoric Ohsidian in the Aegean.* Cambridge: Cambridge University Press.

Tosi, M.
1968 "Excavations at Shahr-i Sokhta: preliminary report on the 2nd campaign september-december 1968," *East and West* 19: 283-86.

Ucko, P.J.
1962 "The interpretation of the Prehistoric Anthropomorphic Figures," *Journal of Royal AnthropologicalInstitute* 92: 38-54.

Virchow, R.
1882 *Alttrojanische Graber und Schädel.* Berlin: Koniglichen Akademie der Wissenchaften.

Vitelli, K.
1989 "Were pots were made for foods?" *World Archaeology* 21: 17-29.

1993 *Franchthi Neolithic Pottery.* Bloomington: Indiana University Press, Excavations at Franchthi Cave, Greece; Fascicle 8.

von Bothmer, D.
1961 *Ancient Art from the New York Private Collections.* New York: Metropolitan Museum of Art

1990 *Glories of the Past: Ancient Art from the Shelby White and Leon Levy Collection.* New York: Metropolitan Museum of Art.

Yakar, J.
1985 *The Later Prehistory of Anatolia. The Late Chalcolithic and Early Bronze Age.* BAR International Series 285.

Wailes, B.
1996 "V. Gordon Childe and the relation of production," in Craft Specialization and Social Evolution: In Memory of V. Gordon Childe, edited by B. Wailes, Philadelphia: University Museum of Archaeology and Anthropology, pp. 3-16.

Warren, P.M.
1969 *Minoan Stone Vases.* London: Cambridge University Press.

Wattenmaker, P.
1994 "State formation and the organization of domestic production at third millennium BC Kurban Höyük, southeast Turkey," in *Archaeological Views from the Countryside. Village Communities in Early Complex Societies,* edited by G.M. Schwartz and S.E. Falconer, Washington, DC: Smithsonian Institution Press, pp. 109-120.

1998 *Household and State in Upper Mesopotamia: Specialized Economy and the Social Uses of Goods in an Early Complex Society.* Washington, DC: Smithsonian Institution Press

Weiner, J.
1981 "Die flintminen von Çakmak. Eine im Aussterben begriffene heute noch produzierende Feuersrtein industrie in Nordwestanatolien," in *5000 jahre Feuersteinbergbau: Die Suche nach dem Stahl der Steinzeit,* edited by G. Weisgerber, Bochum: Deutschen Bergbau-Museum, pp. 383-95

Weishaar, H.J.
1982 "Varna und die Ägäische Bronzezeit," *Archaologisches Korrespondenzblatt* 12: 321-329.

Woodward A.M. and H.A.Ormerod
1910 "A journey in southwestern Asia Minor," *Bulletin of the American School at Athens* 16: 76-136.

Woolley, C.L.
1955 *Alalakh - An Account of the Excavations at Tell Atchana in the Hatay, 1937-1949.* London: Society of Antiquaries.

Wulf, H.E.
1966 *The Traditional Crafts of Persia. Their Development, Technology, Influences on Eastern and Western Civilizations.* Cambridge: M.I.T. Press.

Plates

Plate 1. Upper half of a roughed-out marble pointed beaker with roughly shaped
vertical lugs. Lower illustration shows the drilling mark (**1**)

2 3

4 5 6

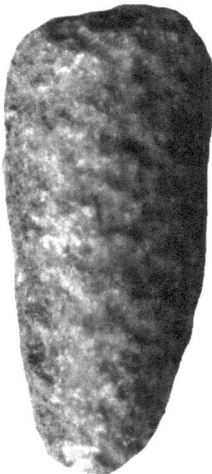
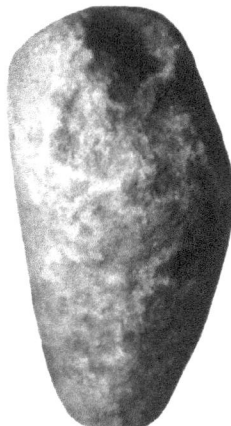

7 8 9

Plate 2. Upper parts (**2-3**) and lower ends (**4-9**) of roughed-out pointed beakers
showing flaking and pecking marks. Examples **8** and **9** were broken during drilling

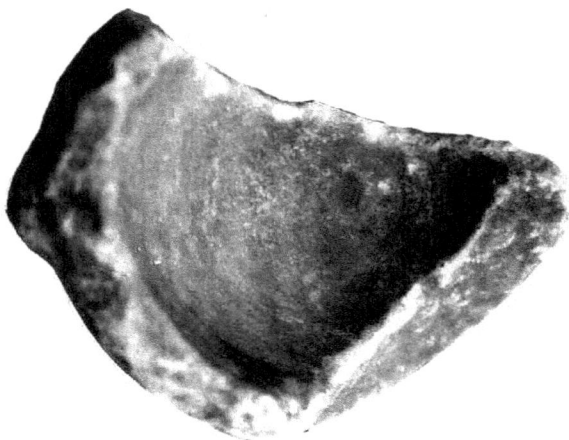

13

Plate 3. Upper part of a roughed-out pointed beaker (13). Upper right illustration shows the
pointed tool marks, while those on the upper left and on the lower
show the lines of rotary drilling.

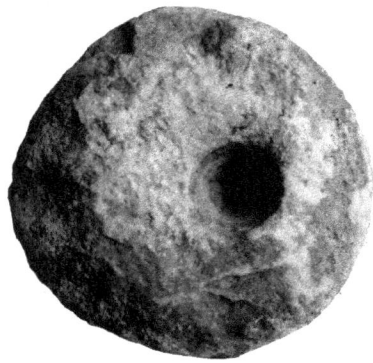

14

15

Plate 4. Lower end fragments of rough out beakers showing off-centered drilling (**14**)
and projection left by a drill-bit (**15**).

16

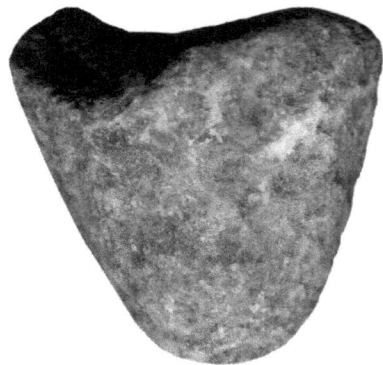

17

Plate 5. Lower ends of pointed beakers showing lines of rotary drilling (**16** and **17**).

30

31

Plate 6. Rim fragments of unfinished marble pointed beakers showing horizontal lines of rotary drilling on their interior and the roughly-shaped vertical lugs on their exterior (**30** and **31**).

12

32

33

Plate 7. Rim fragments (**12**, **32**, **33**) of marble pointed beakers showing pointed tool marks.
The interior of example **33** has heavy calcareous incrustation

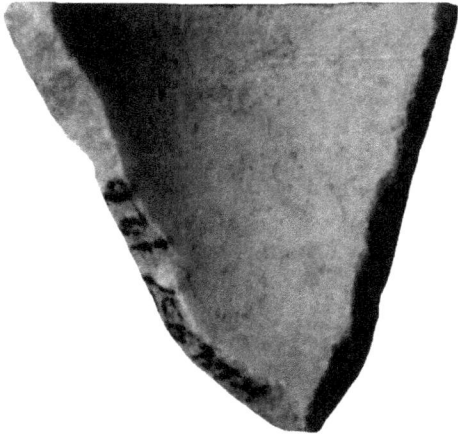

37

41

Plate 8. Rim fragments of pointed beakers showing percussive and abrasive use-wear (37 and 41)

43

44

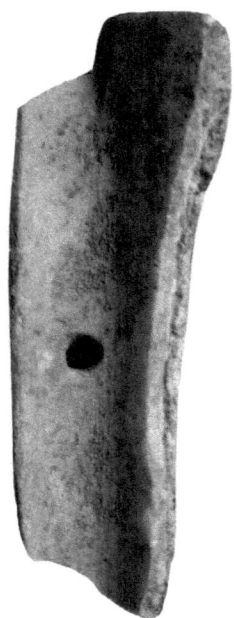

45

Plate 9. Wall (**43**) and rim (**44-45**) fragments of pointed beakers. Example **44** has scratsches on its exterior. Example **45** with pierced lug belongs to a nearly finished pointed beaker

46

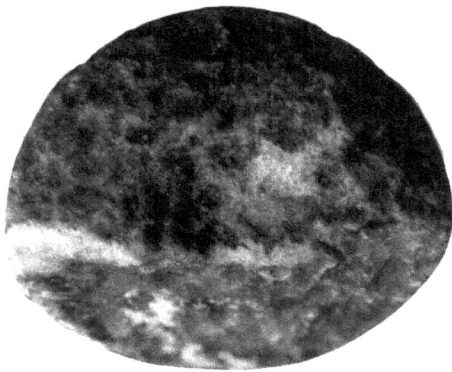
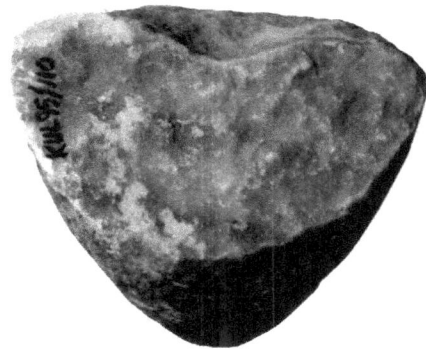

50

Plate 10. Roughed-out pointed bowls (**46** and **50**). Example **50** was split diagonally
during the chipping out of the interior.

60

61

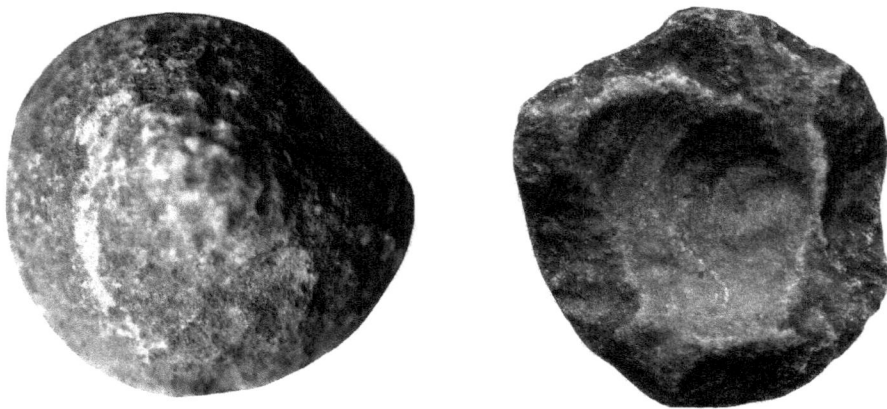

62

Plate 11. Roughed-out pointed bowls showing the use of multiple drill-bits (**60-62**)

58

71

72

Plate 12. Rim fragments of unfinished pointed bowls showing drilling marks (**58**, **71**, **72**)

73

74

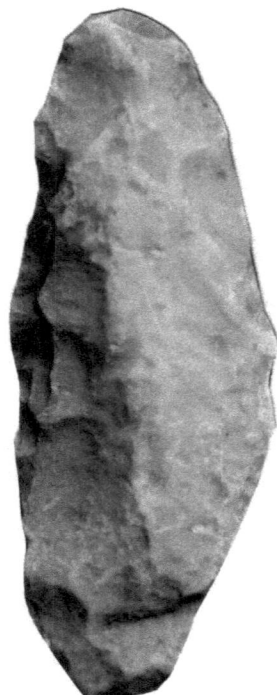

75

76

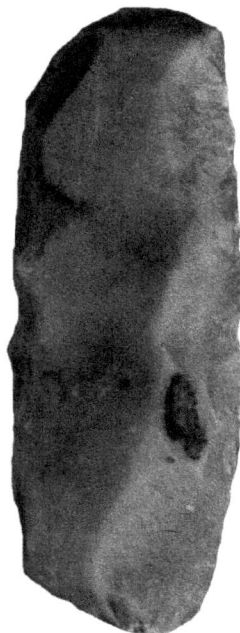

77

78

Plate 13. Marble blanks of figurines with flaking marks (**73-78**)

79

80

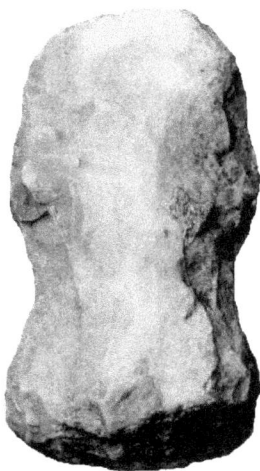
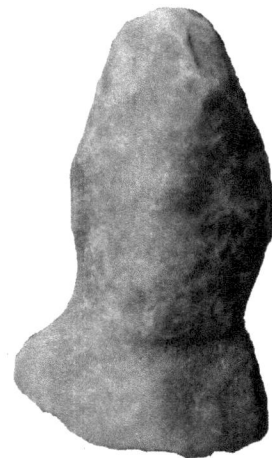

81

82

Plate 14. Figurine blanks with pecking (**79**) and flaking scars (**80**). **81** and **82** are preform fragments showing breakage during the thinning of the neck

83

84

85

87

Plate 15. Lower ends of marble figurine preforms broken off at the waist (**83-85** and **87**)

94

95

 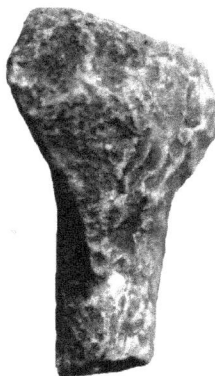

96

Plate 16. Head fragments of Kilia-type figurine preforms broken off at neck (**94-96**)

98

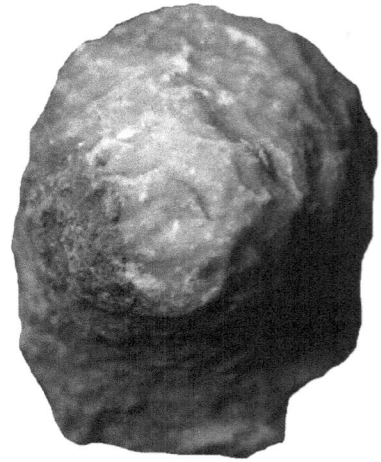

99

100

101

102

Plate 17. Head fragments of marble figurine preforms broken off at neck (**98-102**). Example **102** shows the use of abrasive in differentiating the neck from the head.

104

105

 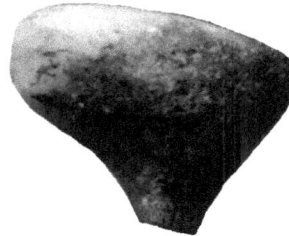

106

111 **112**

Plate 18. Unfinished (**104-106**) and finished (**111** and **112**) fragments of figurines broken off at neck

113

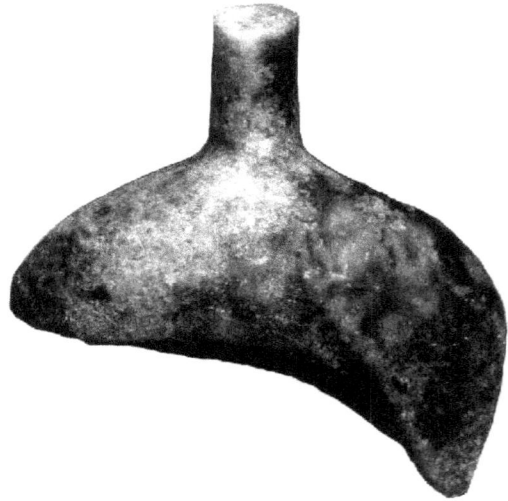

114

115

116

127

130

134

Plate 19. Torso fragments of finished marble figurines showing clefts between bent arms and
body (**113-116**). Examples **127, 130,** and **134** represents lower ends of
nearly-finished figurines.

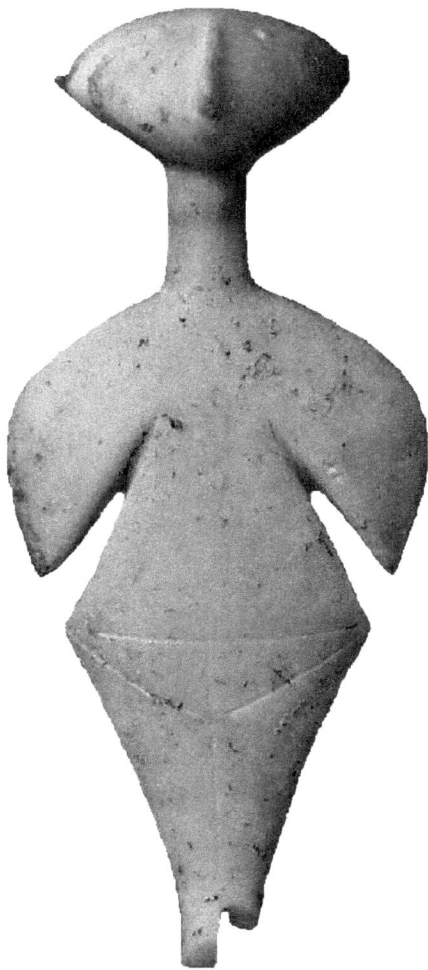
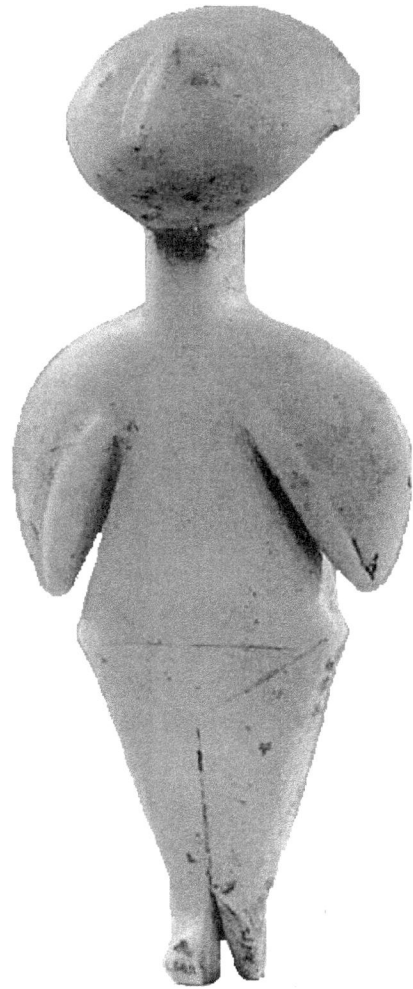

222   **225**

Plate 20. Finished Kilia figurines from Kırşehir (**222**) and Guennol Collection (**225**)
in New York showing minor stylistic variations (After Höckman 1977 and Joukowsky 1986)

93

232

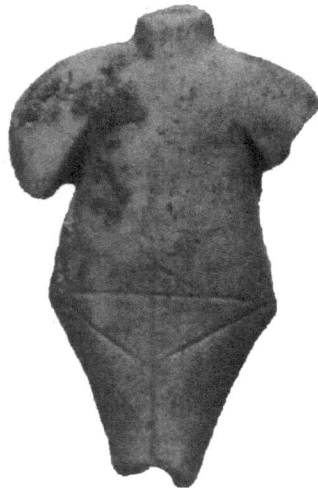

233

246

Plate 21. Finished Kilia figurines from Anatolia with no exact find-places (**232-233**, and **246**)
(After Höckman 1987 and Master Pieces of the Paul Getty Museum 1997)

135

141

136

138

Plate 22. Gabbro (**135**, **141**, and **136**) and basalt (**138**) hammerstones used in flaking and pecking

143

148

152

154

Plate 23. Sandstone crescent-shaped (**143**) and conical (**148**, **152**, and **154**) drill-bits with bevels

145

155

147 **149** **156**

Plate 24. Sanstone crescent-shaped (**145**) and truncated-conical shaped (**147 and 149**) drill-bits with bevels.
Example **156** is probably a drill-head or capstone.

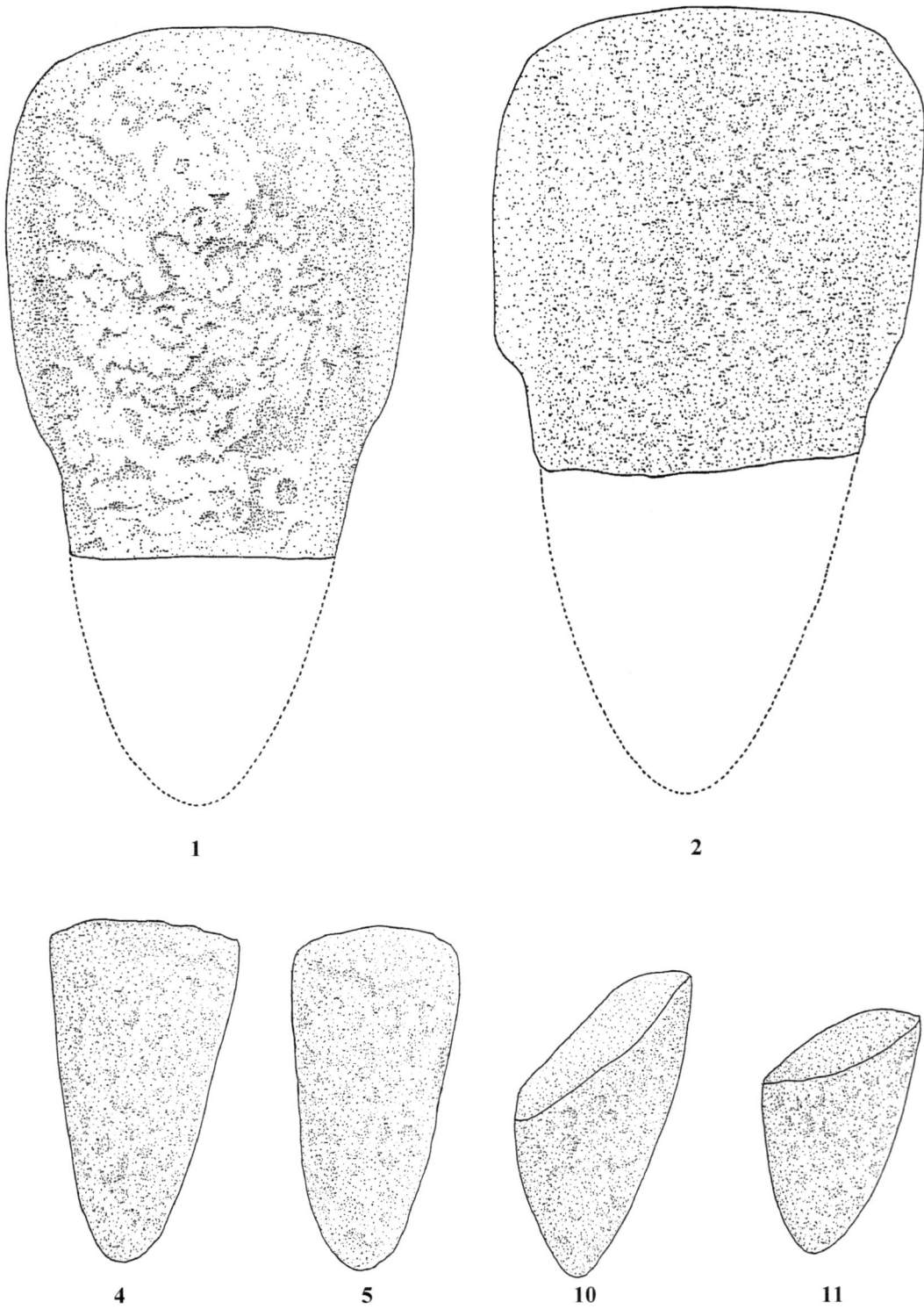

Plate 25. Upper (**1-2**) and lower ends (**4-5** and **10-11**) of pointed beaker preforms broken during the step of pecking (Scale 1:2)

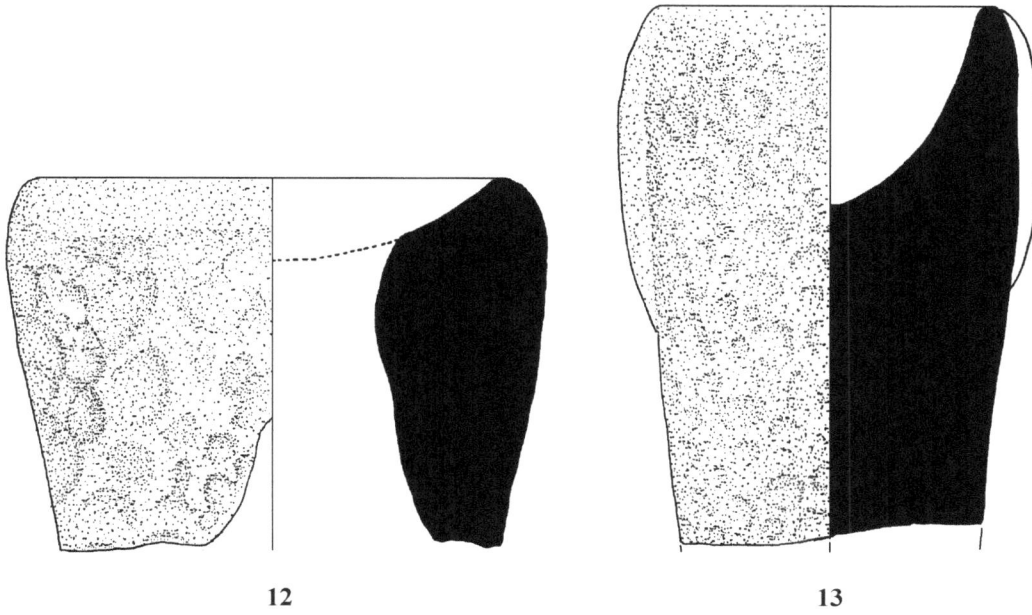

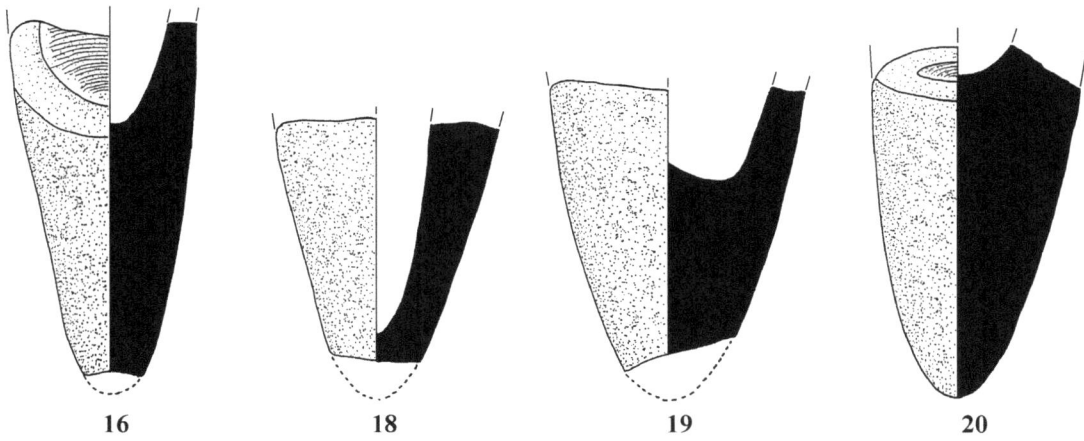

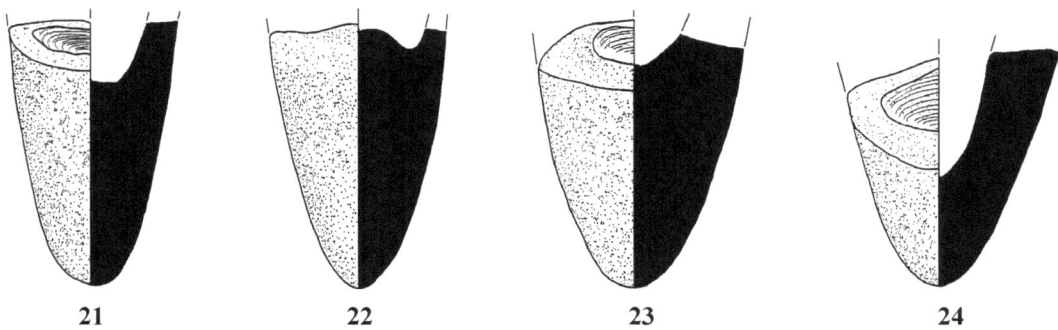

Plate 26. Upper (**12-13**) and lower ends (**16-24**) of pointed beaker preforms broken
during the step of drilling (Scale 1:2)

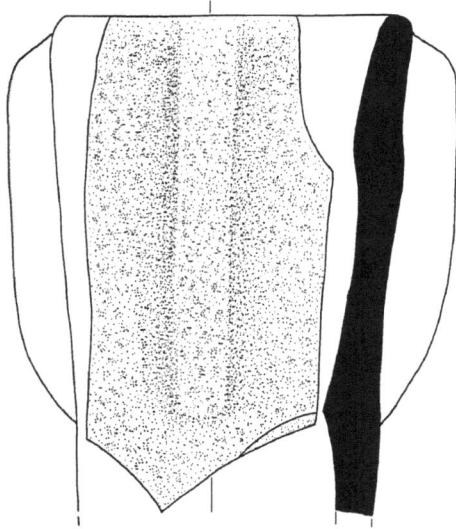

25

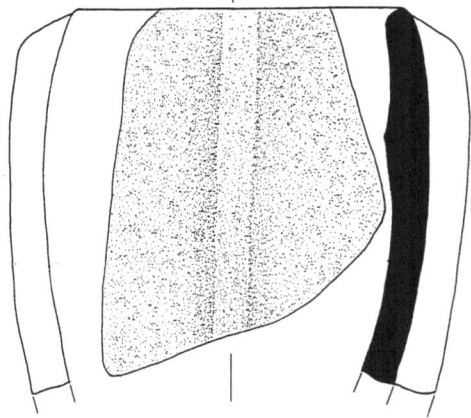

26

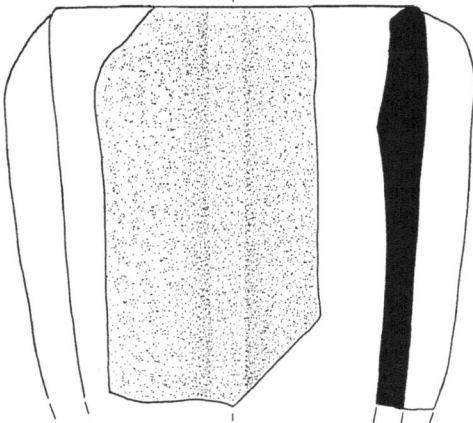

27

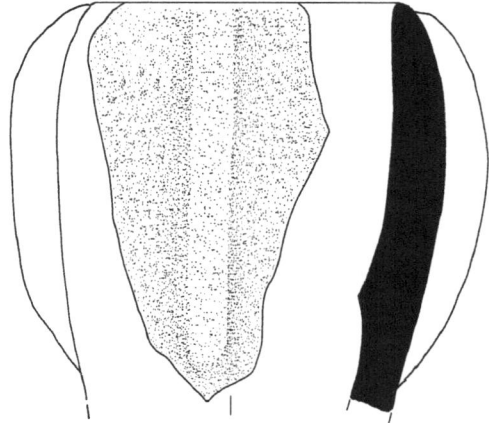

28

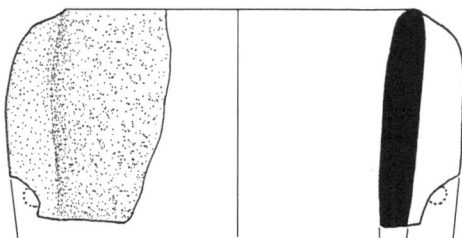

29

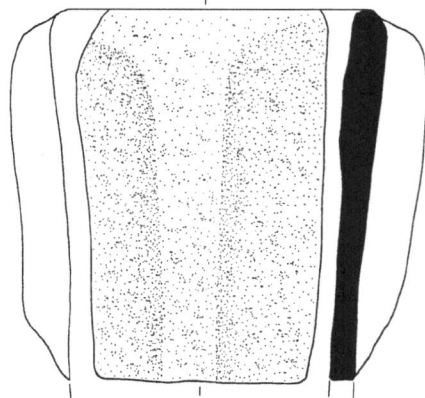

30

Plate 27. Upper parts of roughed-out marble pointed beakers with roughly-shaped vertical lugs broken during the drilling process (**25-30**) (Scale 1:2)

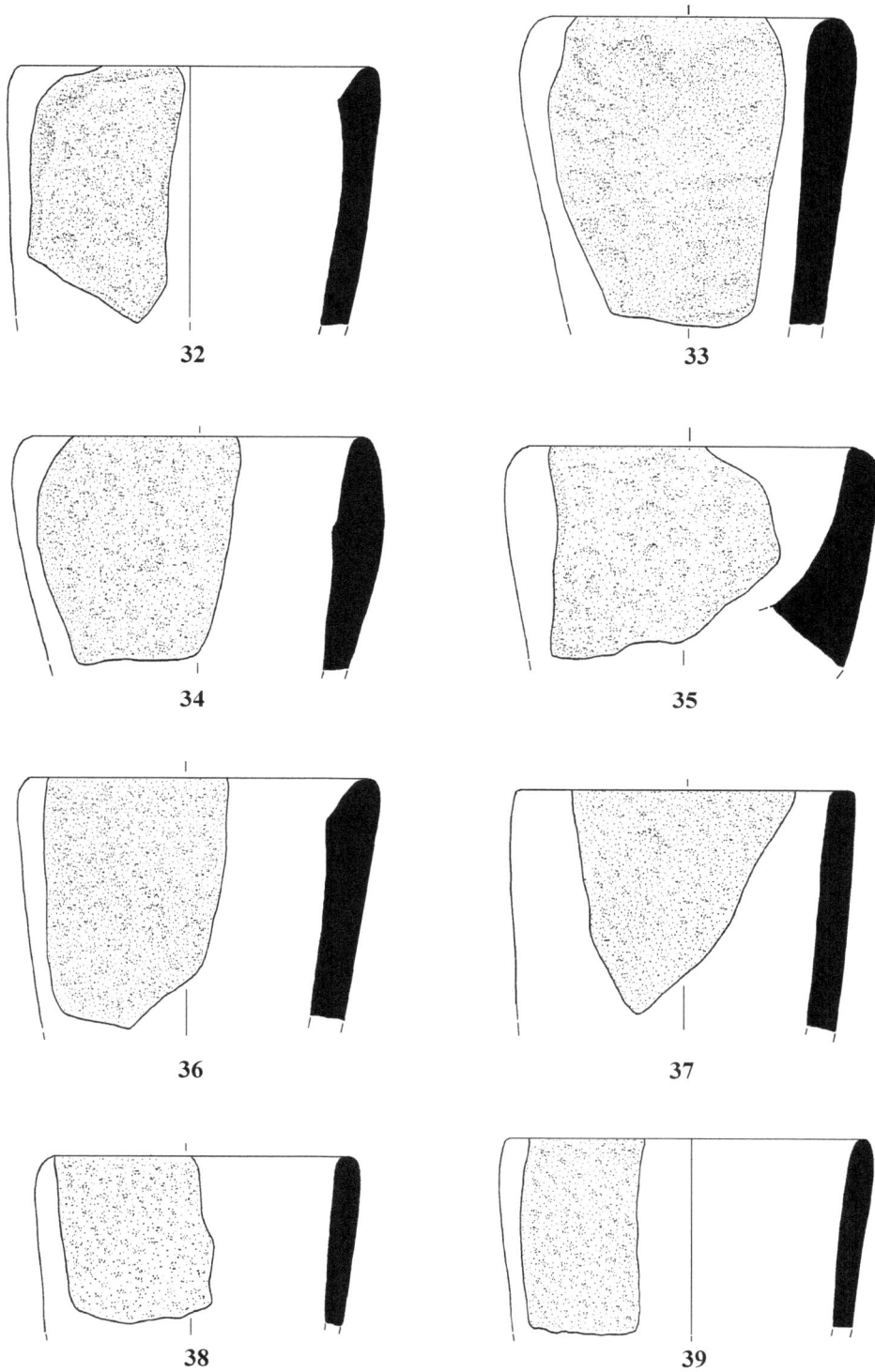

Plate 28. Upper parts of roughed-out marble pointed beakers broken
during the drilling process (**32-39**)(Scale 1:2)

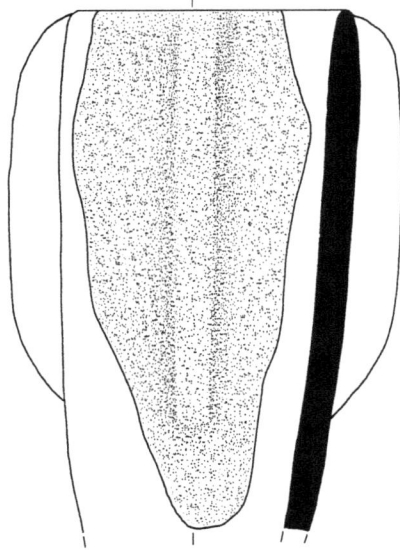

40

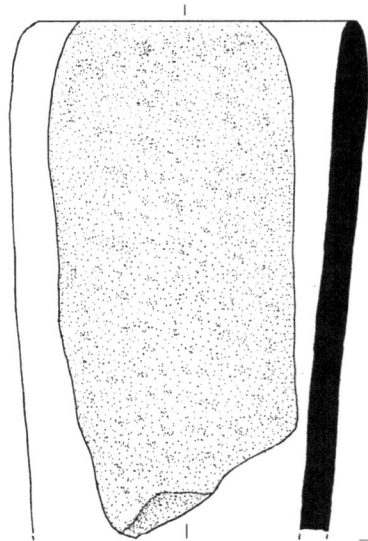

41

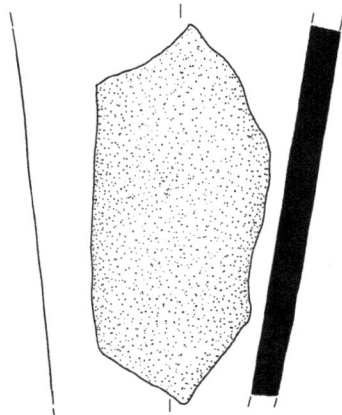

42

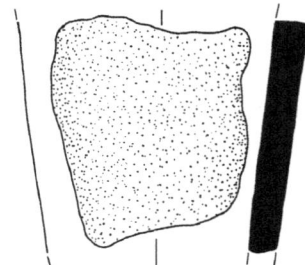

43

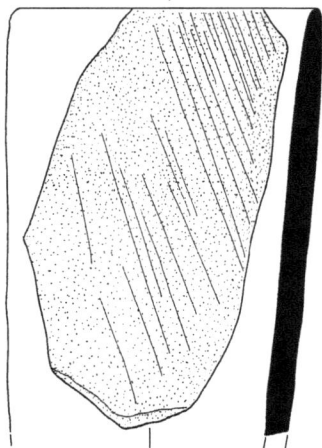

44

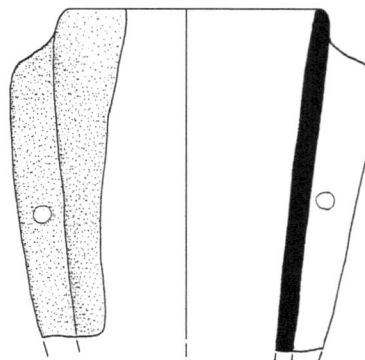

45

Plate 29. Rim and wall fragments of marble pointed beakers broken during the drilling process (**40-45**) (Scale 1:2)

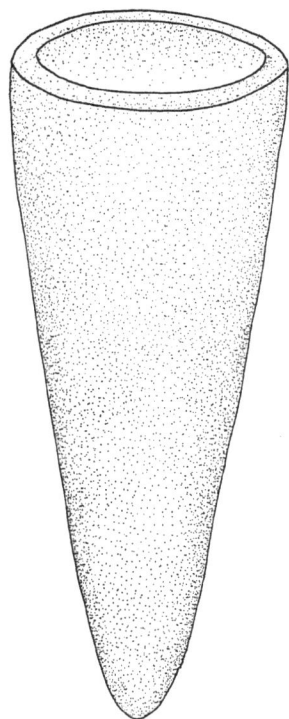
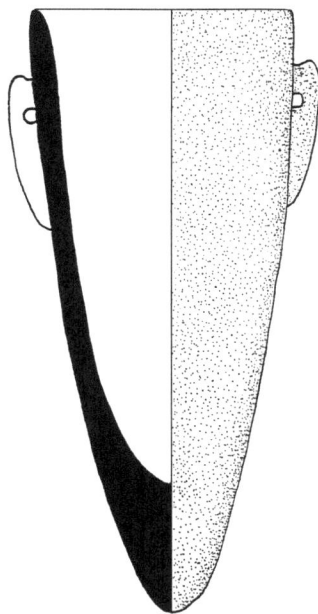
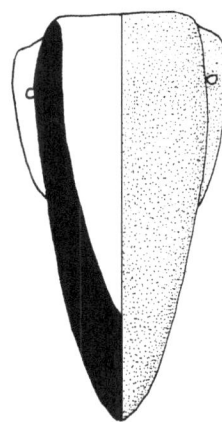

210   211   212

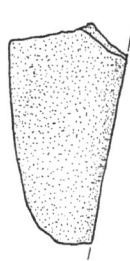
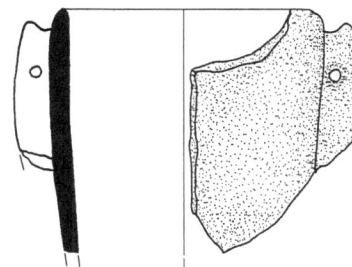

213   214   215

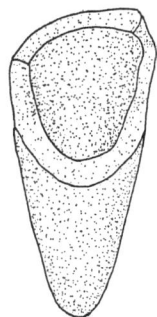
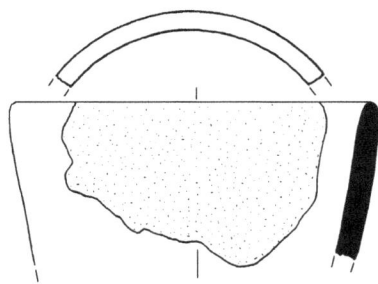
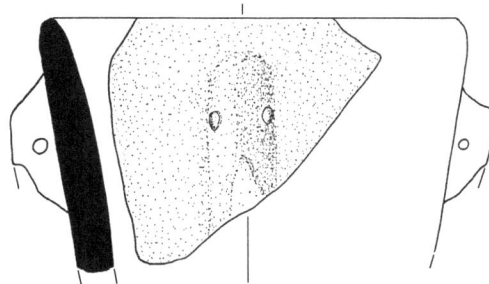

217   218   219

Plate 30. Pointed beakers found at Varna (**210**), Kephala (**211**, **213**), Tigani (**214**, **215**), Naxos (**212**), Kumtepe (**217**), Gülpınar (**218**), and Demircihöyük (**219**) (Scale 1:2)

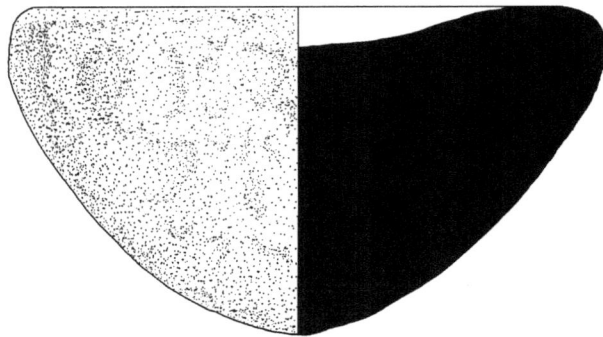

46

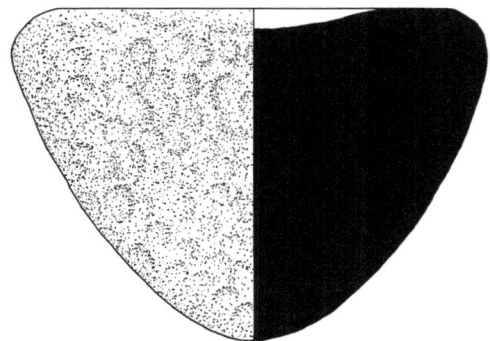

47

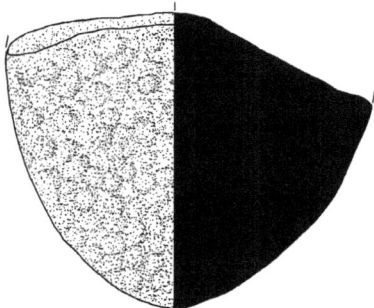

48

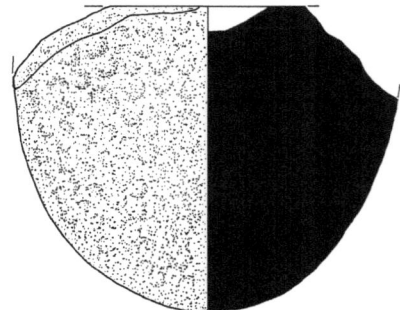

49

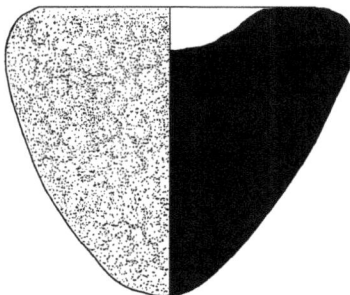

50

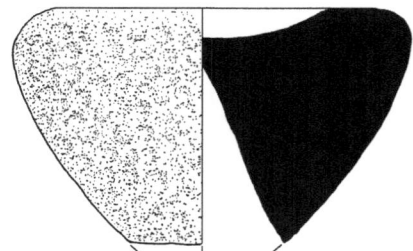

51

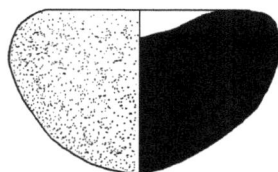

55

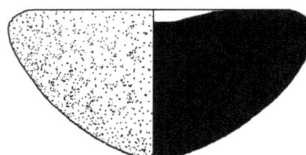

56

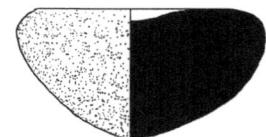

57

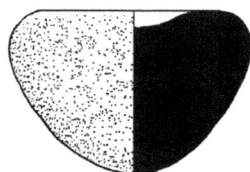

54

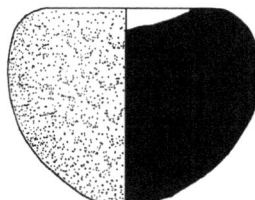

52

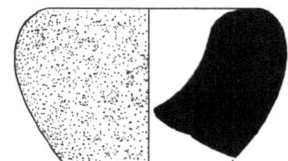

53

Plate 31. Roughed-out marble pointed bowls with slightly chipped out interior (46-53).
Example 53 represents a rim fragment with adrilled interior (Scale 1:2)

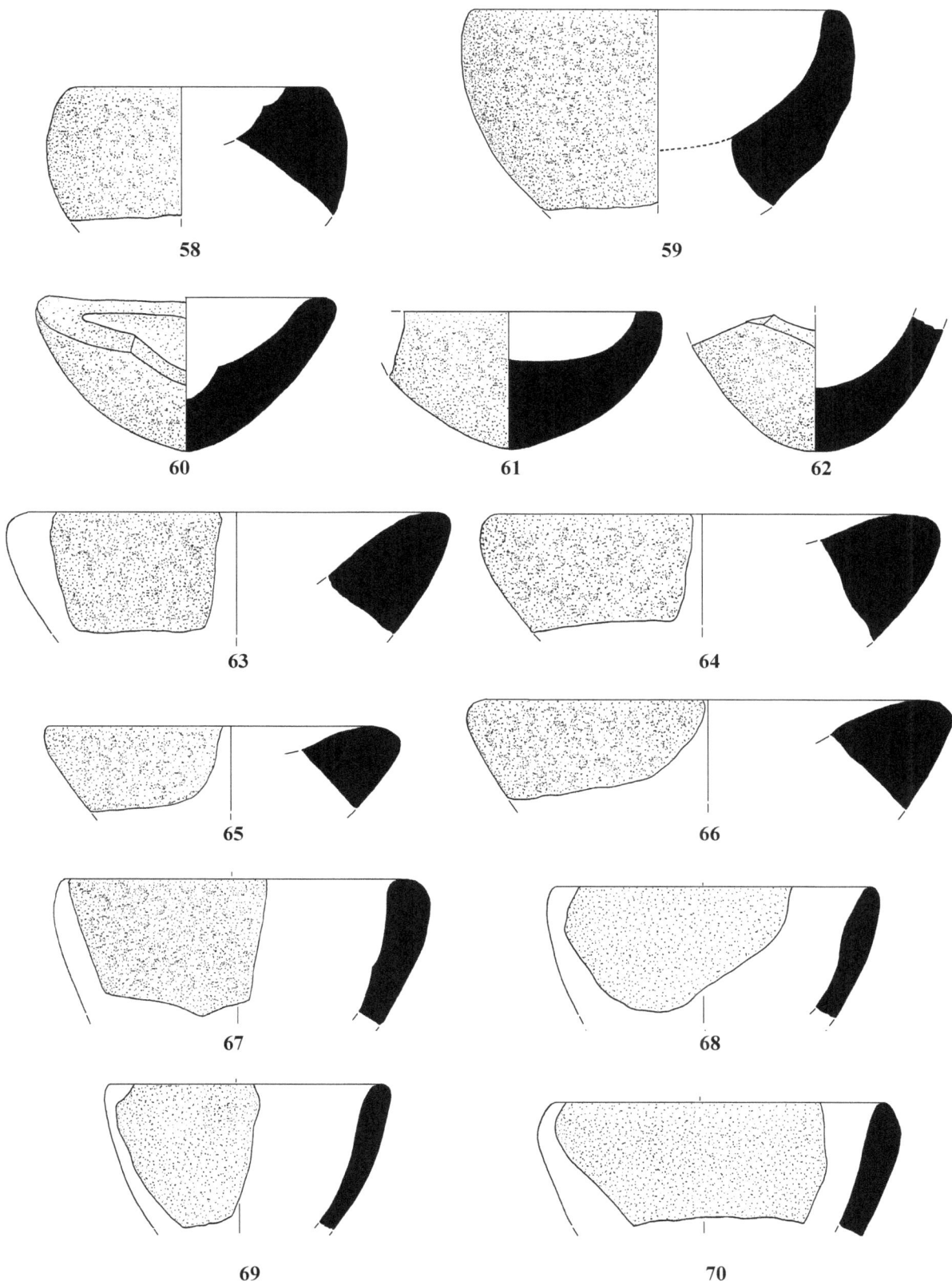

Plate 32. Pointed bowl fragments broken during the drilling process (**58-62** and **67-70**) and chipping out of the interior through pecking (**63-66**) (Scale 1:2)

73

74

79

80

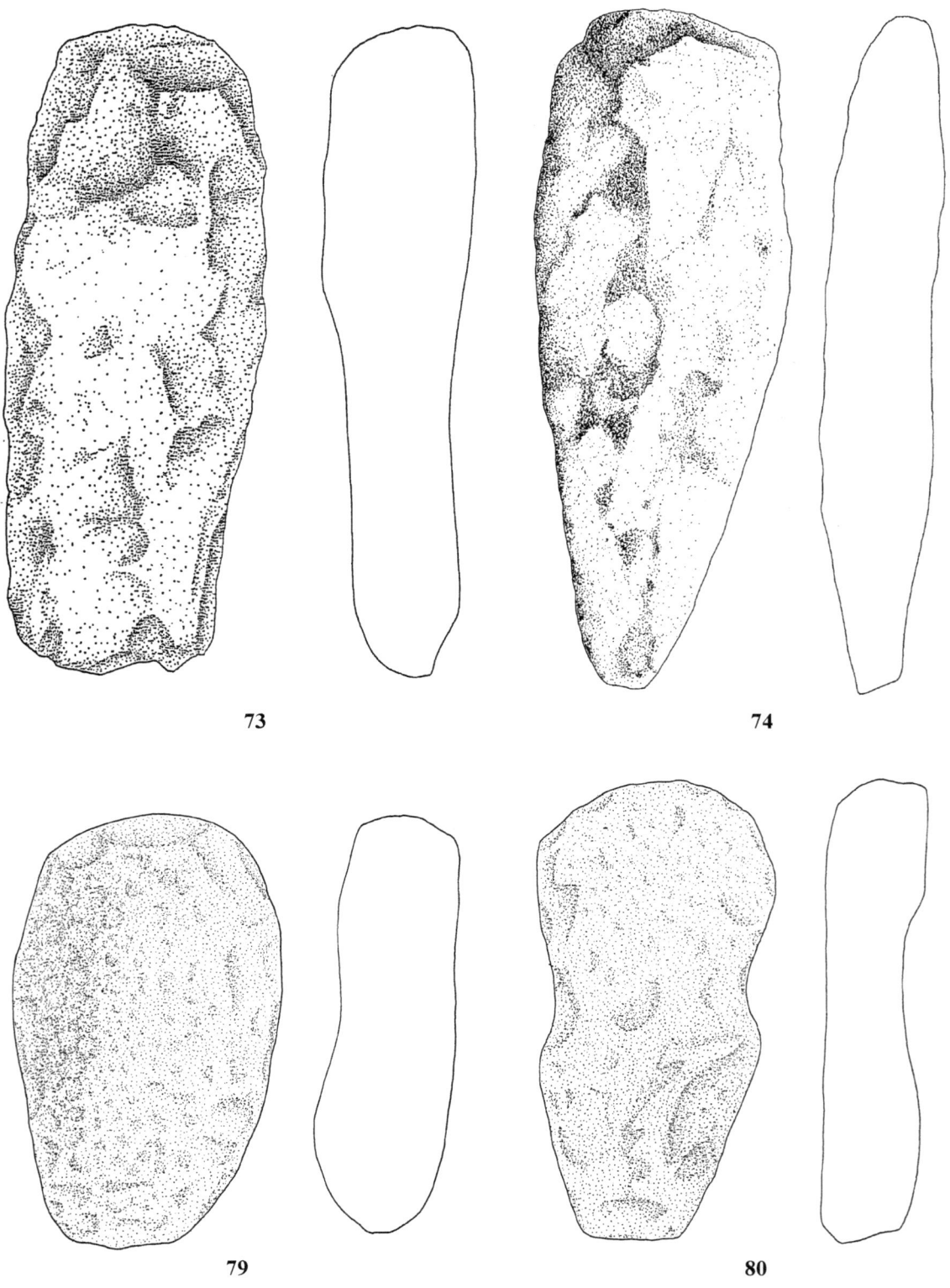

Plate 33. Blanks approaching to the intended sizes of the Kilia figurines (**73-80**) (Scale 1:2)

106

83

84

85

86

88

89

90

91

92

93

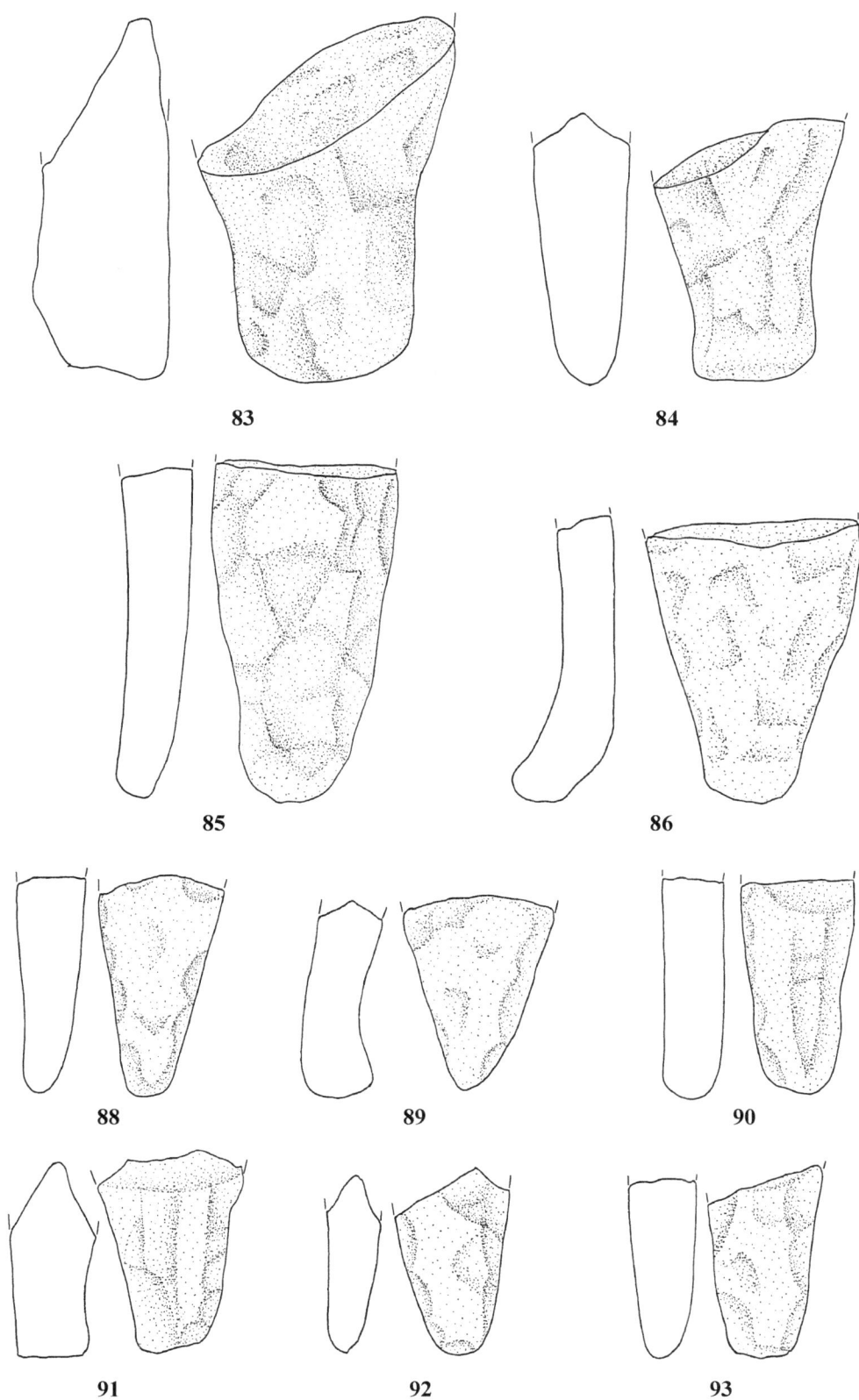

Plate 34. Lower ends of figurine preforms broken during the step of flaking (**83-93**)(Scale 1:2)

94

97

101

103

104

106

107

108

109

110

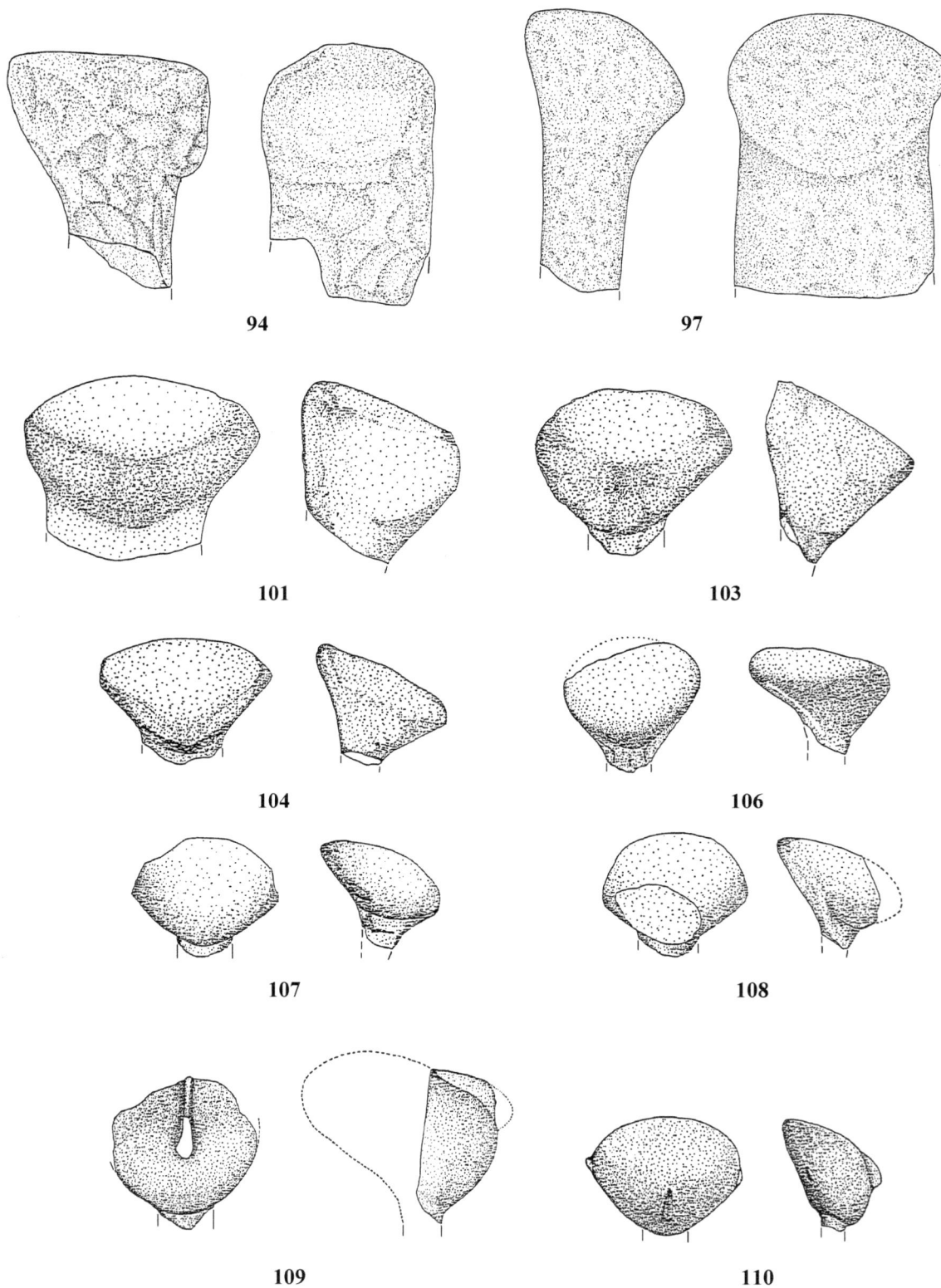

Plate 35. Head fragments of unfinished and finished Kilia figurine broken off at neck (Scale 1:2)

114

115

117

118

119

120

121

122

123

124

125

126

127

128

129

130

131

132

133

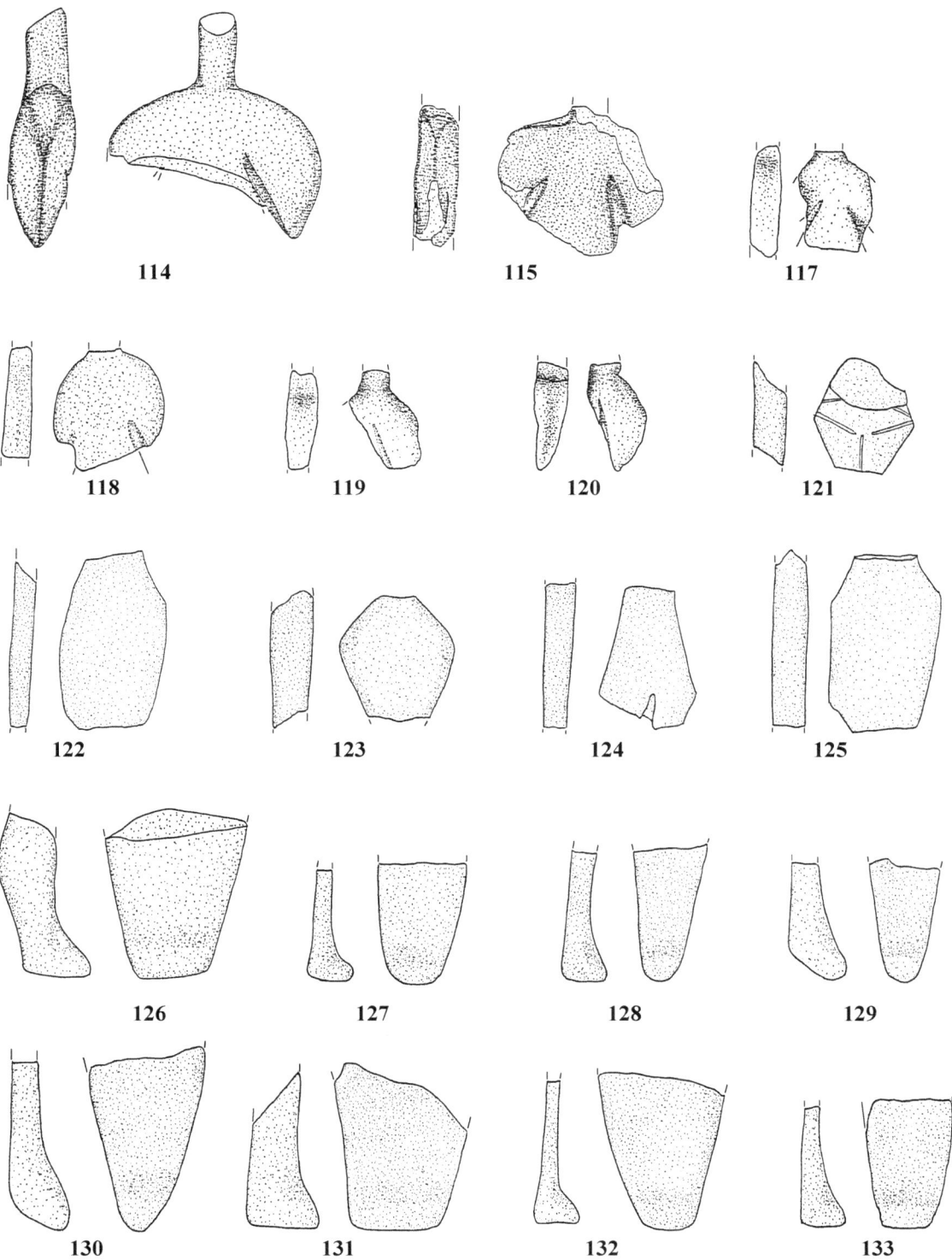

Plate 36. Torso, waist, and lower end fragments of unfinished Kilia figurines (Scale 1:2)

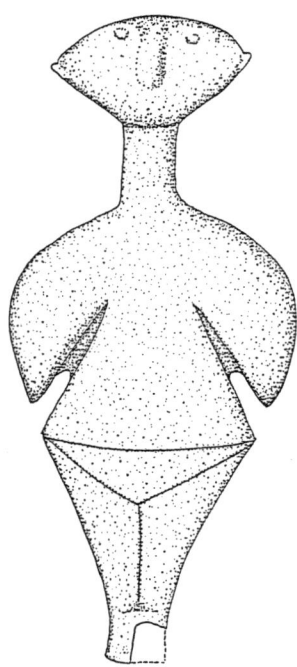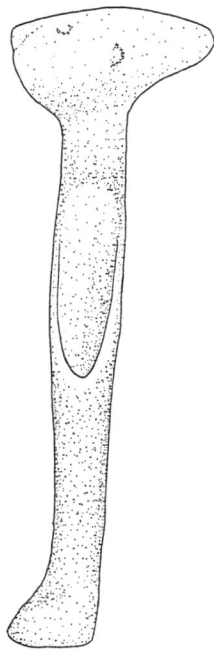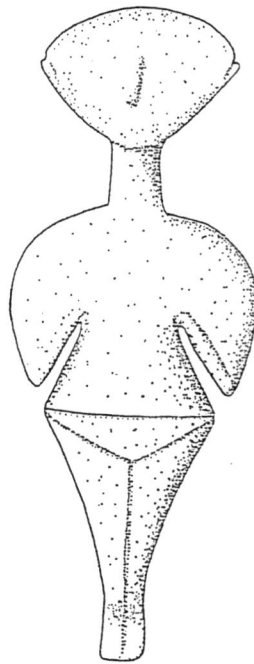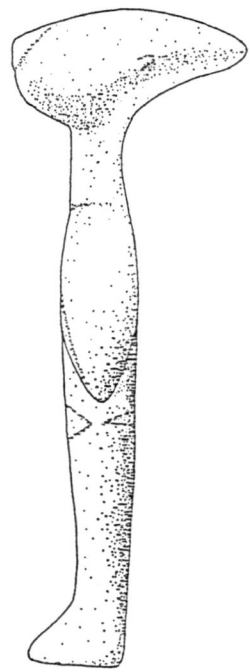

222

223

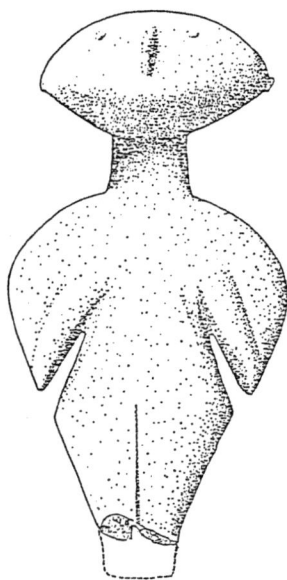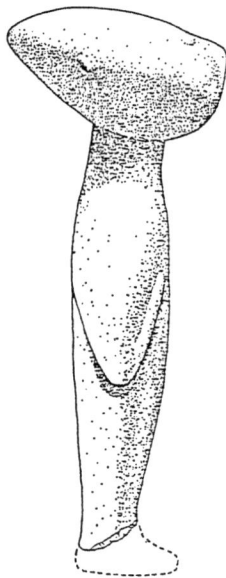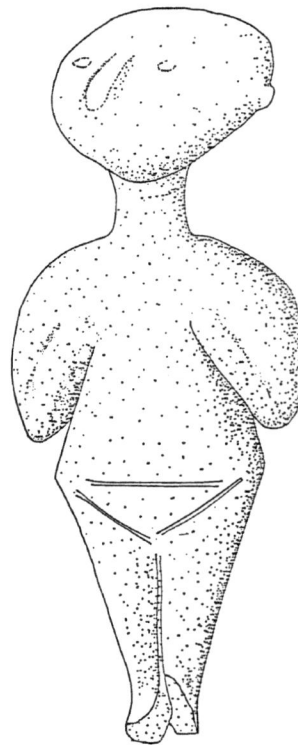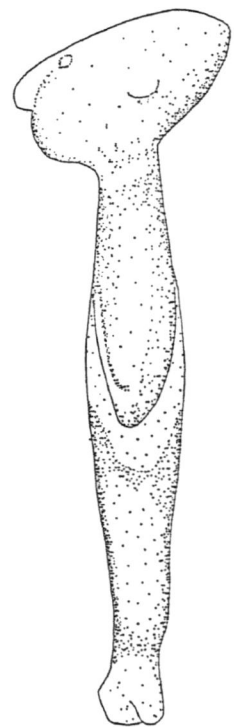

224

225

Plate 37. Kilia figurines from Kırşehir (?) in central Anatolia (**222**, **224**, **225**) and from Kilia Bay area in the Gallipolli Peninsula (**224**) (Scale 1:2)

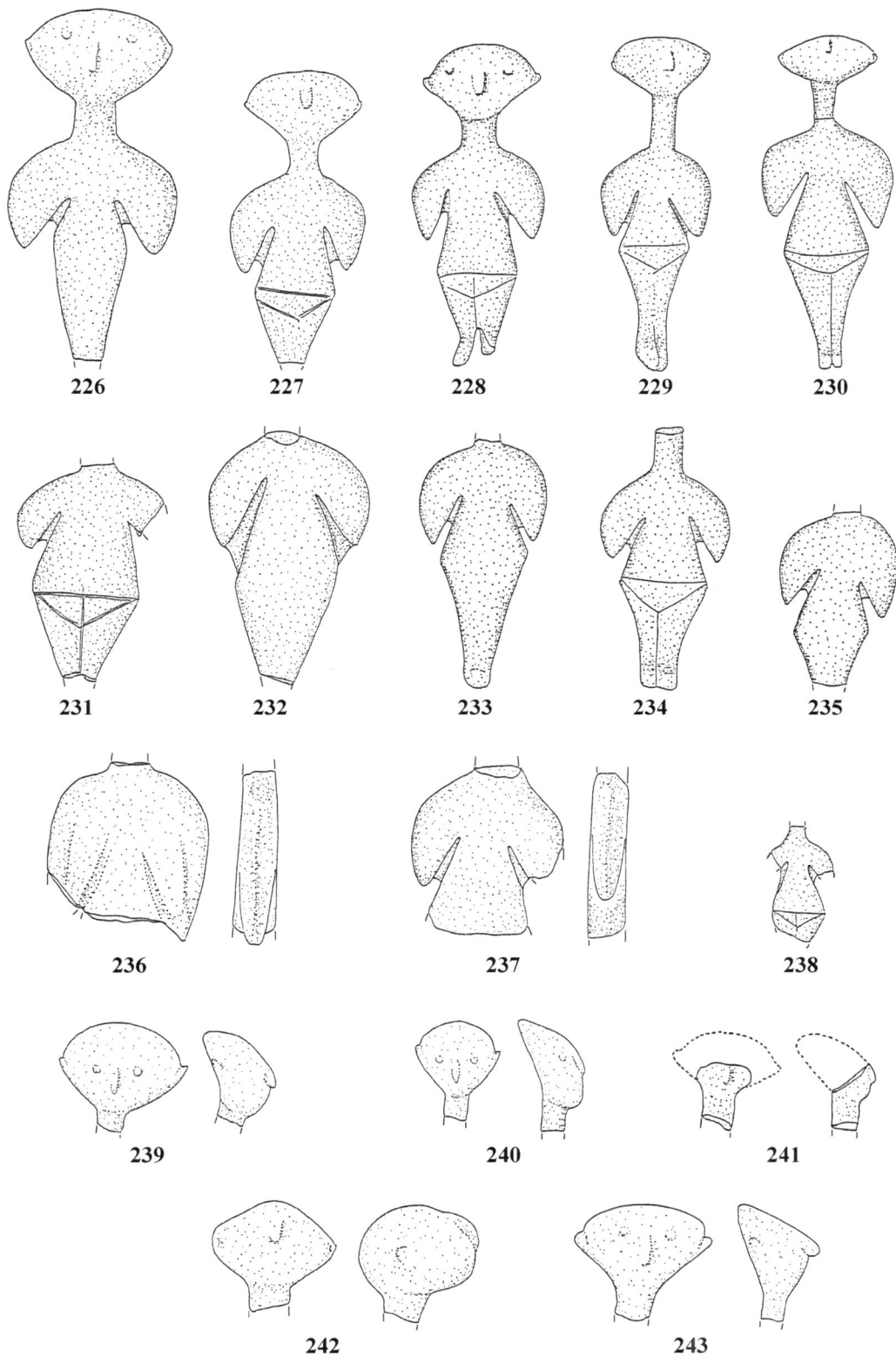

Plate 38. Complete and partially preserved Kilia figurines found at sites in Anatolia.
Example **230** is from Mytilene on Lesbos

135

136

137

138

139

140

141

142

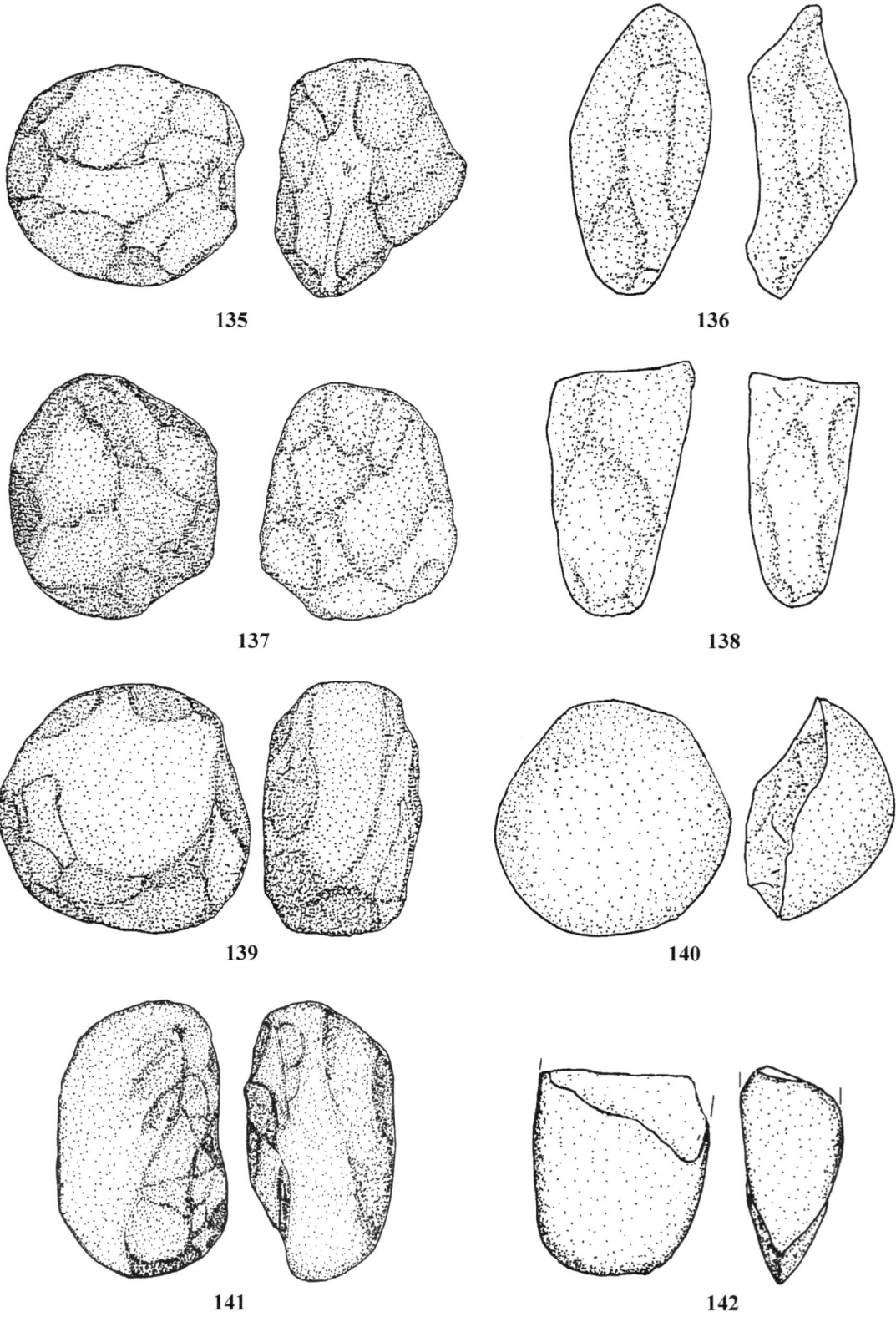

Plate 39. Basalt and gabbro hammer stones with heavy percussion use-wear (**135-142**) (Scale 1:2)

143

144

145

146

147

148

149

150

151

152

153

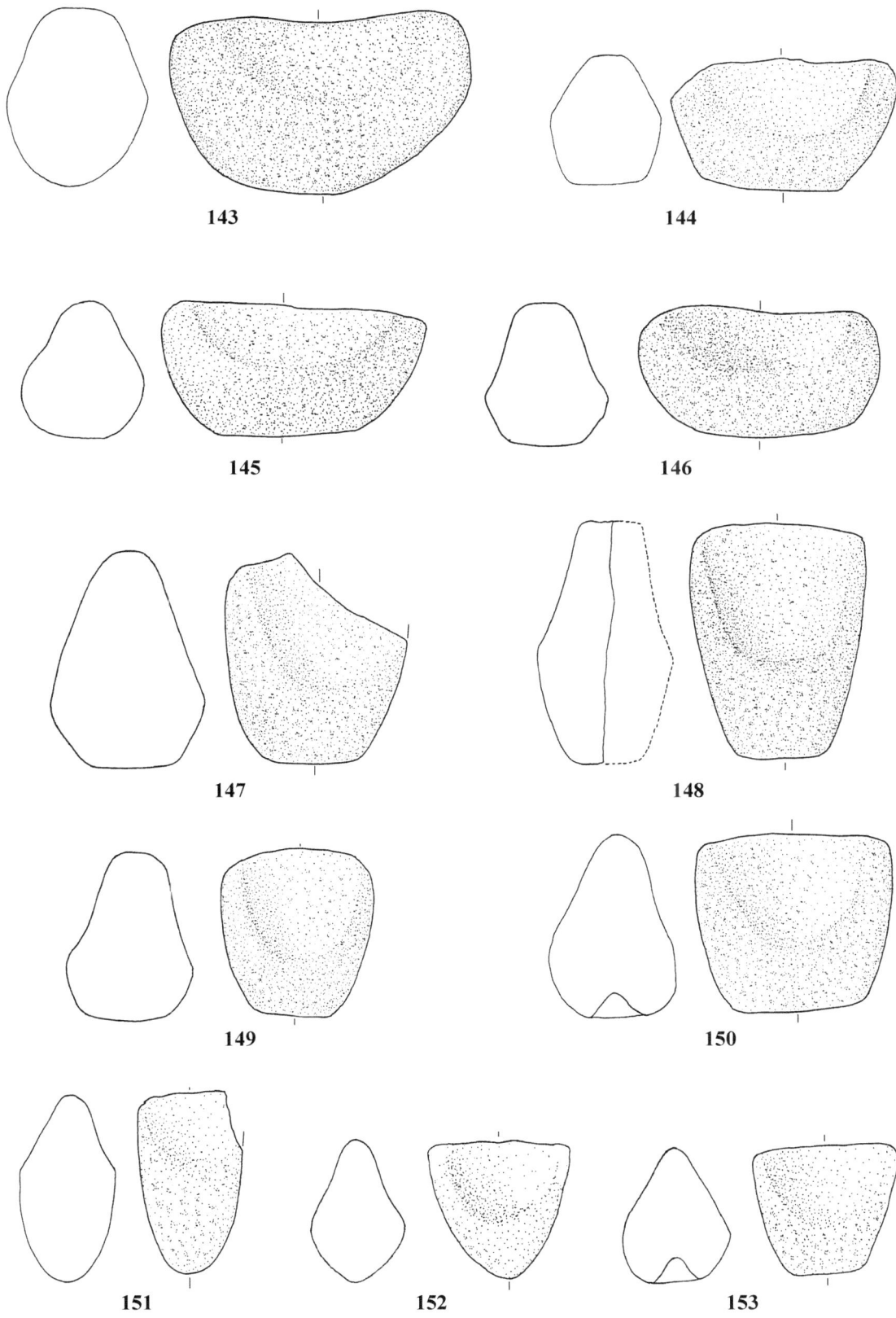

Plate 40. Crescent and conical sandstone drill-bits (**143-153**)(Scale 1:2)

113

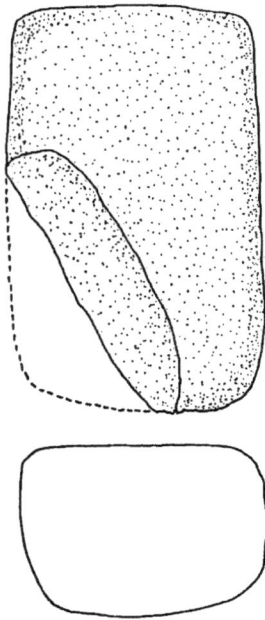

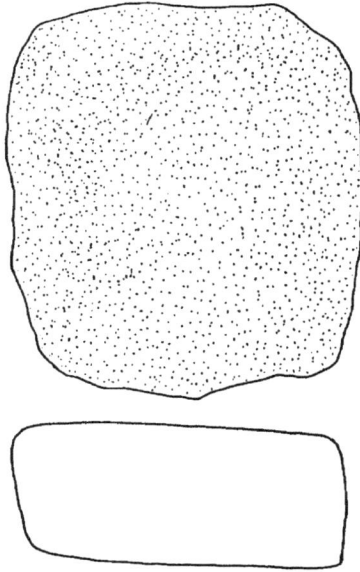

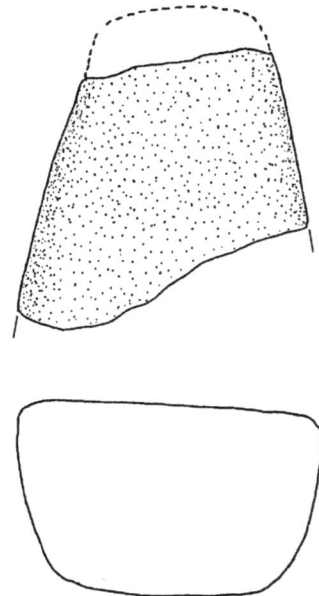

157   **158**   **159**

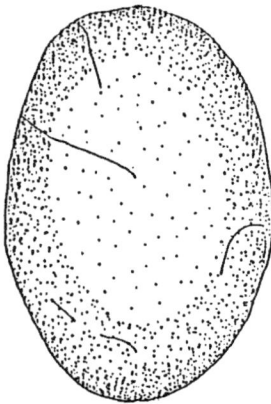

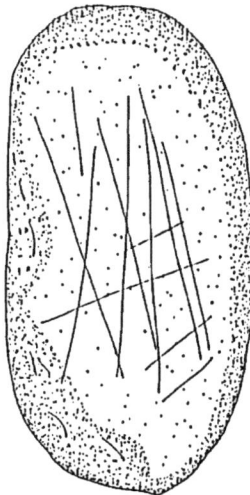

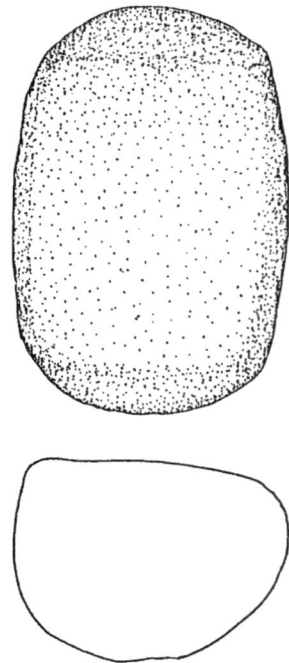

160   **161**   **162**

Plate 41. Andesite abrasives (**157-159**) and river-pebble polishers (**160-162**) (Scale 1:2)

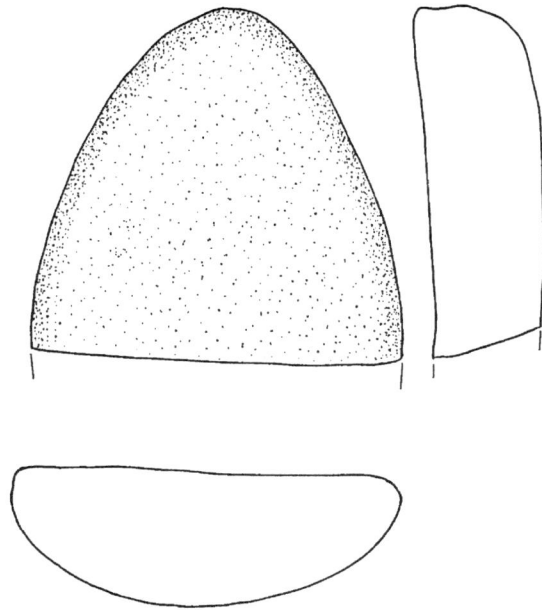
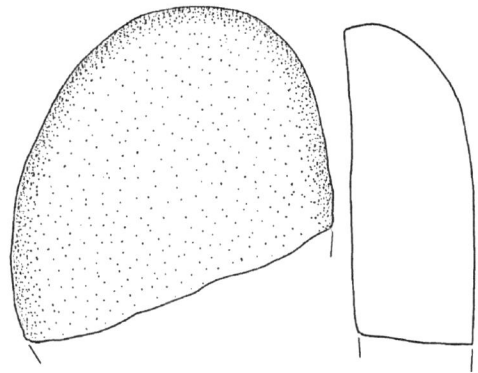
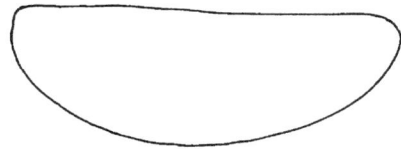

163

164

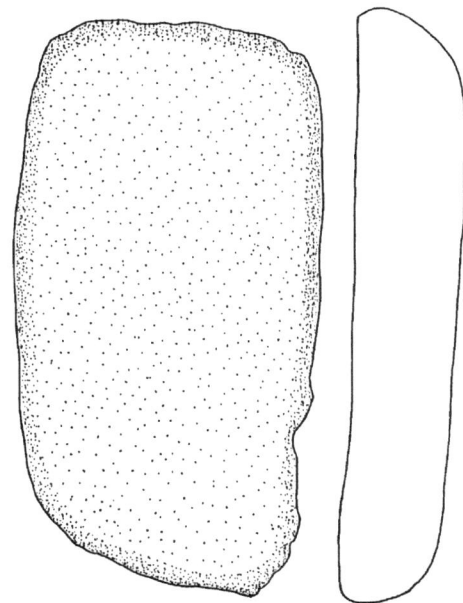
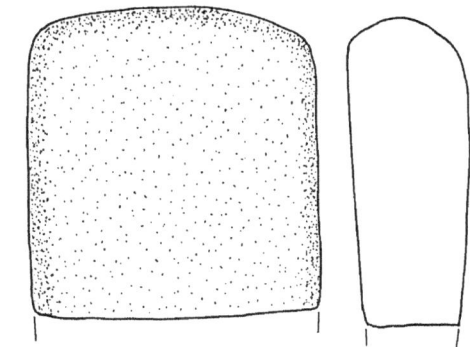
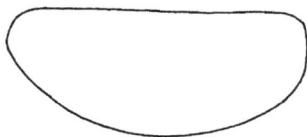

165

166

Plate 42. Andesite saddle querns ovate and rectangular in outline (**163-166**)(Scale 1:3)

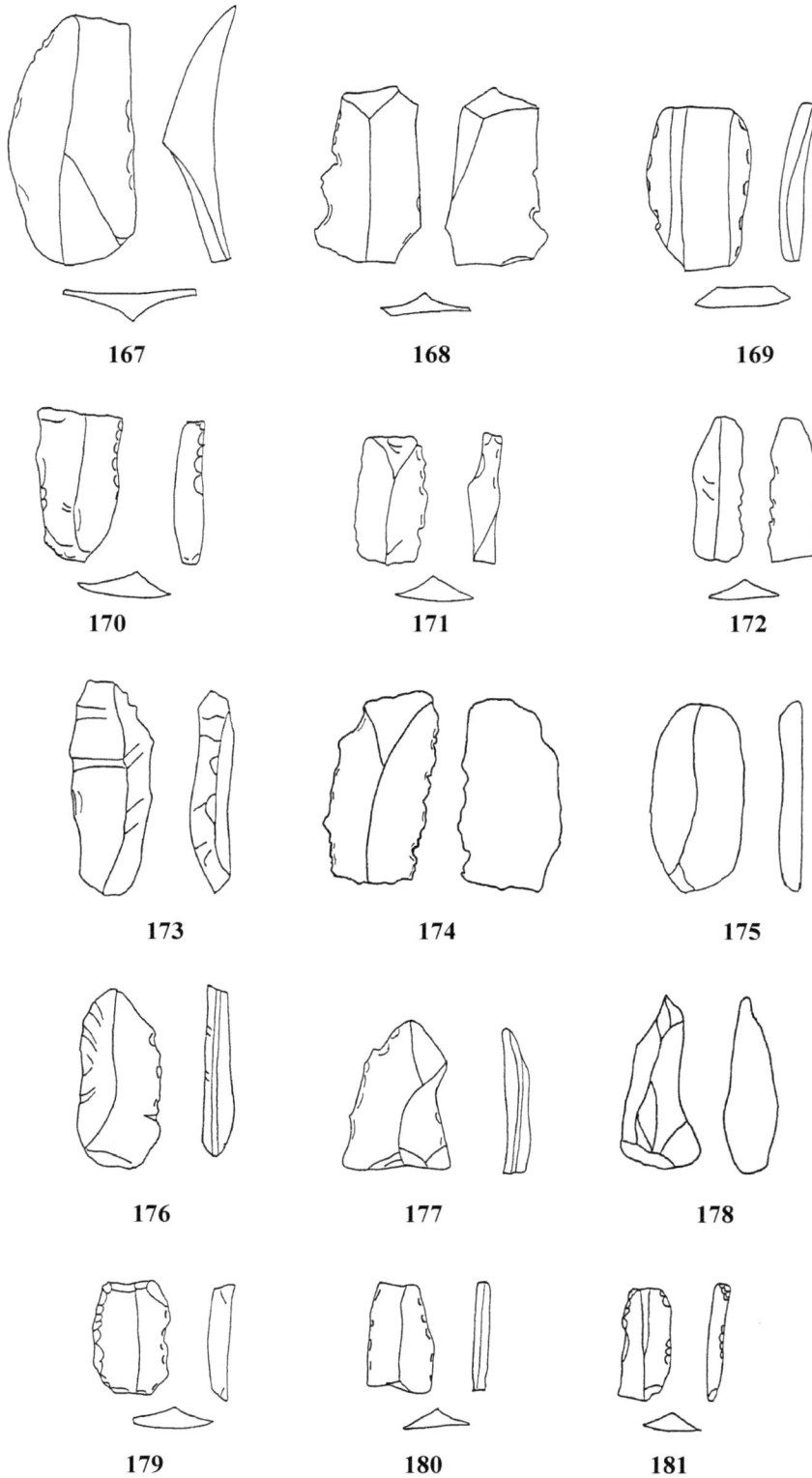

Plate 43. Flint blades showing use-wear along their cutting edges (**167-181**), excluding example **178** which is a flint awl (Scale 1:2)

182   183   184

hole

185   186   187

188   189   190

191   192

193

194

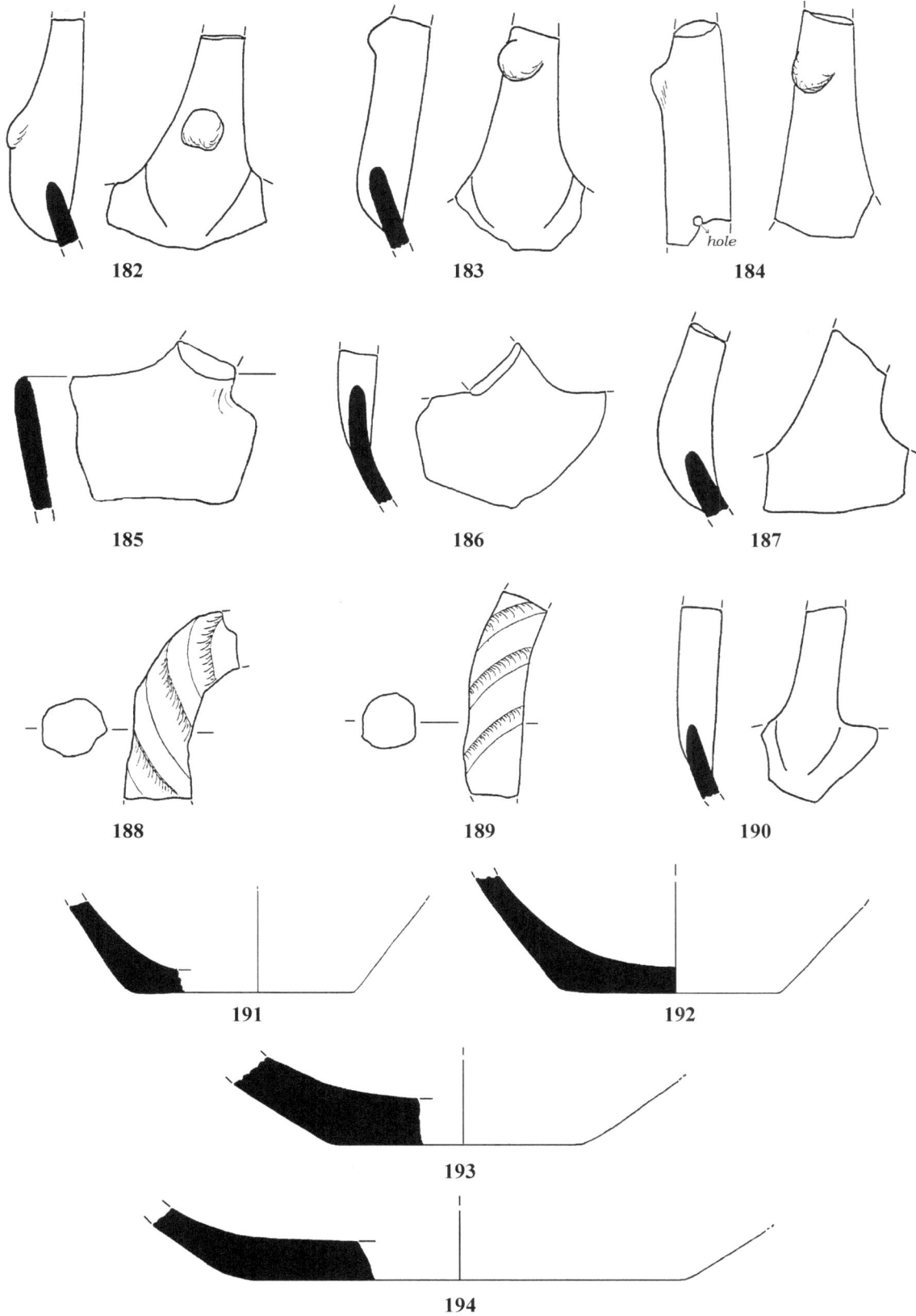

Palte 44. Handle fragments of bowls with high uprising handles (**182-190**).
Examples **191-194** represents flats bases of bowls or jars (Scale 1:2)

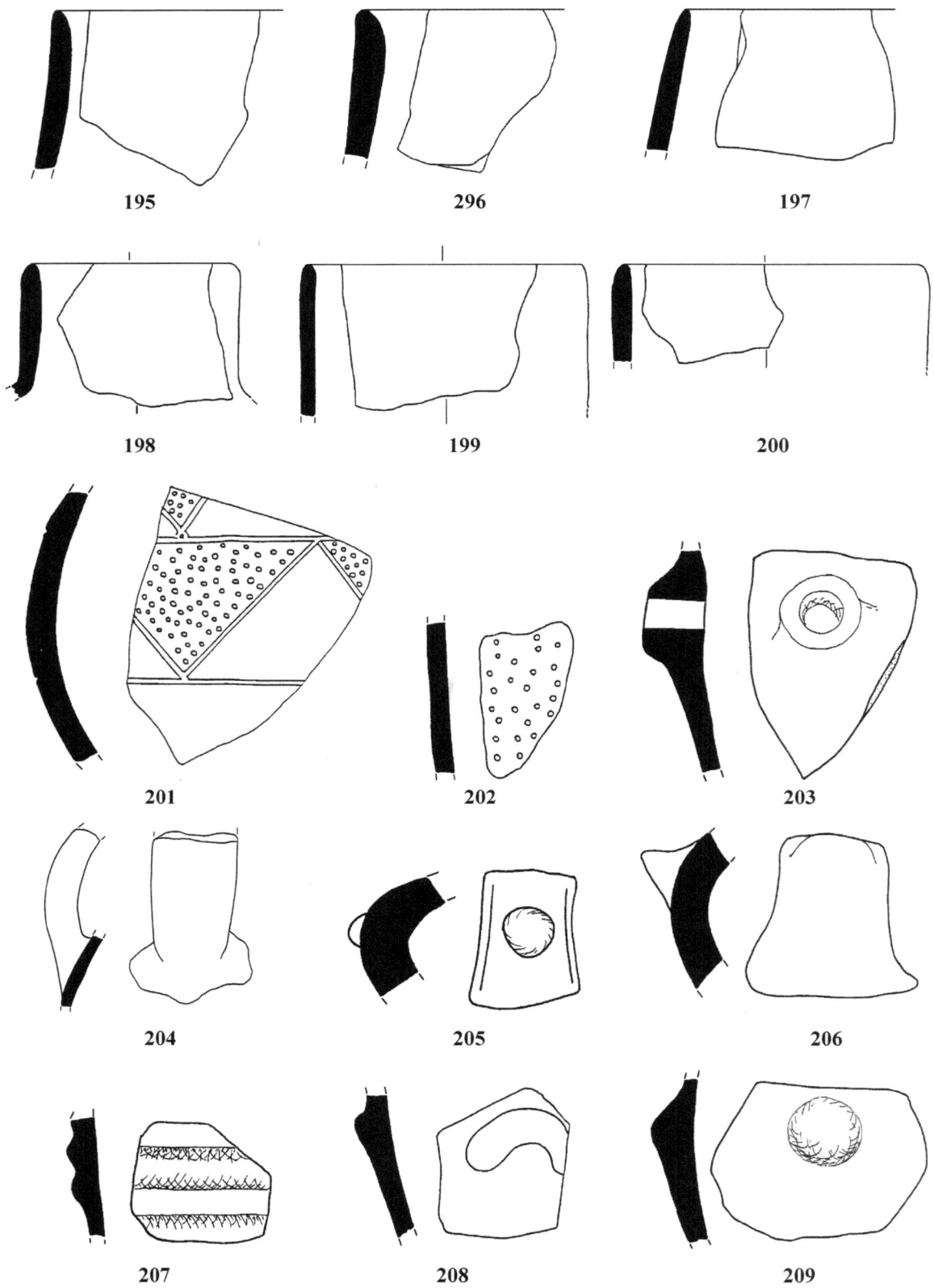

195   296   197

198   199   200

201   202   203

204   205   206

207   208   209

Plate 45. Rim, wall and handle fragments of open and closed-shaped jars (**195-209**) (Scale 1:2)

www.ingramcontent.com/pod-product-compliance
Lightning Source LLC
Chambersburg PA
CBHW061001030426
42334CB00033B/3324